Day Trips® Series

GETAWAYS APPROXIMATELY TWO HOURS AWAY

DAY TRIPS®

FROM **ORLANDO**

Janet Groene *with* **Gordon Groene**

D0712024

The
Globe
Pequot
Press

GUILFORD, CONNECTICUT

Maps by XNR Productions © The Globe Pequot Press

ISSN 1541-0404
ISBN 0-7627-2198-7

Manufactured in the United States of America
First Edition/First Printing

To environmental scientists
Jennifer DuPree and Jason Liddle,
who were wed at
Washington Oaks State Gardens
on April 13, 2002

Help Us Keep This Guide Up to Date

Every effort has been made by the authors and editors to make this guide as accurate and useful as possible. However, many things can change after a guide is published—establishments close, phone numbers change, facilities come under new management, and so on.

We would love to hear from you concerning your experiences with this guide and how you feel it could be improved and kept up to date. While we may not be able to respond to all comments and suggestions, we'll take them to heart and we'll also make certain to share them with the authors. Please send your comments and suggestions to the following address:

The Globe Pequot Press
Reader Response/Editorial Department
P.O. Box 480
Guilford, CT 06437

Or you may e-mail us at:

editorial@globe-pequot.com

Thanks for your input, and happy travels!

CONTENTS

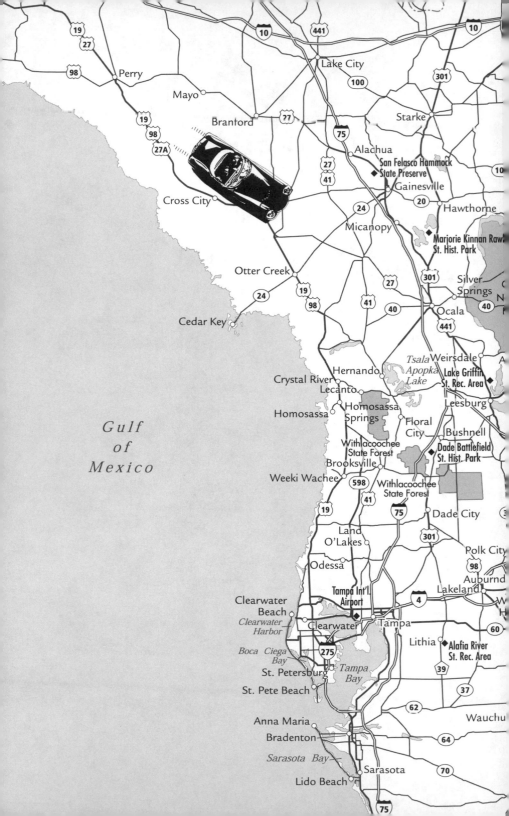

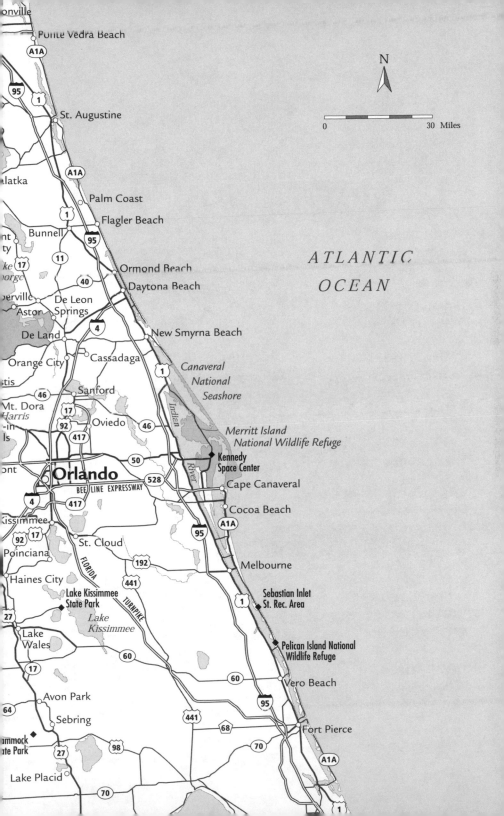

PREFACE

The most-visited tourist attraction in the entire world is Walt Disney World, just south of Orlando in Lake Buena Vista. Whether the theme parks are the focus of your trip to Central Florida or you are a resident in search of side trips from the City Beautiful, we have exciting news for you. In drives of about two hours from Orlando, you can visit America's oldest city, Florida's finest beaches, the birthplace of speed, scuba destinations on offshore wrecks, springs fed by water so clear you can see fish 30 feet down, and miles of country roads that will remind you of sweet yesteryears.

Do we have a favorite day trip? No, because each trip we suggest here has an everyday personality as well as a special event or season that makes it the best place to be: DeLand or Palatka when azaleas bloom, Clermont during the harvest of wine grapes, Clearwater Beach under blue skies, St. Augustine for the reverent Blessing of the Fleet, a spring "run" in a canoe, Ocala National Forest on a brisk winter day, or Alexander Springs on a sweltering summer day for a cooling swim. Come, join us in finding a Florida that is not themes and screams, but is placid, historic, and real.

So much of Florida's treasures are found within two hours of Orlando. In these pages, you'll find villages such as Cassadaga and Lake Helen, where you can lose yourself in a time warp. Check into a posh resort at Ponte Vedra Beach or a 400-year-old inn in St. Augustine. Picnic in Micanopy under an oak tree that was a sapling when this was an Indian village. Walk sacred ground at Crystal River, where unknown tribes buried their dead in enormous mounds.

You'll want to take some of these trips with the children, some alone, some with your lover, and others with parents or grandparents who can tell you about the way things used to be. Whomever you decide to share your day with, take this book in hand, leave Orlando behind—and start day tripping.

TRAVEL TIPS

When is a beach not a beach? Where do Florida residents get special treatment? Here, in alphabetical order, are answers to these questions and others frequently asked about Florida travel. Whether you're an old Florida hand or are visiting for the first time, scan these listings for wrinkles, warnings, shortcuts, and discoveries.

Amtrak: Amtrak serves much of the region covered in this book. For information and schedules, visit www.amtrak.com, or dial (800) USA-RAIL.

Area codes: Area codes are being added throughout Florida at a head-spinning clip. In the 407 area of Greater Orlando, where a new area code—321—is being phased in for new subscribers, ten-digit dialing is required for every call, even if you are dialing next door.

Baseball: Central Florida hosts the following major league teams in March for spring training:

Cleveland Indians—Winter Haven
Detroit Tigers—Lakeland
Kansas City Royals—Baseball City (near Haines City)

Beaches: When reading hotel listings, take the word "beach" with a grain of salt. Some municipalities, such as Daytona Beach, have just one mail address for the entire city; other communities, such as St. Augustine and St. Augustine Beach, have separate names. A Daytona Beach address could be as much as half an hour from anything even resembling a beach. Lodgings that brochures describe as "waterfront" may overlook an oily bay, dirty river, alligator-infested lake, or buggy swamp. "Beachfront" may mean rocks and shell rubble, or waters that you wouldn't let your dog swim in.

When in doubt, look up the address on a good map or in the *Florida Gazetteer,* or simply ask hosts exactly what body of water you're talking about. Florida has some of the best beaches in the world. You don't have to settle for less.

Bicycling: Paved bike paths within two hours of Orlando include the 18-mile West Orange Trail, the 46-mile Withlacochee Trail, the 34-mile Pinellas Trail, the 19.5-mile Flagler County Trail, and the 16-mile Gainesville-Hawthorne State Trail. One of the best guides to Florida bicycling is Jeff Kunerth's *Florida's Paved Bike Trails: An Eco-Tour Guide*, published by University Press of Florida. Also contact the Office of Greenways and Trails (850-488-3701; www.dep.state.us/gwt) or the Florida Trail Association (www.Florida-trail.org). Bicycle tours of the state, some lasting a week or more, are organized by Bike Florida, P.O. Box 451514, Kissimmee, FL 34745; www.bikeflorida.org.

Bird-watching: Florida is one of the major birding states in the nation, offering a huge variety of native, migratory, seasonal, and accidental sightings. Entry fees to Gateway sites on the Great Florida Birding Trail are often free—never more than a few dollars—and loaner optics are often available. Start by visiting www.floridabirdtrail.com or calling (850) 488-8755 to learn where to find Gateway sites. Some trails require reservations or an appointment. Get a map ahead of time and arrive during the right time of year for the species the trail is best known for. Many of the sites are drive-in, suitable for those who have physical challenges.

Camping: Reservations for campsites and cabins in Florida state parks are available by calling (800) 312-3521 or by visiting www.myflorida.com.

Chain motels: Lodging chains offer familiar layouts and facilities. Properties must meet their chains' standards, are usually well located along the highway, and are often an excellent value. Chains located within two hours of Orlando include:

Best Western (800) 528-1234; www.bestwestern.com
Days Inn (800) 329-7466; www.daysinn.com
Holiday Inn (800) 465-4329; www.holiday-inn.com
Howard Johnson (800) 446-4656; www.hojo.com
La Quinta (800) 531-5900; www.laquinta.com
Motel 6 (800) 466-8356; www.motel6.com
Red Carpet Inn (800) 251-1962; www.reservahost.com
Scottish Inn (800) 251-1962; www.reservahost.com

Cruising: Central Florida is not just the theme park capital of the world and a place to stay within a short drive of both Atlantic and Gulf of Mexico beaches. It's also handy to two major and a couple of minor cruise terminals. In-the-know Orlando travelers book a cruise add-on with their Orlando stay.

- From **Port Canaveral**, cruise to the Caribbean or trans-Atlantic with Carnival, Disney Cruise Line, or Royal Caribbean.

- From **Tampa**, sail to the Mexican Riviera with Carnival Cruise Lines or Holland-America.

- *Regal Empress* cruises seasonally out of **Port Manatee** in Sarasota.

A travel agent who specializes in cruises is your key to finding the right ship, cabin, rate, and itinerary.

Fishing and hunting: Florida residents pay $10 for a ten-day saltwater fishing license, $12 for a year and $60 for five years. For non-Floridians licenses are $5.00 for three days, $15.00 for seven days and $30.00 per year. A freshwater fishing license costs $13.50 per year for Floridians or $31.50 for nonresidents, who can also buy a seven-day permit for $16.50. Divers, spearfishers, and people who set traps for marine life need the same licenses as other anglers. Licenses are not required for children under age 16 or Floridians over age 65 with a valid driver's license or registration card.

Fishing licenses can be ordered by phone at (888) 347-4356. A credit card is required and a service fee is charged. Hunting licenses are $12.50 per year for Floridians and $150.50 per year or $26.50 for ten days for out-of-staters.

An excellent guide is *Fishing Secrets*, available free from the Central Florida Visitors & Convention Bureau (863-298-7675 or 800-828-7655). Listed are fishing guides, fish camps, public landings, boat rentals, license centers, fishing piers, and tips on catching largemouth bass, bluegill, shellcracker, crappie, and catfish.

Florida National Scenic Trail: It isn't yet continuous throughout all Florida, but eventually hikers will be able to hike Florida from stem to stern, connecting with other national trails. For now, major segments of the trail can be hiked in state and national forests, in Big Cypress National Preserve, and around the entire circumference of Lake Okeechobee. It's a project of Florida groups and government and the United States Department of Agriculture. Contact the USDA Forest Service, 325 John Knox Road, Suite F-100, Tallahassee, FL 32303. For information on the Florida Division of Forestry's Trailwalker program, call (850) 488-6611 or visit www.fl-dof.com.

Florida residents: When making hotel reservations or buying theme park tickets, always ask if a Florida resident discount applies. Often you can get a price break, albeit sometimes with blackout dates. Some theme park annual passes cost little more than two or three days' admission yet can be used year-round, including special festivals and events.

Getting around: Coastal communities on both the east and west shores of Florida have their own cluster of barrier islands, each with its own beach. Some can be reached by coastal roads that hop from island to island. Others require starting at the mainland and taking the only bridge that serves that particular island. It's fun to drive these coastal roads, but traffic can be stop-and-start and there's always the chance of a long delay for a bridge opening. Consult a good map.

Golf: With its gentle hills and benign weather, central Florida is a natural for golf courses. It's possible to build entire day trips around golf courses in every corner covered in this book. Write to the resources listed in the back of the book, and ask for special brochures on their golf facilities.

Greyhound bus: Second only to a rental car for convenience is traveling Florida's outback by Greyhound. The line serves almost every community listed in this book. Ask about the Florida Pass, which allows unlimited travel for a given time period at a given price. For information call (800) 229-9424; tickets (800) 231-2222.

Handicap access: Thanks to the Americans with Disabilities Act, you no longer have to wonder whether most places have access. Still, it's wise to check ahead to see whether particular facilities suit your needs, because "handicap accessible" may mean only that a wheelchair can get through the door and not that a hotel room has a wheel-in shower, lowered light switches and closet bars, TDD telephone access, information in braille, acceptable facilities for a guide dog, and so on. Check ahead, too, to see what park facilities are available if you need a paved nature trail or a wheelchair-accessible bathroom.

Hurricane season: The chances of a hurricane affecting your day trip are very small. Still, hurricanes happen and should be respected. The three stages of alert are hurricane advisory, watch, and warning. If you travel Florida's coastal areas during hurricane season—roughly June 1 through the end of October—note highway signs indicating EVACUATION ROUTE. If a storm is forecast, follow instructions and evacuate early; it can take many hours to evacuate barrier islands over narrow roads and even narrower bridges or causeways. At the first indication of a hurricane watch, fill the car with gas. Traffic jams can occur on evacuation routes; you could be stuck for hours. Stock up on food and water for the trip home. If a hurricane warning is issued, follow authorities' instructions as quickly as possible. If you have pets, children, or medical problems, prepare even earlier. Pets aren't allowed in most shelters.

Mapping your route: If you want to get to, say, Indian Rocks Beach west of Tampa, you could take the slow, scenic, coastal route—State Road 699—through every hamlet, or take a quicker route via I-4, I-275, and State Road 688 directly to the island. Maps in this book are provided for planning and orientation, but you'll need a good state map or, better still, the *Florida Gazetteer* (DeLorme Publishing), to fine-tune your route. In coastal areas almost every route will be determined by bridges and causeways rather than by a straight-arrow route from here to there.

Pets: It's against Florida law to leave an animal in a closed vehicle, even if a window is cracked to provide ventilation. Temperatures soar quickly in the sunshine, even on a cool day. Animals suffer and die needlessly; you risk a fine or even prosecution.

Sales tax: Some attractions list their prices including tax, others without. Be prepared to pay 6 to 7 percent state sales tax on top of published prices. Hotels rarely include tax or gratuities in their published rates. Hotel rates are plus state sales tax, any county option sales tax, and bed tax—adding 12 to 13 percent to the total tab, not counting tips, service charges, and the occasional surcharge for a special event.

Self-catering: Central Florida is awash in time-shares, suites, condos, apartments, duplexes, and even entire neighborhoods of single-family homes that rent by the night, week, or month. When booking accommodations, understand what services are provided. Resorts usually provide daily maid service, including kitchen cleanup. At other lodgings you may have to make your own bed, do all your own housekeeping, and pay a cleaning-fee deposit in case you don't leave the place clean enough for the next tenant.

Smoking: If you're a smoker, or a nonsmoker who wants to avoid breathing others' smoke, it's wise to call ahead to inquire about a restaurant's smoking policy. Laws and policies are changing, but most restaurants in central Florida permit smoking in at least part of the room. Some, especially gourmet and vegetarian restaurants, allow no smoking at all. Cigars are verboten almost everywhere except in cigar bars.

State parks: Admission to most state parks, gardens, historic sites and recreation areas is by the carload, usually $3.25 to $4.00 for up to eight persons or $1.00 per walk-in or biker. Passes good for all state sites are $31.80 per year for an individual and $63.60 per family.

Swimming safety: It's always best to swim within sight of a lifeguard station. Observe warning flags and signs that may indicate such pests as stinging jellyfish, hazards such as run-outs, or weather problems. In addition to water hazards, Florida is the lightning capital of the United States. When lightning is in the area, get off the beach or golf course or away from other open areas.

Wineries: For a list of Florida wineries that are open to the public, contact the Florida Grape Growers Association, 215 North First Street, Lake Wales FL 33853; (863) 678–0523; www.fgga.org.

USING THIS TRAVEL GUIDE

Highway designations: Federal highways are designated U.S. State routes and are indicated by State Road.

Restaurants: This book uses dollar signs to indicate whether a hotel or restaurant is inexpensive, moderate, or expensive. Assume roughly that you'll pay $10 or less per person for a typical meal at a $ restaurant, $25 or less at $$, or more than $25 at $$$. If $$$$ is indicated, it's likely you'll spend $50 and up per person. Call ahead to see if reservations are accepted or required and to ask about special concerns such as parking, handicap facilities, or the availability of vegetarian meals.

Accommodations: Lodgings priced $50 or less are indicated as $. You'll pay $50 to $100 at $$ rates and $100 and up at $$$ listings. Hotels priced at $$$$ are truly luxury properties where you'll pay $200 or more.

The prices and rates listed in this guidebook were confirmed at press time. We recommend, however, that you call establishments before traveling to obtain current information.

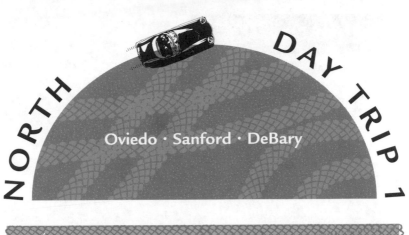

OVIEDO

Barely over the county line north of Orange County, enter Seminole County near Oviedo. You're still in Greater Orlando with its ever-devouring growth, but this is also lake and river country, with some remaining greenspace for the angler, canoeist, and wildlife observer. To reach Oviedo from Orlando, drive east on State Road 50, then north on Highway 434, also known as Alafaya Trail.

WHERE TO GO

Black Hammock. 2316 Black Hammock Fish Camp Road, Oviedo 32765. Black Hammock is a center for boat rentals, nature tours aboard pontoon boats, alligator viewing in a nature exhibit, airboat rides, bait and tackle—and some of the best catfish meals in the South. (407) 365–2201 restaurant; (407) 365–1244 marina.

Gator Ventures. 2536 Black Hammock Fish Camp Road, Oviedo 32765. Come during the day for sight-seeing, fishing, duck hunting, and wildlife watching, or take a night ride for frogging or gator watching. A free alligator exhibit is on the grounds. Ride the wetlands around Lake Jesup, a 10,000-acre wilderness alive with bird life, wild boar, bobcats, and alligators. Adventures are by appointment and are priced by the hour. (407) 977–8235.

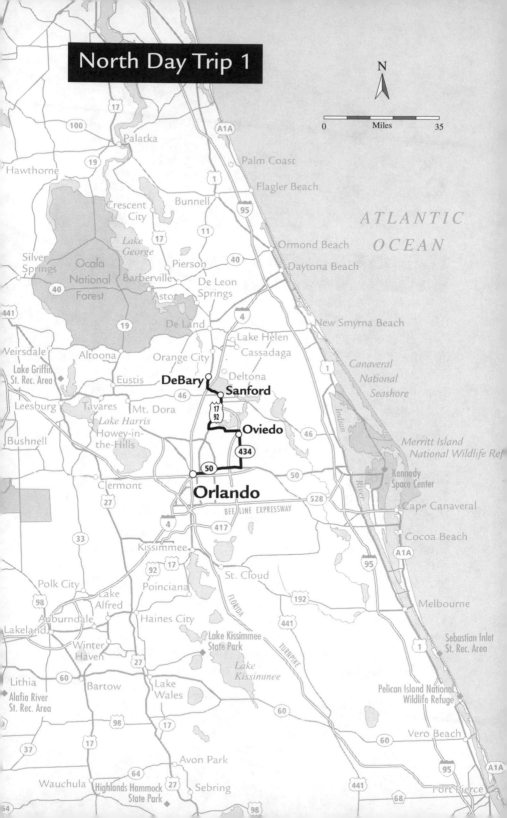

WHERE TO EAT

Black Hammock. 2316 Black Hammock Fish Camp Road, Oviedo 32765. Of the many activities that can be enjoyed here, one of the best is eating. Try farm-raised gator as well as fried or blackened catfish, barbecue, mahi-mahi done your way, burgers, chicken, or steak. The Shrimp Feast features three kinds of shrimp with all the trimmings, or have the Surf 'n' Turf or the Swamp 'n' Turf (steak and gator bites). Prime rib, steak, and chicken are charbroiled. For dessert have the Kentucky Derby pie. Beer is sold by the can, bottle, or pitcher; wine is served by the glass or carafe. On the first and third Sundays of the month, live music starts at 2:00 P.M. in the Tiki Bar. Open Tuesday and Wednesday from 4:00 P.M., Thursday through Sunday from 11:30 A.M. Closed Monday. $–$$. (407) 365-2201 restaurant, (407) 365-1244 marina.

Bills Elbow South. 1802 West Highway 426, Oviedo 32765. This is the spot for a leisurely lunch or an evening out. Have a drink at the full bar, then order from the popular, meat-and-potatoes menu. Open for lunch and dinner every day. $$. (407) 365-2435.

Cha Cha Coconuts. 1275 Oviedo Marketplace Boulevard, Oviedo 32765. This place bounces with Bahamian music and the flavors of goombay. It's one of a popular chain, a gathering spot for drinks, light dining, lunch, dinner, or a late-night bite after a movie. Open daily for lunch and dinner and until 2:00 A.M. on Friday and Saturday. $–$$. (407) 977-4448.

Veppino's Ristorante. 100 Carrigan Avenue, Oviedo 32765. If you're looking for a dressy-casual place to feast on authentically prepared Italian specialties, especially veal and chicken, this is it. There's always a seafood specialty, too, and good steaks. Have a drink from the full bar. Open for lunch and dinner weekdays; dinner only Saturday and Sunday. $$. (407) 365-4774.

SANFORD

Sanford is slipping out of its small-town role and is increasingly perceived as part of Greater Orlando because so many Orlando-bound travelers arrive here at the international airport or at Amtrak's

Auto Train terminus. Many plunge on south to the theme parks, missing out on the treasures that Sanford itself has to offer. Boats with a draft of up to 8 feet can still sail from the Atlantic Ocean all the way to Sanford on the St. Johns River. The city remains an important port, just as it was in the steamboat days when the river was central Florida's chief "highway." Its historic downtown deserves a day or two, and its Lake Monroe is a boating and fishing paradise. To reach Sanford from Oviedo, pop back onto Route 434, exit at U.S. 17–92/Sanford, and continue into Sanford.

WHERE TO GO

Lower Wekiwa River State Preserve. Mailing address: c/o Wekiwa Springs State Park, 1800 Wekiwa Circle, Apopka 32712. Located 9 miles west of Sanford on State Road 46, this preserve covers more than 17,000 acres along the St. Johns River. Access to these fragile wetlands is limited, so be sure to call ahead to inquire about any hiking, primitive camping, horseback camping, or canoeing you want to do. Lucky visitors see black bear, river otters, alligators, wood storks, and sandhill cranes. Except for trails and primitive campsites, there are no facilities. (407) 884–2009.

Museum of Seminole County. 300 Bush Boulevard, Sanford 32771. Because Sanford was a major steamboat stop in the decades before people arrived in Florida by rail or motorcar, the town is drenched in history, and this museum is the place to learn about it. Displays depict agriculture, the steamboat era, a typical country store, hospital memorabilia, and artifacts from the first police and fire stations, and the days when Sanford was the Celery Capital. As you enter the building, note the camphor tree, said to be the third largest in the nation. The building itself began as a home for the indigent and elderly, who became largely self-sufficient through operation of their own orange grove, vegetable garden, chicken farm, and dairy barn. Open Tuesday through Friday 7:00 A.M. to noon and 1:00 to 4:00 P.M. Free. (407) 321–2489.

Rivership Romance. 433 North Palmetto Avenue, Sanford 32771. Your cruise can be a relaxing glide on the St. Johns River or a fun-filled evening of feasting and dancing. On day cruises, bring binoculars for the wildlife show that goes on along the banks of the river. View egrets, herons, and ospreys, sunning alligators and turtles, and perhaps a rare manatee. Dine at your reserved table in the air-conditioned dining room, gazing through a picture window at the passing scene. Menus offer a choice of six entrees, one of them seafood and one vegetarian. Luncheon cruises sail Wednesday, Saturday, and Sunday 11:00 A.M. to 2:00 P.M. and Monday, Tuesday, Thursday, and Friday 11:00 A.M. to 3:00 P.M. Moonlight Dinner cruises with live music and dancing sail Friday and Saturday at 7:30 P.M., docking at 11:00 P.M. Cruises are priced $35 to $50, including the meal. Bar beverages and tips are additional. Reservations are required. (800) 423-7401 or (407) 321-5091; www.rivershipromance.com.

Sanford Museum. 520 East First Street, Sanford 32771. This small effort captures the rich history of "Celery City" with well-displayed mementoes. It's housed in a Mediterranean Revival building on the colorful waterfront. The archives and research library are also open to the public. Admission is free Tuesday through Friday 11:00 A.M. to 4:00 P.M. and Saturday 1:00 to 4:00 P.M. (800) 800-7832.

Sanford Zoo. 4755 Northwest Highway 17-92, Sanford 32747. This small zoo has been a local favorite since 1933. See rare and endangered species from all over the world, as well as an impressive collection of rare Florida native plants. Trained volunteers educate visitors about animals, birds, elephants, big cats, snakes, and much more. Shop for gifts; cold drinks and light meals are sold at the canteen, which can also stage a children's birthday party if you make arrangements in advance. Adults $7.00, children ages 3 to 12 $3.00, and seniors aged 60 and over $4.00. Open every day 9:00 A.M. to 5:00 P.M. (407) 323-4450.

Self-guided walking tour. Write ahead (see Regional Information) for a brochure and map describing the Sanford Historic Downtown District. Picture the city as it was at the turn of the twentieth century, bustling with steamboat traffic and farm wagons laden with produce. Pass the movie palace, the opera house, and buildings that were once the livery stable, saloon, post office, banks, and dime stores. At 1000 East First Street, the old Hotel Forrest Lake is now the home of the New Tribes Mission. The exterior is original.

Wekiwa Springs State Park. 1800 Wekiwa Circle, Apopka 32712. Off State Road 434 or 436, the park takes its name from an Indian word meaning "spring of water." Bring your own horse and ride the 8-mile equestrian trail, or hike 13.5 miles of verdant pathways.

Camp, swim in the springs, picnic, bicycle, or bird-watch for Carolina chickadees, bald eagles, limpkin, hawks, and wood storks. With luck, you may spot a black bear, gray fox, or bobcat. Deer, gopher tortoises, and other critters are more common. Open 8:00 A.M. to sunset every day. State park fees apply. (407) 884-2006.

WHERE TO SHOP

Lady Jayne's. 222 East First Street, Sanford 32771. In this venture into yesteryear, shop for eveningwear, including vintage pieces from the 1940s and 1950s. Deck out in rhinestones, gloves above the elbow, and a romantic hat—styles found nowhere else in town. Hours vary, so call ahead. (407) 323-5167.

Larry's Mart. 215 South Sanford Avenue, Sanford 32771. Located between Second and Third Streets, this is an antiquer's paradise filled with historic treasures, collectibles, contents of entire estates, and an extensive line of fine mahogany reproductions. This is just one of the many antiques shops that add up to hours of happy browsing in downtown Sanford. Hours vary, so call ahead. (407) 322-4132.

WHERE TO EAT

Cactus Bob's. 1566 South French Avenue, Sanford 32771. This is your standard Mexican fun spot serving all the family favorites—quick and uncomplicated, with beer or wine if you wish. Open daily for lunch and dinner. $-$$. (407) 330-1275.

Da Vinci. 107 Magnolia Avenue, Sanford 32771. This is a trendy spot in a cavernous old building with stamped-tin ceilings. Start with crisp calamari or fricassee escargot, or stay with the appetizer menu and make a meal of delectable tidbits. If you're more traditional, start with the house salad (greens in a creamy dressing) and homemade bread followed by meaty osso buco, penne in tomato sauce, duck *au poivre*, or seared salmon draped in paper-thin pancetta. Go with the white chocolate crème brûlée for dessert. Open Tuesday through Friday for lunch and Tuesday through Saturday for dinner. Reservations are suggested. $$-$$$. (407) 323-1388.

Sergio's. 2895 Orlando Drive, Sanford 32771. Italian classics are served with gusto in this locally popular Italian place, found just behind the ABC liquor store north of Lake Mary Boulevard. There are pastas galore, saucy chicken or a steak with a side of spaghetti, juicy veal scalloppini, shrimp diavolo, and desserts such as tiramisu. Start with antipasto or a green salad with vinegar and oil and slabs of the crusty bread. $$-$$$. (407) 323-4040.

DeBary

In the days when steamships brought Northerners to inland Florida for the winter, DeBary caught the eye of Samuel Frederick deBary, who owned his own side-wheelers and made his fortune carrying cargo, including Mumm's champagne. His winter home, once a lonely but elegant outpost on the St. Johns River, is now surrounded by a fast-growing community that bears his name. Continue north on U.S. 17–92 north to DeBary.

WHERE TO GO

DeBary Hall Mansion. 210 East Sunrise Boulevard, DeBary 32713. The mansion is a twenty-room Italianate palace built in 1871 by champagne importer Samuel Frederick deBary and now restored to its original splendor. It's open only on weekends for limited hours, but dedicated volunteers take every opportunity to put the mansion in the spotlight. It's especially lovely at Christmas and during reenactments, balls, and special events. Admission is charged. (407) 749-4340.

    Gemini Springs Park. 37 Dirksen Drive, DeBary 32713. This 210-acre park surrounds one of the springs that Florida is so famous for. There's a boardwalk and nature trails, a picnic area with rest rooms, and swimming in the clear, deep, spring waters. A wading pool for children is 2 feet deep. There's a 2-mile equestrian trail, campsites, a bike trail, canoe rental, and fishing from the fishing dock only. Open sunrise to sunset. Admission is $3.50 per carload. (407) 668-3810.

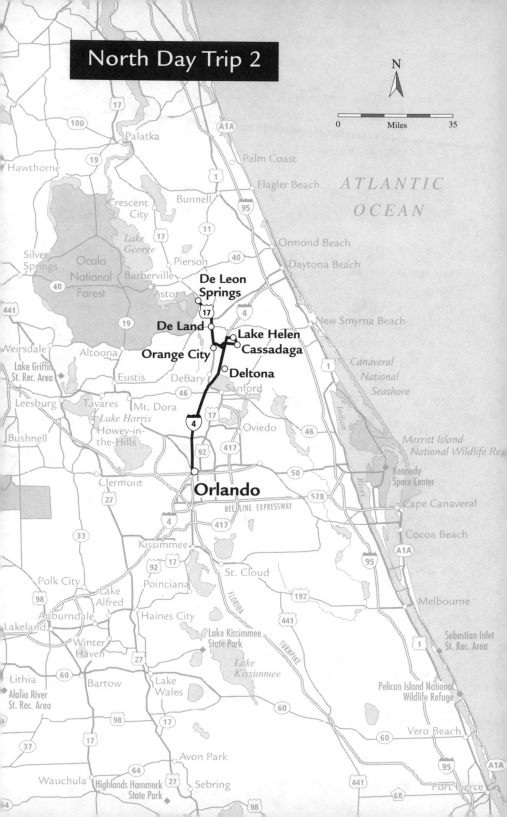

This jaunt covers 10,000 years of history in a nutshell, and you'll want to come back for more. The oldest canoe found in the Western Hemisphere was fished out of DeLeon Springs and sent to a museum in Tallahassee. Today the springs still pour thousands of gallons of water a day into a swimming pool that is the same temperature winter and summer. Ponce de Leon thought he would find the Fountain of Youth in these waters. Some locals swim here daily year-round. Your visit to Cassadaga takes you into the realm of spiritualism. DeLand is a college town abuzz with bustling students; Orange City is the home of Blue Spring. Like DeLeon Springs, the waters here gush up into a crystal pool that spills eventually into the St. Johns River. It's a favorite wintering spot for manatees, who know they'll find shelter and warm water here.

CASSADAGA

Go north from Orlando on I-4 (signs say EAST) toward Daytona Beach. Pass the Deltona exits, then take the DeLand–Orange City exit, turn left on Route 472, then turn right on Martin Luther King Boulevard. Turn right at the sign to Cassadaga, which is on County Road 4139.

The historic hamlet of Cassadaga in Central Florida was settled in 1894 by George P. Colby, a trance medium from New York, and his followers. They established Florida's first spiritualist camp, now known as the Southern Cassadaga Spiritualist Camp Meeting. Half a day does nicely for strolling the streets, having a reading or two if you're into the psychic scene, shopping the book stores for New Age music, and dining at the hotel.

Even if you're immune to superstition and fortune telling, you'll feel the eerie presence here. The homes look like summer camps, unlike any other neighborhood in Florida, and they're packed tightly into one-lane streets. Outside many of them is a sign announcing that a reader, healer, medium, or reverend lives inside. Most will give you a reading for about $50 a half hour. A longer reading or a visit with a departed loved one might run $75. Or you can attend one of the free services, including healing services on Sunday and Wednesday. Mini-readings by students cost only a few dollars, and mediums sometimes offer mini-readings for half the going rate. There's such a crowd on some nights, you have to take a number.

WHERE TO GO

Cassadaga Hotel. 355 Cassadaga Road, Cassadaga 32706. The hotel lies in the heart of this tiny crossroads, and front desk personnel can arrange a reading with one of their resident psychics. The gift shop has a superb selection of New Age paraphernalia and souvenirs. Set a spell on the wide wraparound veranda or in the homey lobby. Start your tour by buying the annual Cassadaga Spiritualist Camp program here or in the other shops. The hotel has a map showing the community's buildings and parks and a schedule of services and events. (386) 228–2323; www.cassadagahotel.com.

Colby Memorial Temple. On Stevens Street, a short walk from the hotel, the temple is the setting for spiritualist services. On Sunday the healing service is at 10:00 A.M., followed by a church service at 10:30. A demonstration message service is held Sunday 12:30 to 1:30 P.M. On Wednesday healing is at 7:00 P.M. There's an admission charge to the message service that follows. On the second Friday of each month, spiritual healing is practiced by candlelight at 7:30 P.M. October through May, the camp also offers adult lyceum every morning, in which teachers instruct in spiritualism and related topics. On the church grounds, note the plaque honoring the founding of Cassadaga. The small six-sided building is the Caesar Forman Healing Center, where healing is held on Sunday 10:00 to

10:30 A.M. and Wednesday 7:00 A.M. to 3:30 P.M. by some of the community's dozen or so Certified Healers. Rites are free, although donations are appreciated. (386) 228-2828 or (386) 228-0067.

Parks dot the little settlement. They all have names and meaning to locals, but for visitors they are just pleasant greenspaces with paths, carefully tended plantings, and sometimes a picnic table. Follow the map in the program mentioned above. Seneca Park, overlooking Spirit Pond, has a gazebo large enough to seat eight to twelve for a picnic.

Self-guided walking tour. Just walk up one street and down the other to soak up the strange atmosphere of a camp community. Occasionally you'll see a patch of the original brick paving peeking through. Roads are still mostly single-lane, lined with homes packed close together, and they're remarkably hilly for flat Central Florida. You'll pass Harmony Hall, Brigham Hall, the temple, several meditation gardens, and Spirit Lake, which has often been dry during Florida's recent droughts.

WHERE TO SHOP

Cassadaga Hotel. Its gift shop is well stocked with New Age books and paraphernalia, incense, unique jewelry, and gifts for followers of the spirit world.

Cassadaga Spiritualist Camp Bookstore. 1112 Stevens Street, Cassadaga 32706. A broad range of New Age philosophies is represented with books, music, trinkets, and icons. You'll also find soaps, scents, writing paper, and other souvenirs. Open daily. (386) 228-2880.

Purple Rose. 1079 Stevens Street, Cassadaga 32706. The shop carries crystals, gems, jewelry, Native American and metaphysical paraphernalia, and butter-soft Minnetonka moccasins. Open every day. (386) 228-3315.

WHERE TO EAT

Lost in Time Cafe. 355 Cassadaga Road, Cassadaga 32706. Located in the Cassadaga Hotel, the cafe is surprisingly conventional in this unusual, spiritualist setting. Choose from a nice variety of sandwiches and hot and cold dishes. You can even get a glass of wine with your meal. Open daily for lunch. $-$$. (386) 228-2323.

WHERE TO STAY

Cassadaga Hotel. 355 Cassadaga Road, Cassadaga 32706. Built in 1927 to replace an even earlier structure that burned, the hotel is beyond quaint. Rooms are small, furnishings defiantly tatty, and bathrooms so minuscule that the tiny pedestal sink may be in the bedroom. Still, baths have all the essential plumbing and are en suite. Window units provide air-conditioning. Some rooms have a tub, balcony, or other special features, but all cost the same. Rates, which are higher on weekends, include continental breakfast. Rooms have no television, phone, radio, or other conveniences, but guests can watch TV in the lobby. The hotel also has a hair salon, a massage therapist—and mediums on call. $$. (386) 228-2323.

Clauser's Bed & Breakfast. 201 East Kicklighter Road, Lake Helen 32744. This AAA three-diamond inn is housed in an 1890s Victorian mansion and carriage house. All rooms are different, so let the hosts know whether you want a soaking tub, in-room Jacuzzi, private veranda, or other feature. A full country breakfast is included. The inn also has an intimate pub, where it's fun to have a quiet drink after dinner. $$. (386) 228-0310 or (800) 220-0310; www.ClauserInn@totcon.com.

ORANGE CITY

A century ago, steamboats stopped at the docks at Blue Spring to load oranges picked in nearby groves. The main drag, U.S. 17–92, has been the main highway from south Florida to the Midwest for almost a century, yet the heart of little Orange City hasn't budged out of the 1950s. Continue west on CR 4139 from Cassadaga. Turn south onto the Martin Luther King Beltway, then CR 4145 west and U.S. 17–92 south to Orange City.

WHERE TO GO

Blue Spring State Park. 2100 West French Avenue, Orange City

33950. The park has a view of the St. Johns River, a clear spring for swimming and snorkeling, an historic home, live oak trees for shade, and a boardwalk that takes you along the spring run to an overlook where, with luck, you'll see manatees. February is usually the top time for these "sea cows" to come in from the cold and live in spring waters that stay the same temperature year-round. The old homestead was built at a time when steamboats brought passengers up river and left here laden with oranges. Bring a picnic lunch. Canoes are rented by the hour or day, and there are a boat launch, showers, and primitive campsites. Admission is $4.00 per vehicle and $1.00 per person for those who arrive on foot or bicycle. Hours are 8:00 A.M. to sunset. (386) 775-3663.

WHERE TO EAT

Harry's. 481 Deltona Boulevard, Deltona 32725. Located in the Best Western Deltona Inn on the way to Orange City, Harry's is a gem of a restaurant that's well worth a special stop for its refreshing lunches and elegant dinners. The lounge is famous for its large selection of martinis; there's live music on special nights. Reservations are strongly advised. The restaurants is open daily for lunch and dinner; breakfast is provided for inn guests. $$-$$$. (386) 860-3000 or (800) 528-1234.

    Stavros Pizza. 413 South Volusia Avenue, Orange City 32763. This is a family favorite for hot grinders, gyros, Greek salad, and all the pasta favorites, from spaghetti and meatballs to lasagna and fettuccine Alfredo. Veal, chicken, or eggplant is served parmigiana, with beer or wine if you wish. Open daily except Monday 11:00 A.M. to 10:00 P.M. $-$$. (386) 775-2066.

WHERE TO STAY

    Best Western Deltona Inn. 481 Deltona Boulevard, Deltona 32725. Located at Deltona exit 53 off I-4, with easy interstate exit and access, this is a twenty-three-acre oasis of calm just off the highway. Rooms have dataports, voice mail, and more than forty channels, including free HBO. The inn is also home to Harry's restaurant, where breakfast is provided for guests. $$-$$$. (386) 860-3000 or (800) 528-1234; www.bestwestern.com.

DeLAND

Originally founded closer to the St. Johns River, the entire community was moved after a long-ago flood. Today a grid of streets shaded with picturesque live oaks, the city is home to Stetson University and an old downtown lined with trendy restaurants and shops. To see the campus, which includes the oldest continuously operating school building in Florida, start 3 blocks from downtown and walk north to the Holiday House restaurant. You'll pass the grand mansion occupied by Stetson's president, historic buildings in a variety of architectural styles, pleasant lawns, and the city's cultural arts center. Peek in to shop the gift shop and to see what's showing in the small museum. Take U.S. 17 north to DeLand.

WHERE TO GO

Beresford Lady. The *Lady* is shy about announcing an address because her home port changes according to water conditions, but the crew will tell you where to meet the boat when you make your reservations, which are essential. Take a three-hour excursion on the St. Johns River aboard this authentic side-wheeler. The boat is air-conditioned and wheelchair accessible and offers lunch and dinner cruises year-round. Reservations are essential. (386) 740–4100 or (888) 740–7523; beresfordlady.net.

DeLand House. 137 West Michigan Avenue, DeLand 32720. This restored home once belonged to Henry DeLand, founder of the city and a benefactor of Stetson University. The house, built in the 1880s, is authentically furnished and filled with memorabilia and research tools for the serious historian. Open Tuesday through Saturday noon to 4:00 P.M. Modest admission is charged. (386) 740–6813.

DeLand Naval Air Station Museum. 910 Biscayne Avenue (in the airport complex), DeLand 32724. Although it's a small, modest effort, this museum looms large in the hearts of aviators, military buffs, and those who learned to fly here during World War II. This airport actually was a naval air station between 1942 and 1946, a training center for dive-bomber pilots. Displays of uniforms, guns, photographs, and aircraft models recall the story. Open Monday through Saturday 1:00 to 4:00 P.M. Free, but donations are accepted. Also on the field and open the same hours is the **DeLand Naval Air Station Historic Hangar,** showing historic war birds and World War II memorabilia. (386) 738–4149.

Gillespie Museum of Minerals. 234 East Michigan Avenue, DeLand 32720. This museum houses one of the largest private gem and mineral collections in the nation, attracting rock hounds from all over the world. See rare, unique, priceless, and gee-whiz rocks and fossils. Open Monday through Friday 9:00 A.M. to 4:00 P.M. Free. (386) 822–7330.

Hontoon Island State Park. 2309 River Ridge Road, DeLand 32720. The park occupies an island in the St. Johns River. Take U.S. 44 west to Hontoon Road, then follow the signs. Timucuan tribes lived here hundreds of years ago, leaving behind an owl totem that wasn't found until 1955. A replica of the original—a rarity because totems were uncommon to Native American tribes in this area—stands on the island today. Take the free ferry to the island to picnic, fish, camp in a rustic cabin or your own tent, observe wildlife, or climb the watchtower for a view of the river for miles around. Allow ninety minutes for the self-guided hiking trail. Free parking is on the mainland; ferries run from 9:00 A.M. to an hour before sundown daily. Bring everything with you; there are no supplies on the island. Dock your boat for the same fee paid by overnight campers. (386) 736–5309.

Manatee Seeker. Take State Road 44 west from DeLand to the Pier 44 Marina. Board a comfortable, wheelchair-accessible, sea-kindly pontoon boat to glide the beautiful St. Johns River. With luck, a manatee will surface beside the boat. See turtles and alligators sunning on the banks, an abundance of wading birds and fish hawks, and perhaps a bald eagle. Every outing is different, depending on Mother Nature's whims. Tours leave daily at 10:00 A.M. and 12:30 and 3:00 P.M. Reservations are strongly recommended. Adults $20; seniors and children $16. (800) 587–7131; www.vis-arts.com/manatee.

WHERE TO SHOP

Angevine's. 2999 South Woodland Boulevard (U.S. 17–92), DeLand 32720. This establishment is the city's oldest antiques dealer, known for its fine silver, estate jewelry, and specialty pieces. Cliff Angevine

Jr. is a Sterling-matching specialist, and Sue Angevine Guess is a graduate gemologist. Open Monday through Saturday 10:00 A.M., closing weekdays at 5:00 P.M. and Saturday at 1:00 P.M.

Doll & Hobby Shop. 138 South Woodland Boulevard, DeLand 32720. This is another of the very special shops that bring tourists to historic downtown DeLand from miles around. Shop for collectible and specialty dolls, everything you need for your Hot Wheels collection, Polar Lights, Barbie, and much more. Open Monday through Friday 10:00 A.M. to 5:00 P.M.; closes 3:00 P.M. on Saturday. (386) 734-3200.

Isadora's. 131 North Woodland Boulevard, DeLand 32720. Isadora's is just one of the many, hard-to-describe specialty shops in historic downtown DeLand. Buyers have an unerring eye for imports, artworks, glassware, china, furniture and "junque." Open Monday through Saturday 10:00 A.M. to 5:00 P.M. (386) 736-4030.

The Muse Book Shop. 112 South Woodland Boulevard, DeLand 32720. The Muse is an old-fashioned book store crammed with books from the latest novels to rare, historic books. Stop in for Florida maps and books as well as to shop for gifts and your own library. Lose yourself among the high stacks, a book lover's paradise. Generally open Monday through Saturday 10:00 A.M. to 5:00 P.M. (386) 734-0278.

Reeve & Howard. 114 North Woodland Boulevard, DeLand 32720. This shop has been a DeLand tradition since 1905, selling fine cards, gifts, collectibles, glassware, china, and pewter. It's just the spot to find special, meaningful gifts and cards. Hours are Monday through Saturday 10:00 A.M. to 5:00 P.M. (386) 734-1227.

Rivertown Antique Mall. 114 South Woodland Boulevard, DeLand 32720. The mall houses more than fifty dealers who offer everything from vintage clothing to furniture, dolls, jewelry, and antiquarian books. Open Monday through Saturday 10:00 A.M. to 5:00 P.M. (386) 738-5111.

Uppity Women. 135 West Plymouth Avenue, DeLand 32724. This big old house is jam-packed with country collectibles, candles, copper, primitives, bath and body products, and a big teacup and teapot collection. It's off the beaten path but worth a special trip several blocks north of downtown center. Take U.S. 17 north, then turn right onto Plymouth Avenue at the Eckerd Drug. Open Monday through Saturday 9:00 A.M. to 5:00 P.M. (386) 736-1117.

Wolfe Contemporary Gallery. 203 North Woodland Boulevard, DeLand 32720. This is one of a growing number of high-quality art galleries in downtown DeLand. Many works are by area artists who are in the national spotlight. Open Monday through Thursday 10:00 A.M. to 6:00 P.M. and Friday and Saturday until 9:00 P.M. The last Thursday of each month is Gallery Night downtown, so come to stroll from gallery to gallery, sipping, dining, hobnobbing, and browsing along the boulevard from 6:00 to 9:00 P.M.

WHERE TO EAT

Belly Busters. 930 North Woodland Boulevard, DeLand 32720. This joint is a delightfully dumpy owner-operated place that loyal locals have been keeping to themselves for more than twenty years. Sandwiches are stuffed with at least a quarter pound of meat. For a cholesterol fix, order the double steak sub with cheese. Buddy and Jerry offer a large menu of subs, soups, and pita sandwiches. The interior is small and has no nonsmoking section, but you can eat on the picnic tables out back or grab a bag of belly busters to take with you for boating or picnicking. $. (386) 734–1611.

DeLand Artisan. 215 North Woodland Boulevard, DeLand 32720. This is the "in" place for lunch (ask for a table overlooking "The Boulevard") or a leisurely dinner in a softly lit dining room backed with the original brick walls. The chef does classic Continental, fusion, Southwest, and Caribbean dishes with flair and finesse. Every day there's a new soup, quiche, sandwich, and specialty of the day featuring fresh seafood or a special cut of meat. There's a full bar, a lounge with live entertainment some evenings, and a comprehensive wine list. Open every day for lunch and dinner. Reservations are highly recommended. $$–$$$. (386) 736–3484; www. delandartisaninn.com.

Holiday House. 704 North Woodland Boulevard, DeLand 32720. This is the original of a small Florida chain of buffet restaurants. It's an interesting concept, with unlimited self-serve for some foods but enough rules and limits that you have to mind your Ps and Qs. You can opt for the full meal (only one serving of meat), hot and cold buffet with no meat, or cold buffet only. The menu is limited but is a good choice for those who don't like buffets. This is basic, home-style Southern family fare. Open daily 11:00 A.M. to

9:00 P.M. They don't take reservations, but call ahead anyway and they'll do their best. On Sunday after church the wait can be long. $-$$. (386) 734-6319.

Le Jardin Restaurant. 103 West Indiana Avenue, DeLand 32720. This restaurant specializes in French-Vietnamese cuisine that locals voted the best Continental food in the county. Order classic noodle dishes, duck, lamb, steak, fresh seafood, or a vegetarian meal, all deftly prepared and prettily presented. Reservations are recommended. Open Monday through Friday for lunch and daily except Sunday 5:00 to 10:00 P.M. for dinner. $$-$$$. (386) 740-0303.

Mr. Phad Thai's. 217 North Woodland Boulevard, DeLand 32720. One-half of a dual-personality restaurant (the other half specializes in sushi), this is a superb place for Thai food. Order a Japanese beer, sushi, or a Thai specialty cooked to order—from unspicy to hot-hot. Open for lunch Monday through Friday and for dinner daily except Sunday. $$. (386) 740-0123.

Yesterday's. 145 North Woodland Boulevard, DeLand 32720. Yesterday's is part hometown eatery, part sports bar, part local hangout for everyone from the college crowd to seniors for lunch, happy hour, dates, and informal dinners. It's the perfect spot for lunch while you are "doing" the shops of the historic downtown district. Have grilled chicken, a chicken Caesar salad, or a BLT with potato salad. The burgers and crab cakes are tops. There's a full bar, famous for its margaritas and daiquiris, with a full choice of cold longnecks, too. Hours are 11:00 A.M. to 9:00 P.M. weekdays and to 10:00 P.M. Friday and Saturday. Closed Sunday. $-$$. (386) 734-1917.

WHERE TO STAY

Comfort Inn. 400 East International Speedway Boulevard, DeLand 32724. The motel is on the east side of DeLand on the highway to Daytona Beach. If you like a familiar, economical chain motel, headquarter here to sightsee both east and west Volusia County. Your day starts with a free continental breakfast; restaurants for lunch and dinner are nearby. Amenities include free cable television, swimming pool, whirlpool, laundry for guest use, and Jacuzzi suites. (386) 736-3100 or (800) 424-6423; www.choicehotels.com.

DeLand Artisan. 215 North Woodland Boulevard, DeLand 32720. The Artisan was built in the 1920s, but you wouldn't guess it from the smart new face. One of the city's most chic places to dine as well as a plush suites hotel, it's within walking distance of the library and downtown's antiques shops, book store, and boutiques. $$–$$$. (386) 736-3484; www.delandartisaninn.com

DeLand Country Inn. 228 West Howry Avenue, DeLand 32720. The inn lies in the heart of the city, within walking distance of downtown restaurants and antiques shops. There's a screened swimming pool, basketball court, and a Florida room where guests can use the television and VCR. Take a single, double, or king room or the two-bedroom cottage that sleeps five. Children are welcome; pets are not. Rates include a full breakfast. $–$$. (386) 736-4244; www.bnbfinder.com.

Howry Manor Holiday Suites. 422 West New York Avenue, DeLand 32720. Across from St. Peter's Roman Catholic Church, this historic home and surrounding buildings have been transformed into a tree-shaded complex offering a variety of lodgings and apartments to sleep everyone from a traveling single or honeymoon couple to a big family. Walk to downtown shops and dining. The Manor's own very British **Sweet Dreams Tea Room** is open Tuesday through Friday 11:00 A.M. to 2:00 P.M. serving such English-themed sandwiches as the Winston Churchill and the Margaret Thatcher. $–$$$. (386) 736-2483.

DeLEON SPRINGS

Today it's a hamlet with little more than a hardware store, convenience store, secondhand shops, a Mexican grocery and a bank, but DeLeon Springs has been a part of Florida history since the earliest explorers. Some historians believe these springs to be the Fountain of Youth that Ponce de Leon sought. Drive north from DeLand on U.S. 17, once the major highway between Florida and Chicago via Chattanooga. You'll still see mom-and-pop motels along the way, some of them derelict and others proudly maintained and still operating. Trains still run on old tracks parallel to the highway, where you'll see the remains of what was once a mighty orange-packing facility.

WHERE TO GO

DeLeon Springs State Recreation Area. 601 Ponce de Leon Boulevard, DeLeon Springs 32130. This beautiful park, with centuries-old live oaks surrounded by azaleas that are a spectacle in February, is best known as the home of the **Old Mill Restaurant.** Once a real mill, the building has a waterwheel, cane grinder, old boiling kettles, and modern machinery for milling flour for the whole-grain breads and pancakes offered here. The tables are centered with grills where you can make your own breakfast or lunch. Rent a canoe, paddleboat or kayak; swim in the clear, sweet spring; and tour the small but excellent museum. Admission is $4.00 per vehicle with up to eight people or $1.00 for walk-in or biker. (386) 985–4212.

Lake Woodruff Wildlife Refuge. Mail address: Box 488, DeLeon Springs 32130. A whopping 18,500-acre wetlands out on County Road 4053, this is one of the best bird-watching spots in the state. Found here are about 200 species of birds and 42 species of animals, plus countless reptiles, amphibians, and fishes. The refuge is remote and there are no facilities, so bring water, food, sun protection and bug repellent—and tell someone where you're going and when you expect to return. If you run into trouble, you might not be found for weeks in this labyrinth of waterways. The area, once known as Spring Garden, has long been considered an Eden. John James Audubon came here to sketch birds almost 200 years ago. The refuge is open during daylight hours. Fishing and primitive hunting are permitted. Look for signs off U.S. 17. (386) 985–4673.

WHERE TO EAT

Karling's Inn. 4640 North U.S. 17, DeLeon Springs 32130. The inn is an Alpine chalet transplanted along a lonely highway more than twenty years ago by a German chef and his wife. The superb food and charming service couldn't be kept a local secret for long, and today it's essential to call ahead for reservations. Meals begin with a wonderful soup from one of the chef's age-old recipes. Try the cucumber salad, then one of the chef's daily specials. At least one game dish and a fresh fish are offered, plus sauerbraten, steaks, chicken, or veal, followed by a roly-poly German dessert. Hours vary seasonally, but the inn is generally open Tuesday through Saturday, from 5:00 to 9:00 P.M. $$–$$$. (386) 985–5535.

Old Mill Restaurant. DeLeon Springs State Park, 601 Ponce de Leon Boulevard, DeLeon Springs 32130. Park admission is required. Explore the grounds of this old mill, which once milled grain thanks to power supplied by the spring run. Then feast on pancakes or sandwiches made from whole grains, or buy some of the breads to take home. Open Monday through Friday 9:00 A.M. to 4:00 P.M. and weekends 8:00 A.M. to 4:00 P.M. Reservations are taken only for groups of ten or more, so waits can be long. $–$$. (386) 985–5644.

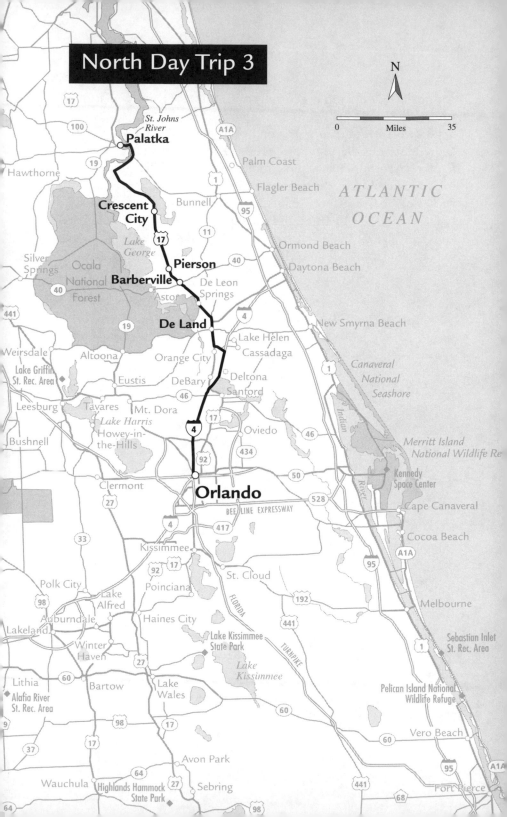

Once upon a time, each of these communities was a waypoint for streams of north-south traffic on the highway, railroad, and river; but the interstates stole their thunder, and there are still long stretches of solitude between them. Barberville is still a mere crossroads. Pierson is the fernery capital of the state and the home of the oldest Swedish Lutheran Church in Florida. It's found on the town's main street, which runs parallel to and 1 block west of U.S. 17. The town itself is tiny, but members come from miles around to attend services at this beloved old landmark. Palatka is an old river town now known for its ravishing azalea gardens, established during the Depression of the 1930s as a public works project.

BARBERVILLE–CRESCENT CITY

Begin your day trip on I-4 east, exit at S.R. 44 (DeLand) and follow U.S. 17 north to Barberville and Crescent City.

WHERE TO GO

Pioneer Center for the Creative Arts. Mail address: P.O. Box 6, Barberville 32105. Located just west of U.S. 17 on State Road 40, the center began with an old wooden schoolhouse, built in 1919 and in session here until 1969. Many of the hardworking volunteers here attended this school, and their love for the land shows in everything from the biscuits they bake to the crops they tend. More than a dozen other buildings have been moved here, creating a community that includes a railroad depot, church, cabins, turpentine still, homes, firehouse, workshops, and stores. Don't miss the special events and reenactments held here. Open Monday through Friday 9:00 A.M. to 4:00 P.M. and Saturday 9:00 A.M. to 2:00 P.M.; usually closed Sunday and holidays. Admission is $2.50 for adults and $1.50 for children age 12 and under. Admission may be higher during special events. (386) 749-2959.

Crescent City. On U.S. 17 between Barberville and Palatka. Write ahead (see "Putnam County" under Regional Information) for a free self-guided walking tour of the little village, which was settled in the mid-1800s high on a bluff overlooking lakes that are part of the St. Johns River system. The settlement flourished thanks to the steamboat trade, abundant orange crops, and the patronage of wealthy Northerners who wintered here. Old homes, churches, and commercial buildings are privately owned, but you can walk the streets to ponder the history of American architecture. The brochure explains who built each structure and when.

Take a ferry ride on an ancient ferry that has transported people, wagons, horses, and vehicles across this part of the St. Johns River since 1856, saving travelers the 45-mile trip to the Palatka Bridge. From Crescent City, go west on County Road 308 to County Road 309, then north to Mount Royal Avenue; follow the signs to the Fort Gates Ferry. The ferry runs 7:00 A.M. to 5:30 P.M. daily except Tuesday. One-way fare is $9.00 per vehicle.

WHERE TO EAT AND STAY

Sprague House Inn & Restaurant. 125 Central Avenue, Crescent City 32112. The Sprague House is a rambling wooden hotel just a block from the lake, on a quiet street that hasn't changed much since the turn of the twentieth century except for the addition of highlights of city history that someone carved in the sidewalk. Rent a boat, fish from the dock, or take a walking or bicycling tour of streets that time forgot. The standard room has twin beds, cable TV, and private bath. Children should be age 12 or older. Suites are sweetly old-fashioned; the honeymoon suite has a tiled bathroom with stained-glass windows, bidet, and a shower big enough for two. $$–$$$, including breakfast. The restaurant is open for lunch and dinner daily except Monday, offering a large choice of hot and cold dishes. Fresh seafood is a house specialty. End your meal with the hot peach cobbler. $$–$$$. Don't miss the old-fashioned bar and the antiques shop. Sailors and street ladies are reminded to use the back entrance. (386) 698–2430.

PALATKA

Continue north on U.S. 17 through layers of history laid down by the river, then the railroad, and finally by the motorcar. Palatka was founded on the banks of the St. Johns in 1821 and named for an Indian word meaning "crossing." The settlement was burned in the Seminole War of 1836 and rebuilt as Fort Shannon. Among notables who served here were Winfield Scott, Zachary Taylor, and William T. Sherman. The city was occupied by the North during the Civil War. After the war, Yankees returned here in winter to soak up the Southern sun. The old downtown has seen better days, but empty storefronts are slowly finding new owners with drive, brains, and a love for these old buildings. Ask anyone in town how to find Angels, which dates to 1932 and is one of the state's oldest diners, and stop in for grits and gravy.

WHERE TO GO

Bronson-Mullholland House. 100 Madison Street, Palatka 32178. Hours for this Greek Revival home filled with period furnishings and relics from the city's past are 2:00 to 5:00 P.M. Tuesday, Thursday, and Sunday. A modest admission is charged. (386) 329–0140.

Ravine State Gardens. 1600 Twigg Street, Palatka 32178. This geological wonder was formed by nature's forces, as swirling waters sculpted deep ravines like no other in the state. In time, grasses and shrubs took root, slowing the erosion. In 1933 the federal Works Projects Administration set up a work camp to make the ravine a botanical showplace. Hundreds of azaleas were planted, some of them now house-high. Camellias bloom through the winter, to be replaced in early spring by a symphony of azaleas that inspire an annual Azalea Festival. Drive the 1.8-mile loop road, or stroll trails along a spring-fed creek. The gardens are at their busiest and most beautiful in February and March, but they're worth walking through any time to see the wildlife and enjoy the cool green of the magnolia, live oak, hickory, and sweet gum trees. Open daylight hours. Admission is $3.25 per vehicle. (386) 329–3721.

WHERE TO SHOP

Fifth Street Emporium. 500 Reid Street (U.S. 17), Palatka 32178. This is one of the city's leading antiques dealers. Open Tuesday through Friday 10:00 A.M. to 5:30 P.M. and Saturday 10:00 A.M. to 5:00 P.M.; closed Sunday and Monday. (386) 325–5377.

Palatka Antique & Art Mall. 111 North Fourth Street, Palatka 32178. The mall is filled with individual stalls operated by dealers, each with his or her personal interests and specialties. Hours vary seasonally, but the mall is generally open Monday through Saturday 10:00 A.M. to 5:00 P.M., Sunday afternoon November through May, and Sunday by appointment only May to October. (386) 329–9669.

River City Gallery. 710 Reid Street (U.S. 17), Palatka 32178. The gallery sells fine antiques, collectibles, and works of ark. Open Monday through Friday 10:00 A.M. to 5:30 P.M., Saturday 10:00 A.M. to 5:00 P.M., and Sunday noon to 5:00 P.M. November to May. Open other times by appointment. (386) 328–1001.

WHERE TO EAT

Corky Bell's Seafood of Palatka. 211 Comfort Road, Palatka 32178. This restaurant is one of a small chain known for its big menu of fresh seafood served up with coleslaw, onion rings, hush puppies, and french fries. There isn't much here for vegetarians, but some offerings can be ordered broiled to cut down on the calories. This place is enormously popular and doesn't accept reservations, so expect long waits at peak hours. Call for hours, which vary seasonally. $–$$. (386) 325–1094.

Lori's Restaurant. 2401 Crill Avenue, Palatka 32178. Lori's is the quintessential small-town beanery, beloved for its home-style cooking and its early hours for farm and fishing folk. Lori offers a good choice of sandwiches, hot lunches, and hearty breakfast fare. Open Monday through Friday 6:00 A.M. to 3:00 P.M.; breakfast is served until 11:00 A.M. Saturday hours are 6:00 A.M. to 2:00 P.M., and breakfast is served all day. $. (386) 328–9769.

Southwell's Restaurant & Lounge. 118 North Nineteenth Street, Palatka 32178. You can start the day with biscuits and gravy and end with a great steak, hand-cut in Southwell's own kitchen. Seafood is brought in from the Atlantic, and there's also catfish and crab from local waters. Everything is served with fresh vegetables. There's a separate lounge, or order a cocktail at your table. Hours are 6:00 A.M. to 8:30 P.M. weekdays and till 9:30 P.M. on Friday and Saturday; closed Sunday. $–$$. (396) 328–9261.

WHERE TO STAY

Azalea House. 220 Madison Street, Palatka 32177. This establishment is for those who prefer a historic setting and the personal service of a bed-and-breakfast inn. The 1878 Queen Anne house has a pool and spa in its secluded garden. Breakfast can be served on the pool deck if you like. Rates also include cookies at bedtime and a picnic lunch. The house has four guest rooms, three of them with private bath. Children under age twelve and pets aren't accommodated; smoking is permitted only outdoors. Ask about packages that include dinner at a nearby restaurant or a romance package that includes dinner, chocolate, roses, and champagne. $$–$$$. (386) 325–4547.

Best Western Inn of Palatka. 119 Highway 17 South, East Palatka 32131. This is one of a respected, reliable chain known for clean, spacious rooms and a generous continental breakfast at no added charge. Enjoy the swimming pool and whirlpool, use the guest laundry, and walk only half a block to the river. Suites have a wet bar with minirefrigerator, coffeemaker, and microwave. Golf packages are available, and a public boat launch is nearby. $$. (386) 325–7800 or (888) 325–7801.

Holiday Inn Riverfront. 201 North First Street, Palatka 32178. Book a room with a view of the St. Johns River, and dine in the waterfront restaurant. There's also a full-service lounge, with live music on some nights. Arrive by car or boat. Docks and fishing guides are available. $$. (386) 328–3481.

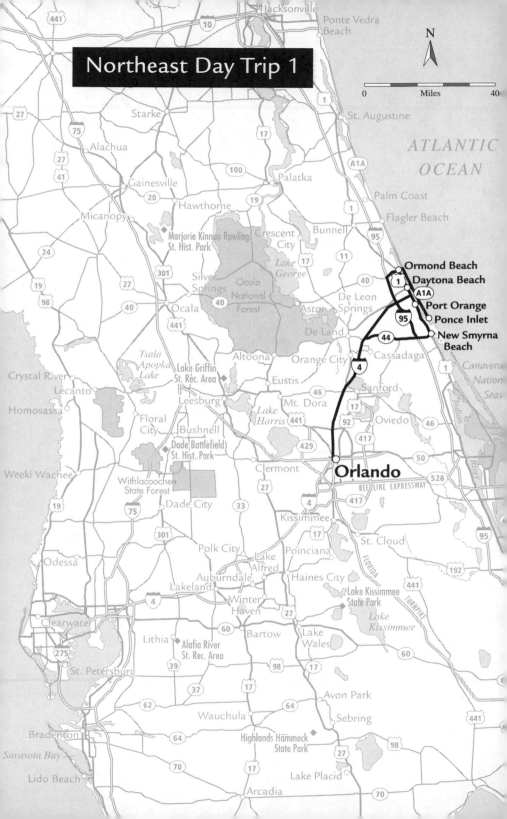

Ormond Beach · Port Orange ·
Ponce Inlet · New Smyrna Beach

Drive up I-4 from Orlando to I-95, then north to State Road 40, which goes east to Ormond Beach. If you start here, you can work your way south past Daytona—saving it for another day trip—to Port Orange, Ponce Inlet, and New Smyrna Beach via I-95, U.S. 1, or Highway A1A.

This string of communities has attracted beachgoers to their shores for more than a century—some to speed across the flat sands in their racecars, others to find new lives in the New World, and most to vacation in sun-warmed communities that haven't yet succumbed to the tourism stampede. Although Daytona's special events spill over and you may not be able to book a room during those times, these Atlantic-front communities should be explored one by one by beach-starved Orlandoans.

ORMOND BEACH

The city calls itself the Birthplace of Speed because of early motorcar speed records that were set on the beach by the likes of Barney Oldfield and R. E. Olds. Ormond Beach started as a retirement community in the 1880s, when an enormous wooden hotel was built overlooking the Halifax River. An early resident was John D. Rockefeller, who loved the area so much that he built his own home across the street. (The hotel fell to the wrecker's ball, but his mansion remains.)

If you're an RV traveler, skip Ormond Beach. Strict laws apply to where and how long you can park (including your own driveway), and many shopping centers have NO RV PARKING signs.

WHERE TO GO

The Casements. 25 Riverside Drive, Ormond Beach 32176. This mansion was once the winter home of John D. Rockefeller. Indoors, see vestiges of the opulent life lived by the powerful tycoon, as well as a Boy Scout Museum and a museum of Hungarian folk art. Special events often take place on the grassy riverfront grounds. Stroll them to view lush greenery and giant live oaks. Open Monday through Friday and Saturday morning. Donations are appreciated. (386) 676-3216.

Ormond Memorial Art Museum and Garden. 78 East Granada Boulevard, Ormond Beach 32174. This small but important museum is surrounded by lush gardens, waterfalls, and a koi pond. The building itself is of historic interest, and it's filled with the works of Florida artists. Admission is $2.00. Open Monday through Friday 10:00 A.M. to 4:00 P.M. and weekends noon to 4:00 P.M. (386) 676-3347.

Tomoka State Park. 2099 North Beach Street, Ormond Beach 32174. This greenspace at the confluence of the Halifax and Tomoka Rivers is a place where Native Americans once powwowed under the enormous live oak trees. Spanish explorers visited the settlement in 1605, a story told in the visitor center's museum and art gallery. Rent a canoe, fish, picnic, boat, camp, or walk the nature trail. The park is open 8:00 A.M. to sunset daily. State park fees apply. (386) 676-4050.

WHERE TO EAT

Barnacle's Restaurant & Lounge. 869 South Atlantic Avenue, Ormond Beach 32176. This place has a whopping big seafood menu and plenty of steaks, baby-back ribs, prime rib, and pasta specialties. Create your own combination platter. The salad bar is one of the city's biggest and best, and the children's menu offers treats for kids. Early-bird specials and happy hour are offered every day. $-$$. (386) 673-1070.

Frappes North. 123 West Granada Boulevard, Ormond Beach 32176. A consistent award-winner, from soup to the sinful desserts, Frappes is offbeat and innovative. Go conventional with the Black Angus burger and bistro fries, or go gourmet with the walnut-crusted chicken breast with goat cheese and spinach or the veal chop Milanese with sage butter, rosemary potatoes, and balsamic organic greens. Open for lunch and dinner. Call for hours and reservations, which are highly recommended. $-$$ ($$$ with an expensive wine). (386) 615-4888.

La Crepe en Haut. 142 East Granada Boulevard, Ormond Beach 32176. Yes, they serve crepes, but the gourmet menu offers much more—all prepared in French classic style and served in an elegant setting. Start with French onion soup or ravioli with porcini mushrooms, then the *salade maison* and an entree of veal medallions with Maine lobster, filet *au poivre*, salmon in almond crust, or duck a l'orange. Have a strawberry or praline crepe for dessert, or splurge on the bananas Foster, prepared tableside for two. Choose from the selection of French vintages. Open for lunch Tuesday through Friday and for dinner daily except Monday. $$$. (386) 673-1999.

Marco's Oceanview Restaurant. 1900 Oceanshore Boulevard, Ormond Beach 32176. Marco's has been a beachside fixture for more than twenty-five years, serving some of the best Greek food in an area that has a long history of Greek settlement. Fresh seafood tops the menu; pasta dishes are a close second. Choose from a long list of fresh, local fish cooked to order or traditional spaghetti, lasagna, and linguini dishes. Early-bird specials are bargain priced. Hours vary seasonally, but it's usually open 4:00 to 10:00 P.M. Monday through Saturday and 11:00 A.M. to 10:00 P.M. Sunday. Call ahead for carryout. $$. (386) 441-1333.

Stonewood Tavern & Grill. 140 South Atlantic Avenue, Ormond Beach 32176. This is a familiar name because the founders have restaurants in other Florida locales. The setting is warm mahogany, with good smells coming from the oak-burning grill. Aged steaks are hand cut; seafood comes fresh from local fleets or is flown in from Chesapeake Bay or the Pacific. Try herb-crusted rack of lamb, pork Adirondack, or big, herb-basted black tiger shrimp. Chicken potpie and pot roast are comfort-food classics; quesadillas are made with hand-made flour tortillas, and the chef does a fantastic pasta with fire-roasted vegetables. Add chicken or shrimp if you like. There's a modest, well-selected wine list. Open for dinner only; call for reservations. $$. (386) 677-1167.

WHERE TO STAY

Makai Beach Lodge. 707 South Atlantic Avenue, Ormond Beach 32176. The lodge has a refrigerator and safe in every room, ocean views from half the rooms, and an owner-operator who keeps things running smoothly. Swim in the ocean or the heated pool. Pets are permitted, and there is a coin laundry for guest use. $$. (386) 677-8060; www.makailodge.com.

Quality Inn & Suites. 251 South Atlantic Avenue, Ormond Beach 32176. This property is a high-rise on the ocean, with a huge swimming pool, outdoor spa, kids' pool, sundeck, and outdoor dining area. Take a room, efficiency, bridal suite, or spa suite, and ask for a private balcony overlooking the sea. Dine in the full-service restaurant. There's live entertainment in the lounge and Tiki Bar. $$-$$$. (386) 672-8510 or (800) 227-7220; www.qualityinndaytona.com.

PORT ORANGE

Rich, black soil attracted early settlers to these lands north of Spruce Creek. They planted acres of sugarcane and thrived until the Seminole Wars, when every plantation south of St. Augustine was put to the torch. Today their ruins are one of the community's most compelling attractions.

WHERE TO GO

Sugar Mill Gardens. 950 Old Sugar Mill Road, Port Orange 32127. Towering trees and flowering shrubs surround the ruins of a sugar plantation with botanical glory. Bring your camera; it's a favorite of fashion photographers. The sugar mill was burned out during the Seminole Wars, but troops stayed on this land during the Civil War. A century later, an attempt was made to turn it into a dinosaur theme park. Huge old statues of prehistoric creatures still sit incongruously amid the rusted boilers, live oaks, and tangled shrubs. Picnics and bicycles are prohibited. Admission is free; open sunrise to sunset every day. (386) 767-1735.

Sunny Daze & Starry Nights. Dunlawton at U.S. 1, Port Orange 32127 (at Aunt Catfish's Restaurant). Cruise down the Halifax River and into its creeks and tributaries to observe the wildlife that makes up a fascinating ecosystem. The skipper knows the natural world as well as area history and spins fascinating yarns while you enjoy the breezes, sparkling waters, and sightings. Bring your binoculars. Reservations are essential because times vary. A one-hour cruise is $9.00; $14 for two hours. A half-day tour that includes the historic lighthouse at Ponce Inlet is $30. Seniors and children get a discount for the two longer tours. (386) 253-1796.

WHERE TO EAT

Marko's Chick-fil-A Heritage Inn. 5420 South Ridgewood Road (U.S. 1), Port Orange 32127. Birthplace of the popular fast-food chain, this one's located in an old farmhouse—with a museum thrown in. See racecars, antiques, and Remington statues. Dining rooms are themed for race fans, motorcycle fans, beach vacationers, and families. Serve yourself from the soup and salad bar, or order one of the tasty Chick-fil-A specialties or a hand-cut steak, fresh seafood, chicken and dumplings, a smoothie, or one of the scrumptious desserts. Open for lunch and dinner daily except Sunday. $–$$. (386) 756-1004.

PONCE INLET

Ponce Inlet lies east of Port Orange, a residential community. The easiest way to reach it is to hop back on I-95 and cruise south to the Taylor Road–Dunlawton exit, then south on Nova Road to U.S. 1. Both U.S. 1 and Highway 1A are clogged with local traffic and should be avoided on this day trip as a way of getting through Daytona Beach.

WHERE TO GO

Ponce de Leon Inlet Lighthouse. 4931 South Peninsula Drive, Ponce Inlet 32127. This is one of the East's most scenic lighthouses.

Climb 203 steps to the top for a bird's-eye view; tour buildings and the grounds for a glimpse of the life of a lighthouse keeper at the turn of the twentieth century. (The beacon was first lit in 1887.) See the 600-pound bronze bell recovered from a sunken sea buoy, the oil storage house built in 1887 with a unique double ventilation system, the old radio shack dating to just before World War II, keeper's quarters, and much more. Shop the gift shop for souvenirs and lighthouse memorabilia. Open 10:00 A.M. daily until 8:00 P.M. in summer and 4:00 P.M. in winter. Admission is $5.00 for adults and $2.00 for children age 11 and younger. (386) 761-1821.

WHERE TO EAT

Down the Hatch. 4894 Front Street, Ponce Inlet 32127. This long-running, family-operated local favorite overlooks the inlet. Dine indoors or out in a laid-back, calypso setting where a clean T-shirt does for dress-up. Anglers gather here for breakfast, and the salty scene goes on through spectacular sunsets and into a starlit night. The catch of the day is always a good bet, right off the boat. There are also daily specials, burgers, chicken, and steaks. Vegetarians will have to get by with salad and potatoes. Open every day 7:00 A.M. to 10:00 P.M. $-$$. (386) 761-4831.

    Inlet Harbor Marina & Restaurant. 133 Inlet Harbor Road, Ponce Inlet 32127. This is a local favorite, not just for great seafood fresh from the restaurant's own fleet but also for a 1,000-foot river walk with nonstop nature watching and a view of the romantic Ponce de Leon Inlet Lighthouse. Arrive in time for the spectacular sunset and dine indoors in air-conditioned comfort or outside on the breezy RiverDance Deck. Start with the smoked fish dip and crisp crackers, then have peel-and-eat shrimp, snow crab, or fresh fish cooked your way and served with all the trimmings. Chicken, wings, steak, and ribs they call Bimini Bones also highlight the menu. For dessert enjoy Chocolate Suicide, Key lime pie, mud pie, or the cheesecake of the week. This popular hangout also has shopping for arts and crafts, so plan to arrive early and linger late, dancing to live music on the deck. Charter fishing by the day and half day can be arranged through the restaurant by calling (386) 767-5705. Open daily except Monday at 11:00 A.M.; closes 10:00 P.M., later on Friday and Saturday. $$. (386) 767-5590.

NEW SMYRNA BEACH

The first Greek settlement in the Americas, this area has a fascinating history filled with intrigue. People from Minorca were brought here as indentured servants by Scottish entrepreneur and medical doctor Andrew Turnbull in 1768. Florida was a British colony and events in far-away Boston and Philadelphia, where a revolution was brewing, were remote and irrelevant. The more than 1,200 immigrants who were brought in to work Turnbull's land grant fled to St. Augustine after years of disease, crop failures, and Indian attacks. Archaeologists are still cataloging and uncovering the marvelous works the immigrants created out of wilderness. Resettlement didn't begin in earnest here until after the Civil War.

New Smyrna Beach calls itself the redfish capital of the world, so wet a line on your own or book a guided outing. Surf fishing, backwater and river fishing, and deep-sea fishing are all on the menu here. From New Smyrna Beach, drive west on State Road 44 to I-4 and south to Orlando to complete the loop.

WHERE TO GO

Chamber of Commerce. 115 Canal Street, New Smyrna Beach 32168. Stop in for information, including a brochure describing a self-guided walking tour of the historic area. Two dozen buildings are highlighted and described. You'll see the history of small-town American architecture in old movie palaces, stores, a library that houses a museum of local memorabilia, and the park where Dr. Turnbull's home once stood. (800) 541–9521. (Also useful is a self-guided tour brochure published by the Southeast Volusia Historical Society, P.O. Box 968, New Smyrna Beach 32170.) Chamber personnel can also provide a current list of outfitters and guides who will take you to Turtle Mound or along the backwaters of Canaveral National Seashore, the Intracoastal Waterway (Halifax River), or the St. Johns River.

Historic Conner Library Museum. 201 Sams Avenue (in Old Fort Park), New Smyrna Beach 32168. See a permanent display depicting the Turnbull Colony, early settlers from Minorca. One or two temporary displays are always worth seeing, too, based on Florida arts, history, or nature. Free. Open 10:00 A.M. to 2:00 P.M. Tuesday through Saturday. (386) 424-2196.

Smyrna Dunes Park. At the north trip of Highway A1A, New Smyrna Beach. Take State Road 44 east, then left at the park. This windswept stretch of dunes and creamy surf is on the south end of Ponce Inlet. A boardwalk lets you walk over the impressive dunes without damaging the delicate sea oats. Bring a picnic lunch and spend the day nature watching, walking the seaside and trails, fishing from the jetty or in the surf, and enjoying the view from the observation tower. Rangers guide nature walks every Saturday at 11:00 A.M. No lifeguards are on duty, so swim with caution. Admission is $3.50 per vehicle, $1.00 per person for more than eight passengers, or $30/$50 for an annual resident/nonresident pass. (386) 424-2935; www.volusia.org/park.

WHERE TO SHOP

Arts on Douglas. 123 Douglas Street, New Smyrna Beach 32168. This superb gallery in a community known as an art colony is home to many artists, sculptors, photographers, and potters. Open Tuesday through Saturday 11:00 A.M. to 6:00 P.M. and by appointment. (386) 428-1133. Other galleries include the **Clay Gallery,** 302 South Riverside Drive (386-427-2903), and **Artist Workshop Gallery,** 114 Canal Street (386-424-9254).

Flagler Avenue is the historic heart of New Smyrna, with many of the boutiques and specialty shops open every day. Come here to browse for unusual gifts, swimwear, accessories, and souvenirs. You'll find funky places to dine, nosh, or have a coffee. Sometimes the street fills with street parties and entertainers.

WHERE TO EAT

Heavenly Sandwiches & Smoothies. 115 Flagler Avenue, New Smyrna Beach 32168. This establishment is part of the historic downtown scene. Breakfast begins at 8:00 A.M., and the goodness goes on through early dinner. Drive through if you like. Dine on healthy alternatives to burgers and fries. Have a fruit smoothie, a refreshing salad, a wrap, or soup of the day. $. (386) 427-7475.

Norwood's Restaurant & Wine Shop. South Causeway, New Smyrna Beach 32168. Norwood's is known for its fine cellar as well as Continental cuisine with a Florida spin. Have the catch of the day, steak, chicken, or the chef's most recent whim. Dine indoors or out. Kids can order from their own menu. Open 11:30 A.M. to 10:00 P.M. daily. Reservations strongly suggested. $$–$$$. (386) 428–4621.

Riverview Restaurant. 101 Flagler Avenue, New Smyrna Beach 32169. Start with sundowners at happy hour prices on the deck of this rambling waterfront place along the Intracoastal Waterway. The menu is extensive and includes such house specialties as Riverview Wellington en croute, bourbon molasses New York strip, sesame-encrusted chicken breast, and stuffed pork loin. The filet mignon is always a good bet, as are the fresh seafood dishes, especially Kelsey's Grouper Gourmet, crusty with almonds and topped with artichoke pesto. For dessert, have bananas Foster and flaming citrus coffee followed by dancing and nightcaps serenaded by live music. Owner-hosts Jim and Christa Kelsey, formerly of the landmark Faro Blanco Resort in the Keys, took over the old Riverview Charlie's, and this popular spot shines brighter than ever. Reservations are suggested. Open for lunch and dinner daily until 9:00 P.M., later on Friday and Saturday. Call about happy hour specials and Sunday brunch, one of the area's best. After dessert, visit the quaint gift shop. $$. (386) 428–1865; www.restaurant.com/riverview.

WHERE TO STAY

Buena Vista Inn. 500 North Causeway, New Smyrna Beach 32168. The inn is so close to the Indian River that you can walk out the back porch and straight out on the fishing pier. They'll also provide bikes to get to the beach, 5 blocks away. One-room units have refrigerators; one-bedroom units have complete kitchens. Pets are welcome for a modest extra fee. Children under age 12 stay free. The office and reservations are open only 9:00 A.M. to 8:00 P.M. $$. (877) 428–5565 or (386) 428–5565.

Corodado del Mar. 701 South Atlantic Avenue, New Smyrna Beach 32169. This is an excellent value if you don't mind doing your own housekeeping. Every unit at this oceanfront condo offers an Atlantic view from the balcony. Kitchens are fully equipped, or you can walk to restaurants as well as to the beach, tennis courts, and shops. Units have two bedrooms and two or two-and-a-half baths and rent by the week. It's an ideal meeting point for families who want to get together on the beach. $-$$$. (800) 700-9445 or (386) 428-2970.

Little River Inn Bed & Breakfast. 532 North Riverside Drive, New Smyrna Beach 32168. The original home was built in 1883 on a two-acre estate overlooking Indian River Lagoon. Stroll the grounds and gardens, play tennis, or just sit on the veranda and watch the passing scene. Each of the six king or queen rooms has its own bathroom. Gourmet breakfast is included. $$-$$$. (888) 424-0102 or (386) 424-0100; www.little-river-inn.com.

Night Swan Bed & Breakfast. 512 South Riverside Drive at Anderson Street, New Smyrna Beach 32168. Chuck and Martha Nightswonger host this stately mansion along the Intracoastal Waterway. Rooms are all different, but all have private bath, telephone, and cable television. There's also a private cottage with a Florida room. Breakfast is included in all rates, and the proprietors can also arrange a catered dinner for one to four couples, a sweetheart package with surprises for your loved one, in-room massages, bicycle rental, and a good choice of fishing and sight-seeing outings. $$-$$$. (386) 423-4940; www.NightSwan.com.

Oceania Plaza Condo Hotel. 425 South Atlantic Avenue, New Smyrna Beach, 32169. This property puts you in a two-bedroom, two-bath, all electric home away from home that accommodates four to six people. Full kitchens have full-size appliances and everything you'll need for cooking breakfast, snacks, or complete meals to eat on your balcony overlooking the Atlantic. The swimming pool is heated. Rentals are by the night or week; higher rates and a three-night minimum apply during race and bike weeks. $$-$$$. (386) 427-4636; www.oceaniaplaza.com.

Riverview Hotel. 103 Flagler Avenue, New Smyrna Beach 32169. The Riverview is an elegantly restored relic of the flamboyant Flagler era, when tourists came to Florida on the new railroad to winter in big hotels with spacious quarters for themselves and their servants. Built as a hunting and fishing lodge in 1885, it became the River View Hotel in 1924. Rates include a generous continental breakfast—served in your room or on your private patio—use of bathrobes, bicycles, and evening turndown. Beach towels are provided at the heated swimming pool. The hotel is a few blocks from the ocean on the Intracoastal Waterway and has a popular restaurant overlooking the water. Stay in a standard hotel room, suite, or a two-bedroom cottage that sleeps four. If you arrive by boat, you can dock overnight for 75 cents per foot. $$. (800) 945–7416 or (386) 428–5858; www.riverviewhotel.com.

Somerset Bed & Breakfast. 502 South Riverside Drive, New Smyrna Beach 32168. Enjoy a veranda as wide as a smile, overlooking the Intracoastal Waterway and a private boat dock. Built in 1916, the house is furnished in period pieces. Docking, breakfast, and evening wine are included in rates. Ask about packages. $$–$$$. (386) 423–3839 or (888) 700–1449; www.somersetbb.com.

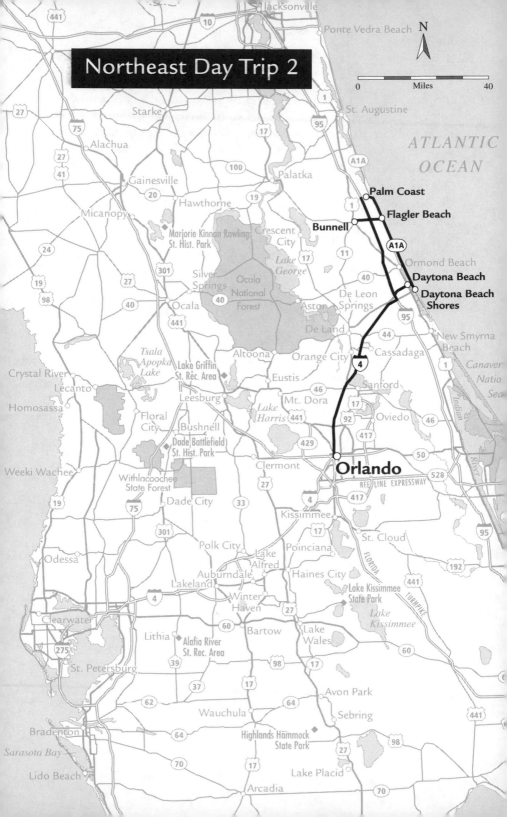

Daytona Beach ·
Flagler Beach–Palm Coast

Take I-4 north (the signs say EAST) from Orlando to the Daytona Beach exit, where I-4 ends. From here, I-95, U.S. 1, or Highway A1A takes you north to Flagler Beach and Palm Coast.

DAYTONA BEACH

Most visitors look at this area as one, long beach playground from Ormond Beach south to Ponce Inlet. Other little communities are found along the way, with such names as Wilbur-by-the-Sea, Holly Hill, and Daytona Beach Shores, but it's all strung together like beads on a chain. U.S. 1, Highway A1A, and I-95 provide easy access to beachside hotels and restaurants. Inland are attractions galore and some of the best golf courses in the state, including the home of the Ladies Professional Golf Association.

Daytona calls itself the World's Most Famous Beach because, in addition to its boardwalk, it's one of the few beaches in the world with sands firm enough to drive on. It's a right zealously guarded by some beachgoers and bitterly contested by others. If you like the idea of driving to the water's edge to offload your cooler and beach umbrella, that's good. If you don't want to sunbathe on a beach where cars are permitted, well, that's bad.

If you aren't quite sure what to make of Daytona Beach, you're not alone. To some tourists it's a place for a cheap drunk during Spring Break. To others it's nothing but auto racing. Still others associate it with motorcycle mania. Critics call it "binge" tourism. Unless you're here to participate, give Daytona Beach a wide berth when these events are held. Traffic congeals, hotel rates rise out of all proportion—and many locals flee town to get away from the melee.

In short, Daytona Beach is a different city depending on when you are here, so choose your dates carefully. However, the city has enormous variety to offer and is not to be missed. Take I-4 northeast from Orlando to the Daytona Beach exit, which brings you into town on U.S. 92.

WHERE TO GO

A Tiny Cruise Line. 425 South Beach Street, Halifax Harbor Marina, Daytona Beach 32114. This company's cruises are always different, always a delight, thanks to a nonstop nature show that can't be predicted. The little boat itself is a replica of a fantail launch once used to ferry early hotel guests. Take a midday waterway cruise, a look at estates that front the water, a combination nature and sightseeing cruise, or the sunset cruise. Prices range from $9.66 to $15.32 for adults and $6.12 to $8.00 for children. Call ahead for reservations, or walk in and take your chances for any but the sunset cruise, which includes a snack and soda, or you can BYOB. Cruises sail every day but Monday. (386) 226-2343.

Adventure Landing. 601 Earl Street, Daytona Beach 32114. Have your fill of fun at one of the state's best water parks as well as an entertainment center with video games, go-karts, miniature golf, and fun food. The best part for people on a budget is that you pay for only the features that you want. Kids will want to spend the whole day here. Open every day 11:00 A.M. to 10:00 P.M. April through Labor Day. Water park admission is $19.99 for adults and $16.99 for children under 42 inches. Children under age 3 are free with paying adults. A Nite Splash is $12.99. Arcade tokens are 25 cents each; miniature golf starts at $5.00, and go-karts start at $6.00. (386) 258-0071.

Daytona Beach Drive-in Christian Church. 3140 South Atlantic Avenue, Daytona Beach Shores 32116. Drive-in movies have all but disappeared, but Florida still has a few drive-in churches like this one. Services are held Sunday at 8:30 and 10:00 A.M. Drive in and tune your radio to 680 AM or 88.5 FM. Nursery and toddler care are available in the church building for both services. (386) 767-2292 (fax only).

Daytona USA. 1801 West International Speedway Boulevard, Daytona Beach 32114. From I-95 or I-4, take the U.S. 92 exit and go east. Expect a sizzling half day of fast-paced fun, even if you're not a race fan. Start with the larger-than-life movie, then join a pit crew to change a tire. View displays of historic cars and drivers, make a recording of your report on a race, and try the "virtual" race machines. Tickets—$16.00 for adults, $13.00 for seniors, and $8.00 for children—pay for the indoor attractions and a tour of the Speedway and track when weather and conditions allow. The Richard Petty Driving Experience ($105) lets you take three laps at 150 miles per hour or more. Shop the gift store for NASCAR collectibles. Open daily except Christmas 9:00 A.M. to 7:00 P.M., sometimes later. (386) 253-7223; www.daytonausa.com.

Halifax Historical Museum. 252 South Beach Street, Daytona Beach 32114. The museum is worth visiting once to see the displays and often thereafter to participate in special events such as moonlight river walks or candlelight museum nights. It's housed in one of Daytona's earliest buildings in a row of shops, an architectural delight, now filled with specialty items. Admission is $3.00 for adults and $1.00 for children under age 12. Open Tuesday through Saturday 10:00 A.M. to 4:00 P.M. (386) 255-6976; www.halifaxhistorical.org.

Klassix Auto Attraction. 2909 West International Speedway Boulevard, Daytona Beach 32124. Located a mile west of the Speedway and across from the Daytona Flea Market, Klassix is a treat for gearheads of all ages. Or stop in for a treat at the old-fashioned ice cream parlor (no admission necessary). See classic and collectible cars and motorcycles and famous cars from the movies and television, such as the Munsters' Drag-ula and the TV Batmobile. Open daily 9:00 A.M. to 6:00 P.M. Admission is $9.00 for adults and $4.50 for children. (386) 252-3800; www.klassixautom.com.

LPGA International. 300 Champions Drive, Daytona Beach 32124. This is just one of the many, many golf courses in the area, but it ranks as one of *Golf Magazine*'s "Top 10 You Can Play" public-access courses. It's the headquarters of the Ladies Professional Golf Association, but men can also play this eighteen-hole, par 72 championship course. Collared shirts are required. Greens fees and other fees apply. The course's restaurant is a fun little place for lunch. (386) 274-5742.

Main Street Pier. At the end of Main Street at the ocean is a fishing pier and an old-fashioned honky-tonk waterfront loaded with fun. Ride the Sky Lift, climb the Space Needle for an eagle's view of the sea, or rent tackle and go fishing. $–$$. (386) 238–1212.

Museum of Arts and Sciences. 1040 Museum Boulevard, Daytona Beach 32124. This is one of the state's finest small museums and home to three blockbuster attractions. One is the largest and most complete giant sloth skeleton ever found. This 150,000-year-old leviathan was found in a clay pit near here. Second is the largest collection of Cuban art in the free world. Third is the Root collection of railroad cars and memorabilia, Coca-Cola memorabilia, and quilts. The museum also has a sculpture garden, Florida wing, and galleries filled with permanent exhibits and a changing panorama of special shows. The children's wing, filled with hands-on exhibits, is worth a special trip with the kids. Admission is $5.00 for adults and $1.00 for children; planetarium shows are $3.00 and $2.00. Open daily except Monday. (386) 255–0285.

Arrange through the museum to tour the **Gamble Place** on the 175-acre Spruce Creek Nature Preserve. Built in 1907 by James N. Gamble of Proctor & Gamble fame, the estate has a typical old Florida house with antiques and exhibits, gardens, a citrus packing house, acres of primeval wetlands, and a whimsical playhouse built in 1938 following 1937's popular *Snow White and the Seven Dwarfs*.

Ocean Waters Spa. 600 North Atlantic Avenue, Daytona Beach 32118. Located in the Plaza Resort & Spa, this is a place to get away from it all for a day or half day. Construct your own day from a menu of eight massages, nine facials, salon treatments for men and women, nails, waxing, body wraps, tanning, or therapies. They're all priced a la cart; for example, $60 for a fifty-minute Swedish massage or $75 for a fifty-minute seaweed wrap. By appointment only. (800) 767–4471 or (386) 255–4471.

Seaside Music Theater. 1200 West International Speedway Boulevard, Daytona Beach 32118. The Seaside is in the Daytona Beach Community College Theater Center. Some performances are also held in the theater downtown at 176 North Beach Street. See Broadway favorites, enthusiastically performed. Ask your concierge what's playing. (386) 252–6200 or (800) 854–5592.

World's Most Famous Beach. Accessed at multiple spots along Highway A1A, the beach allows cars in some areas, so you can drive to a good spot and off-load the beach umbrella and playpen without having to haul everything from the parking lot. Swim near a lifeguard station (run-outs, stinging jellyfish, and sharks have been a problem), and observe the 10 mph speed limit. No alcohol, pets, or loud music allowed. Hours vary through the year. Beach access is $5.00 except for those with handicap ID. Nonresident passes are $40. The beach hot line is (386) 239–SURF.

WHERE TO SHOP

Angell & Phelps. 154 South Beach Street, Daytona Beach 32118. This has been a downtown icon since 1925. Let your nose guide you to a domain drenched in luscious chocolate sights and smells. Take a free guided tour Monday through Friday between 10:00 A.M. and 3:00 P.M. (call ahead), or shop Monday through Saturday 9:30 A.M. to 5:30 P.M. for fine chocolates, ice cream, and gifts for the chocoholic in your life. (386) 252-6531 or (800) 969-2634.

    Daytona Flea and Farmers' Market. U.S. 92 at I-95, Daytona Beach 32114. This is one of the world's biggest and best flea markets, as well as a place to shop for fresh produce and plants. Antiques are sold in an air-conditioned building. The two restaurants are also air-conditioned, and nine snack bars dot the massive complex. Admission is free. Open Friday through Sunday. (386) 253-3330.

WHERE TO EAT

Martini's On Bay Cafe. 101 Bay Street, Daytona Beach 32118. Martini's features multicultural fusion cuisine. Nightly specials feature food (surf and turf on Monday), discounted drinks, music (a DJ on Friday and Saturday spins acid jazz and Euro beats), or special treats (free chair massages on Thursday). This is where Generation X and older Generation Y hang out. Open 11:00 A.M. to 10:00 P.M., later on weekends. The martini bar is open daily until 3:00 A.M. $$. (386) 258-1212.

    Ocean Deck. 127 South Ocean Avenue, Daytona Beach 32118. This is a locally popular place for lunch, drinks at sundown, or after-dark noshing on seafood, sandwich platters, or pastas featuring sauces so popular that they're for sale by the jar. For snacks order a frigate of fries with chili and cheese, nachos, salsa and chips, or onion rings. Almost everything on the menu is under $10—but for a whimsical touch, you can add a bottle of Dom Perignon champagne for $125. Park behind the Reggae Republic. Open daily from 11:00 A.M. $. (396) 253-5224.

Park's Seafood Restaurant. 951 North Beach Street, Daytona Beach 32114. Just north of the Seabreeze Bridge, this place has been family owned and operated since 1976, a longtime local favorite for fresh seafood and steaks. Start with cocktails on the deck overlooking the Halifax River. It's also a fresh-fish market where you can pick out dinner to cook on your grill. Open daily for dinner; the market is closed Sunday. $$. (386) 258-7272.

Teauila's Hawaii Dinner Show. 2301 South Atlantic Avenue, Daytona Beach Shores 32116. Located in the Hawaiian Inn, this is one of the area's longest-running hits, and it never fails to charm. You'll dine on American and Polynesian foods while a whirl of hula, fire dancing, and sweet music surrounds you. It's a treat for all ages. Call for reservations for dinner or matinee shows. $$. (386) 255-5411 or (800) 922-3023.

WHERE TO STAY

Adam's Mark Daytona Beach Resort. 100 North Atlantic Avenue, Daytona Beach 32118. One of the finest hotels on the "world's most famous beach," this is the center of the massive new oceanfront complex called the Ocean Walk Resort. The complex begins with the beach, fishing pier and historic band shell and spreads over acres of hotel rooms, shopping space, dining venues, and entertainment. Rooms are smartly furnished and have in-room movies, hair dryer, iron and ironing board, minibar, dataports, and coffeemaker. The hotel has bars, lounges with entertainment, and casual and fine dining; or order from room service and dine on your balcony overlooking the sea. No cars are permitted on this part of the beach. $$-$$$. (386) 254-8200 or (800) 444-2326; www.adamsmark.com.

Best Western Mayan Inn Beachfront. 103 South Ocean Avenue, Daytona Beach 32118. It's hard to beat the value offered by this chain hotel, especially when you can find one right on the beach with a bountiful breakfast thrown in. All 112 rooms have an ocean view, and most have a balcony. Kitchens and Jacuzzi suites are available. Every room has a coffeemaker, free stays for kids under age 18 with parents or grandparents, cable TV with premium channels, in-room safe, and dataport. The pool is heated, which is a plus during Daytona's occasional cold spells. $-$$. (386) 252-BEST or (800) 443-5323.

Hilton Daytona Beach Oceanfront Resort. 2637 South Atlantic Avenue, Daytona Beach 32118. This high-rise hotel is right on the beach, with a sparkling pool, a wide swath of pristine sand, and the Atlantic beyond. Amenities include a kids' pool, whirlpool, gift shop, and fine dining or quick deli bites. Have a drink in the Blue Water Lounge overlooking the ocean. Every guest room has a refrigerator, voice mail, dataport, cable TV with pay-per-view movies, iron and ironing board, hair dryer, safe, and coffeemaker with free supplies. Balcony rooms are available, and the hotel also has six suites. $$-$$$. (386) 767-7350 or (800) HILTONS.

Key West Village. 1901 South Atlantic Avenue, Daytona Beach Shores 32118. This apartment hotel offers suites with one or two bedrooms, kitchen, living room with balcony overlooking the ocean, and a swimming pool surrounded by nice greenery. Children under age 12 stay free in parents' room; extra persons are $10 per day. $$. (800) 207-5420 or (386) 255-5394; www.anchoragebeachsuites.com.

Sun Viking Lodge. 2411 South Atlantic Avenue, Daytona Beach Shores 32118. This family resort offers free accommodations to children under age 17 in their parents' room. You don't have to worry about rowdy spring breakers here. Singles under age 25 aren't accommodated. Cribs are free, rollaways are $10 extra, and some of the units have sofa beds. Choose from a wide range of layouts ranging from a motel room with two queen beds to a three-bedroom cottage with full kitchen and beds for up to eight persons. The lodge lies on a sugar-sand beach where you can walk or ride a bicycle for miles. Planned activities include children's programs and a family ice cream social on Tuesday. Swim indoors or out, soak in the hot tub, and use Nautilus equipment in the fitness room. Dining and shopping are close by. Ask about packages, including golf deals. $-$$$. (800) 874-4469 or (386) 252-6252; www.sunviking.com.

Tropical Manor Beach Motel. 2237 South Atlantic Avenue, Daytona Beach 32118. Located on Highway A1A, this is one of Daytona's many small, resident owner-managed resorts. Other than having a refrigerator, all rooms are different, ranging from motel rooms to efficiencies, suites, and a fully furnished cottage that sleeps up to eleven. Balcony suites overlooking the Atlantic are perfect for a romantic weekend. Walk a block to a supermarket, or drive to a nearby fishing pier, charter boats, golf courses, and the Speedway. Restaurants are as near as next door. Picnic tables, chaises, barbecues, a gazebo, chairs, and tables with umbrellas are on the grounds for guest use. Adult and kiddy pools on the oceanfront are heated. $–$$ (ask about weekly rates). (386) 252–4920 or (800) 253–4920; www.tropicalmanor.com.

PALM COAST–FLAGLER BEACH

Barely a dot on the map a decade ago, Palm Coast has mushroomed into a major community, with miles and miles of residential streets filled with moderately priced homes. Older neighborhoods are along the coast and waterway. Both Flagler Beach and Palm Coast are north of Daytona Beach via I-95. Nearby Bunnell is on U.S. 1 just west of Flagler Beach.

WHERE TO GO

Bulow Plantation Ruins State Historic Site. Mail address: P.O. Box 655, Bunnell 32110. Find this wilderness on Old Kings Road, 3 miles west of Flagler Beach off County 2001 between State Road 100 and Old Dixie Highway. Major Charles Bulow was master of a 4,600-acre wetland along a tidal creek where sugarcane, cotton, and rice flourished. One of the rich planter's visitors was John James Audubon, who was charmed by the abundance of bird life here. By the outbreak of the Second Seminole War, the major was dead and his son in charge of the plantation. As the Seminoles became more hostile, Bulow and his slaves fled the property, which was subsequently burned by the Seminoles. Heartbroken, the twenty-six-year-old Bulow fled to Paris, where he died three months later. Hike among the ruins of the house, sugar mill, and slave quarters; have a picnic, or launch your boat in Bulow Creek, a state canoe trail. The park is open daily 9:00 A.M. to 5:00 P.M. Entry is $2.00 per vehicle. (386) 517–2084.

Gamble Rogers Memorial State Recreation Area. 3100 South Highway A1A, Flagler Beach 32136. On this barrier island bordered by the Atlantic to the east and the Intracoastal Waterway to the west, walk a nature trail through coastal scrub. Swim in the ocean, or fish in the creamy surf. Launch your boat on the ICW, picnic, or camp. Shelling can be good, especially at low tide. Watch shorebirds pick their way through the restless waterline, pecking at meaty morsels while pelicans soar in updrafts. May through September, sea turtles come ashore here to lay their eggs. Hiking trails, rest rooms, and picnic shelters are provided. Open 8:00 A.M. until sundown. State park fees apply. (386) 517–2086.

Princess Place Reserve. Princess Place Road (no mail address). From U.S. 1, take Old Kings Road (a dirt road) east, following signs. While this reserve isn't the most polished or accessible in the state, it has a fascinating story and is the home of the oldest existing homesteads in the county. The King of Spain granted this land to Francisco Pellicer in 1791. Later a settler planted orange groves, and in 1886 a wealthy New England sportsman, Henry Cutting, bought the grove and surrounding property along Pellicer Creek. His hunting lodge is said to be the only Adirondack Camp–style structure in the state. It has stables, tennis courts, and the first in-ground swimming pool in the state. Cutting died and his widow married an exiled Russian prince, thus becoming a princess. They returned to the grove, known ever since as Princess Place. Because the reserve is at the confluence of Pellicer Creek and the Matanzas River, it's alive with birds, small mammals, and a profusion of plant life. Bring a picnic lunch; there are no facilities. The reserve is open during daylight hours. Taking shape here is the Florida Agricultural Museum, so facilities will gradually be added. Call the Flagler Beach Chamber of Commerce at (800) 881–1022 or the Flagler County Chamber at (800) 298–0995 for information. The museum's number is (386) 446–7630.

Washington Oaks State Gardens. 6400 North Oceanshore Boulevard, Palm Coast 32137. This 400-acre preserve on Highway A1A is built around flourishing gardens that were established for a private home in the 1930s. Picnic, walk along a bouldery shoreline pounded by surf, or stroll along the river under towering live oaks past azaleas and mirrored ponds. Stop at the interpretive center, housed in the original 1930s home, to learn about natural flora and fauna, then hike the nature trails. Open daily 8:00 A.M. to sunset. Admission is $3.50 per vehicle. (386) 446–6780.

WHERE TO EAT

Chicken Pantry. U.S. 1 South, Bunnell 32110. This is a country place that reels in the city folk for mountains of Southern fried chicken, black-eyed peas, green beans, squash, eggplant, and all the trimmings. Turkey with dressing is served on Thursday; fresh St. Augustine shrimp or macaroni and cheese leads the fare on Friday. For lunch have a club sandwich and a platter of onion rings. Open for breakfast, lunch, and dinner 7:00 A.M. to 8:00 P.M. daily except Sunday. $–$$. (386) 437–3316.

 Cracker Barrel. 4 Kingswood Drive, Palm Coast 32136. This is an outlet of the popular roadside chain that everyone loves for the rustic decor and modest prices. Order your favorite comfort food: chicken and dumplings, eggs and grits, Salisbury steak with real mashed potatoes, or roast pork with applesauce, followed by a slab of pie. It's open most of the time and can be crowded at peak times, but it's big and well organized so waits are usually bearable—especially if you shop the country store until your name is called. $–$$. (386) 445–2127.

 Flagler's. 300 Clubhouse Drive, Palm Coast 32136. Located in the Palm Cost Golf Resort, Flagler's is a haven of elegance and cool after a vigorous day on the golf course or tennis courts. The cuisine is New American, focusing on fresh ingredients, local seafood and produce, and hints of unusual herbs and spices. There's live entertainment on weekends. Open for breakfast, lunch, and dinner, with a terrific Sunday brunch. Reservations are recommended. $$$. (386) 445–6357.

 Topaz Cafe and Porch. 1224 South Oceanshore Boulevard, Flagler Beach 32136. One of the most popular restaurants between Jacksonville and Daytona Beach, the Topaz is known for its varied and unpredictable menu, fine wine list, and creative, eye-popping desserts. The chef might be offering chateaubriand for two, the fresh catch of the day prepared in a new way, vegetable strudel, or rack of lamb. Start with one of the toothsome appetizers, such as macadamia shrimp with pineapple salsa. Come here for an unforgettable evening of fine dining, with live music on weekends. Hours vary according to the season, so call ahead and make reservations, which are essential. $$$. (386) 439-3275.

Wings Sports Bar & Grill. State Road 100 (between I-95 and U.S. 1), Bunnell 32110. Located at the Flagler County Airport, this is a favorite hangout for aviation groupies and sky divers who are serious about their burgers, fries, local seafood, pies, and a good cuppa joe. Listen to the buzz, watch a takeoff or two, photograph a colorful sky filled with 'chutes, and eat hearty, not fancy. Open for breakfast, lunch, and an early dinner. Call ahead for hours. $-$$. (386) 437-0410.

WHERE TO STAY

Best Western Plantation Inn. 2251 Old Dixie Highway, Bunnell 32110. This is a reliable, traveler-friendly roadside inn handy to exit 90 off I-95. Stop in for a swim, a meal in the restaurant, and a restful night at modest prices. Continental breakfast is included. Pets are permitted. $$. (396) 437-3737; www.bestwestern.com.

Palm Coast Golf Resort. 300 Clubhouse Drive, Palm Coast 32137. This 154-room country retreat is located in the still-quiet corridor north of Daytona Beach. Play the highly rated Palm Coast Players Racquet Club and the Ocean Hammock Golf Course designed by Jack Nicklaus, who designed six holes overlooking the Atlantic. There's also a choice of courses designed by Arnold Palmer, Ed Seay, Gary Player, and Bill Amick. The resort has three swimming pools, a marina, weight room, spa, and miles of jogging paths. All suites have French balconies, oversize baths, double-sink vanities, and Roman tubs. Dine in the stately Flagler's, known for its fine seafood, steaks, and luncheon buffets. It's open for breakfast, lunch, early-bird dinner, and dinner. $$-$$$. (386) 445-3000 or (800) 654-6538; www.palmcoastresort.com.

Topaz Motel & Hotel. 1224 South Highway A1A, Flagler Beach 32136. This property has been here since the flapper era but in recent years has become very "in," a favorite weekend hideaway for job-weary fugitives from nearby cities. Rooms overlook the Atlantic; the restaurant, the Topaz Cafe, has been listed by *Florida Trend* as one of the top 200 restaurants in the state. The motel consists of standard rooms that are predictable, clean, and comfortable. The hotel, by contrast, is more of a B&B, furnished in antiques. Discuss your preferences when you make reservations, because so many different accommodations are available. Pets are welcome in the motel but not the hotel. $$–$$$. (386) 439-2545 or (877) 635-5535.

White Orchid Bed & Breakfast. 1104 South Oceanshore Boulevard, Flagler Beach 32136. Located on Highway A1A, this romantic spa getaway on the ocean has a heated swimming pool and an extensive menu of spa treatments and services, ranging from LaStone Therapy ($110) to a Chakra Radiance Facial ($75), plus packages that include half a dozen or more services. Included in the rates are a full breakfast and wine with afternoon snacks. Ask for a room with a two-person Jacuzzi, and let your hosts arrange everything else you'll need, from fine dining to suggested sight-seeing. Bicycles are available for guest use. All spa packages include use of the mineral pool. $$$. (386) 439-4944; www.whiteorchidinn.com.

ST. AUGUSTINE

From Orlando, zip northeast on I-4 to Daytona Beach, where you pick up I-95 and a quick route northward to America's oldest city and, just north of it, one of Florida's least known but most exclusive beach communities. The scenic route is Highway A1A, which you might pick up at Flagler Beach, Crescent Beach, or Palm Coast. It takes you past Marineland, no longer the tourist attraction it once was as Florida's first marine park but now a development and research station. Beaches, beach overlooks, parks, beach motels, and beach restaurants line the route and make the going slower but more interesting than the interstate. The beaches of St. Johns County alone (Marineland to Ponte Vedra) stretch for 42 miles.

Timucuan Indians lived well in this area, tending crops and harvesting shellfish, until the coming of the Spanish in 1513, more than seventy years before Sir Walter Raleigh founded his English settlement on what is now the Outer Banks of North Carolina. By 1565 French Huguenots had arrived. Massacre followed, with the Catholic Spaniards driving out the Protestant French. Sir Frances Drake burned St. Augustine in 1586, but the strongly fortified Spanish settlement held until 1763, when Florida was ceded to Great Britain by Spain under the terms of the Treaty of Paris, which ended the French and Indian War. Twenty years later, another treaty gave Florida back to Spain for almost forty years before it became a U.S. territory.

Ponte Vedra Beach

A1A

Vilano Beach
St. Augustine
St. Augustine Beach

Crescent Beach

95

A1A

Northeast Day Trip 3

N

0   Miles

History can be confusing; the following St. Augustine timeline will help:

Amerindian Period	Prehistory to mid-1500s
First Spanish Period	1513–1763
British Period	1763–1783
Second Spanish Period	1783–1821
U.S. Territory Period	1821–1845
U.S. Statehood Period	1845–1861
Confederate Period	1861–1865
Reconstruction Period	1865–1877

Visitors come back to St. Augustine time and again to try the great variety of accommodations, from lavish beach and golf resorts to bed-and-breakfast inns housed in 400-year-old buildings. You can spend years of weekends just trying the B&Bs. World Golf Village is new and trendsetting. Casa Monica, which dates to the flamboyant Flagler railroad era, is a luxury hotel steeped in rich history.

The Marriott at Sawgrass Resort alone has ninety-nine holes of world-class golf. World Golf Village is home to the Senior PGA Tour's Legends of Golf Tournament. The Ponte Vedra Inn & Club is the home of a 1974 Robert Trent Jones classic course, and the eighteen-hole course at the Radisson Ponce de Leon Golf and Conference Center was designed by Donald Ross himself. In fact, the whole area is such a golf destination that there's a separate booking number just for golf vacations: (800) 653–1489; www.Getaway4Golf.com.

In the "living history" attractions, people go about their daily tasks as though it's still the seventeenth or eighteenth century, so visits here are always new, always absorbing. During reenactments, which occur often throughout the year, it's a time warp to be entered time and again. Wear period clothing and join in. Driving is difficult, parking impossible, so park at the visitor center and sightsee on foot, in a horse-drawn carriage, or on the trolley.

In addition to the hot spots listed in the next section, take time to visit the historic churches and cemeteries, where the thoughtful traveler will find the real history and passion of this centuries-old city. Christian Indians were buried in the Tolomato Cemetery across from the Castillo; the National Cemetery on Marine Street has been used as a burial ground since 1763 and is the resting place of soldiers killed during the Second Seminole War. The Huguenot Cemetery, a burying place for Protestants, who weren't permitted burial in the Catholic city, was probably named for the French Huguenots who arrived in 1564. All the churches have a story, a monument, a shrine, or a placard that will enrich your understanding of St. Augustine's history. The Cathedral of St. Augustine, Memorial Presbyterian Church, St. Photios Chapel, and Trinity Episcopal are usually open for sight-seeing. Ancient City Baptist, Grace United Methodist, and St. Ambrose Catholic Church are historically significant churches that are usually open only during worship services.

Note that Anastasia Island and St. Augustine Beach are the same community. The names are used interchangeably and have the same ZIP code. A car is required to get to the historic area from the island.

WHERE TO GO

Castillo de San Marcos National Monument. 1 South Castillo Drive, St. Augustine 32085. This is the heart of the city, a fortress with echoing dungeons and walls that never fell to enemy invasion. It's the oldest masonry fort in the nation, dating to 1672. Allow an hour or more for exploring the rambling ramparts, seeing exhibits, chatting with costumed characters, and photographing sea views from the highest towers. Admission is $5.00 for adults and $2.00 for children ages 6 to16. Open daily except Christmas 8:45 A.M. to 4:45 P.M. (904) 829-6506.

Faver-Dykes State Park. 1000 Faver-Dykes Road, St. Augustine 32086. The park follows wildly beautiful Pellicer Creek through pine flatwoods and mesic hammock, 15 miles south of St. Augustine. The park offers family camping with electric hookups, picnic tables, rental canoes by reservation, fishing, and nature walks. State park fees apply. Open 8:00 A.M. to sundown daily. (904) 794-0997.

Fort Mose. Two miles north of St. Augustine off U.S. 1; watch for signs. There isn't a lot to see here, but you'll feel the powerful history of a community of free blacks who escaped from their owners in the Carolinas and took refuge in Florida, where slavery was not practiced under Spanish rule. When the British attacked from Georgia, blacks fought on the Spanish side; when the British won Florida in a European treaty deal, most blacks fled to Cuba. The fort is open during daylight hours; admission is free. (800) OLD-CITY.

Fountain of Youth. 155 Magnolia Avenue, St. Augustine 32084. Touristy but with a serious, archaeological side, this was the site of the Indian village of Seloy, noted by Ponce de Leon. See the old spring, the burial grounds for Indian Christians, and the site of the first settlement of St. Augustine. Take the tram or walk the park. Hours vary seasonally, so call ahead. Admission is charged. (904) 829-3168.

A Ghostly Experience walking tour. The tour starts at the north end of St. George Street at 8:00 P.M. nightly. A 500-year-old city is sure to have a lot of ghosts, legends, and juicy stories, which are described by lantern light as you walk with a guide for ninety minutes of spooky, good fun. It's G-rated, so don't hesitate to bring Grandma and the kids. Everyone pays $8.00 except children under age 6, who walk free. (888) 461-1009; www.ghosttoursofstaugustine.com.

Government House Museum. 48 King Street, St. Augustine 32084. This museum takes you through the city's history from early Native American settlements through the Flagler era. See gold and silver from Spanish shipwrecks, archeological treasures, and presentations that walk you through the city's culture, history, and economy in quick and digestible bites. Open every day except Christmas 9:00 A.M. to 6:00 P.M. (904) 825-5033.

Kayak in the rivers and wetlands that surround St. Augustine. For lessons and canoe or kayak rents, call Anastasia State Park Canoe and Kayak Concession (904-471-9463); Coastal Kayaks (904-471-4414); Outdoor Adventures (904-393-9030); or Whole Earth Outfitters (904-824-6161). For information about area water sports, hiking, and outdoor adventures, request the *Recreation Guide* from the St. Johns County Visitors & Convention Bureau. (See Regional Information).

Lightner Museum. King Street, St. Augustine 32085. Located in the City Hall Complex, this museum offers a gilt trip into an ornate Victorian era. Housed in what was built in 1888 as a luxury hotel, the museum shows antique musical instruments, costumes, furniture, and works of Louis Comfort Tiffany. See the hotel's old casino, grand ballroom, and what was once an indoor swimming pool. Admission is $6.00 for adults and $2.00 for children ages 12 to 18. Children under age 12 are admitted free with an adult. Hours vary seasonally, so check ahead. (904) 824-2874; www.lightnermuseum.org.

Memorial Presbyterian Church. 36 Sevilla Street, St. Augustine 32084. The church was built by a grief-stricken Henry Flagler after he received word that his daughter, Jennie, had died delivering his first grandchild. Workers toiled around the clock to finish this magnificent structure in one year, and it opened on the first anniversary of her death. Flagler and his family are buried here in the magnificent Venetian Renaissance structure. Open daily 8:30 A.M. to 4:30 P.M. Free. (904) 829–6451.

Old St. Augustine Village Museum. 250 St. George Street, St. Augustine 32084. The main entrance is on Bridge Street. A complex of nine ancient buildings, galleries, and gardens, this is a place to spend half a day. Costumed interpreters pose as French pirates, Spanish conquistadors, seventeenth-century cooks, storekeepers, and Cracker cow hunters in an era when Florida was a rawboned frontier. Check the *Village Almanac* to see what's doing today and where. One of the houses was once the home of Napoleon's nephew, Prince Murat, a place where Ralph Waldo Emerson wrote and movie star Greta Garbo dined. On the grounds are the ruins of a colonial fort, the oldest hospital, and one of the oldest bridges in the United States. Open daily except Christmas 9:00 A.M. to 5:00 P.M. Admission is $7.00 for adults, $6.00 for seniors, and $5.00 for children. (904) 823–9722.

St. Augustine Trolley Tours are arranged through your hotel or at the Old Jail Complex, 167 San Marco Avenue, St. Augustine 33084. The 7-mile narrated tour is the best way to get oriented in the city before striking out on your own. Tours run 8:30 A.M. to 5:00 P.M., and you can get off and on as you please. There's a wide range of prices and options, $12 to $70, depending on whether a package includes admissions. All tickets are good for three days. (904) 829–3800 or (800) 397–4071.

St. Augustine Alligator Farm and Zoological Park. Highway A1A South, St. Augustine Beach (mail address: P.O. Drawer 9005, St. Augustine 32085). Cross the Bridge of Lions, then turn right on A1A. One of Florida's oldest attractions, this has evolved from a mere curiosity to an important refuge and breeding ground for gators, which were once overhunted to the point where they needed protection. Spend the day. Walk boardwalks through wetlands to see nature's harmony in birds, buzzing insects, small mammals, monkeys, and slithery alligators. Special shows and exhibits highlight a spectrum of Florida wildlife from parrots to snakes, plus imports from all over the world. Bring the children to learn about nature's beasts, including one of the world's greatest collections of crocodilians. Admission is $14.25 adults and $8.50 children; under age 5 free. Discounts for AAA and seniors. (904) 824–3337.

Spanish Quarter Museum. Mailing address: P.O. Box 210, St. Augustine 32085. The complex spreads along St. George Street from Government House Museum to the Spanish Quarter Museum. Start at Government House to see exhibits explaining 500 years of city history, then go to the Spanish Quarter to see them come alive. "Townspeople" in authentic costumes go about their daily lives as merchants, carpenters, soldiers, homemakers, gardeners, and idlers. They'll be glad to talk to you about their concerns with hunger, homesickness, the fear of English invasion, or the next attack of malaria or yellow fever. Admission is $2.50 for adults and $1.00 for children for Government House and $6.50 adults, $5.50 seniors, and $4.00 for children ages 6 and up for the Spanish Quarter Museum. Open daily except Christmas 9:00 A.M. to 5:30 P.M. (904) 825–5033; www.historicstaugustine.com.

St. Augustine Sight-seeing Trains. 170 San Marco Avenue, St. Augustine 32084. These narrated tours are the best way to get your bearings and some background before you set out on your own. Park at the visitor center just north of the Castillo, one of the few places in the historic area with ample parking, and see the orientation films, then take a tour. Trains cover 7 miles, with twenty scheduled stops where you can get off, stay as long as you like, then reboard. Tickets are good for three days. Call for rates for seven different tour plans. Admissions to attractions are extra. (904) 829–6545 or (800) 226–6545; www.redtrains.com. A number of other tours are available, from flight-seeing to individually guided tours on foot or by carriage. Ask about them while you're at the visitor center, or call (800) OLD–CITY.

St. Augustine Lighthouse & Museum. Red Cox Road, St. Augustine Beach. Climb to the top of this 165-foot tower off Highway A1A for a bird's-eye view of the area. See artifacts from shipwrecks including the British sloop *Industry*, which was lost on St. Augustine Bar on May 6, 1764. See the working Fresnel lens, hear the story of the "mission impossible" restoration of the damaged light, see the lighthouse keeper's quarters, and shop for lighthouse memorabilia in the gift store. Hours are daily 9:00 A.M. to 6:00 P.M., with longer hours in summer. Admission is $6.50 for adults, $5.50 for seniors age 55 and over, and $4.00 for children ages 7 to 11. Note that children must be at least 7 years old and 48 inches tall to climb the 219 steps to the tower. Free museum admission and activities are offered to children under age 7 with an accompanying adult. (904) 829-0745.

San Sebastian Winery. 157 King Street, St. Augustine 32084. This is a surprising find in a state that has so few wineries. Taste the wines, including a delightful cream sherry, then shop for wine by the case, wine gifts and accessories, and gourmet foods. There's plenty of parking for cars and even big RVs. Admission is free. Open Monday through Saturday 10:00 A.M. to 6:00 P.M. and Sunday 11:00 A.M. to 6:00 P.M. (904) 826-1594 or (800) 352-9463.

Victory 111 sails out of the Municipal Marina south of the Bridge of Lions on a seventy-five-minute cruise of the waters just off the Old City. She's skippered by members of a family that has been here for 500 years, so the narration is informative and exciting. See the shore as seen by the earliest Spanish and English settlers. You'll also see a world of wildlife and, with luck, bottlenose dolphins. Adults are $9.50, $7.00 for ages 13 to 18, and $5.00 for children ages 4 to 12. Sailings are daily except Christmas, but schedules vary seasonally. (904) 824-1806 or (800) 542-8316.

World Golf Village. 21 World Golf Place, St. Augustine 32092. An entire community devoted to golf, it's the home of the PGA Tour Golf Academy, a 300-seat IMAX theater, the World Golf Hall of Fame, two par-72 golf courses, plus restaurants and resorts. (see Where to Stay). Play The King & The Bear golf course, designed by Arnold Palmer and Jack Nicklaus, or The Slammer and The Squire, designed by Gene Sarazen and Sam Snead. Walk the half-mile-long Walk of Champions around Kelly Lake on granite slabs signed by members of the World Golf Hall of Fame. Play the eighteen-hole putting course, and dare the 132-yard Island Challenge Hole. Dine in the **Murray Brothers' Caddy Shack, Sam Snead's Tavern,** or the many hotel restaurants; and shop for golf memorabilia, including autographed mementos, at the museum store. The village also has a toy shop, art studio, ice cream and fudge, a travel shop, and a fly-fishing center where you can buy supplies or take lessons in fly-tying or casting.

Sign on for lessons from top professionals at the PGA Tour Golf Academy, then try your skills in the Full Swing Golf Simulator in the Renaissance Resort. If you stay on the grounds, excursions can be booked for the historic area. (800) WGV-GOLF or (904) 940-4000.

WHERE TO SHOP

Belz Factory Outlet World. 500 Belz Outlet Boulevard, St. Augustine 32095. From I-95, take the State Road 16 exit. Seventy-five stores are spread under one roof here. Shop for bargains in such brands as Fossil, Zales, Samsonite, Nike, Timberland, Black & Decker, Le Creuset, Royal Doulton, Polo Ralph Lauren, Coleman camping equipment, Tommy Hilfiger, and many more. When you're hungry, choose among the snack shops and fast-food places. Open daily. (904) 826-1311. Also at this exit, the **St. Augustine Outlet Center** offers ninety-five more stores and a trolley to take you around. Shop for books, Harry & David, Levis, Jockey, Van Heusen, Seiko, L'Eggs/Hanes, and dozens of other famous names. Open daily except Thanksgiving and Christmas; limited hours on Easter. (904) 825-1555.

Old City Farmers' Market in the St. Augustine Amphitheater, Highway A1A South, Anastasia Island 32084. The market is open Saturday morning only, selling home-grown produce, homemade baked goods, and lovingly tended plants. Free programs on nature and wildlife are also offered. On Tuesday morning, the same spot hosts a combination farmers' market and flea market. (904) 824-8247. A farmers' market is held on Wednesday morning, rain or shine, at 370 Beach Boulevard, St. Augustine Beach. (904) 471-8267.

Whetstone Chocolate Factory. 2 Coke Road, St. Augustine 32084. This is a working chocolate factory where you can see a video, take a self-guided tour, and shop for delectable chocolates and souvenirs in the Factory Outlet Store. Open Monday through Saturday 10:00 A.M. to 5:00 P.M. (904) 825-1700.

World Golf Village. 1 World Golf Place, St. Augustine 32092. This is one of the largest and most complete golf-related shops in the state. Shop for clothing, logo merchandise, gifts, souvenirs, golf-theme accessories and furnishings for the home, and the finest golf equipment. Hours vary, so call ahead. (904) 940-4000; www.wgv.com.

WHERE TO EAT

Aruanno's. Highway A1A at D Street, St. Augustine Beach 32080. Aruanno's has been a local favorite since 1982, specializing in seafood, veal, and steak with an Italian accent. The long appetizer list offers calamari, minestrone, escargot in mushroom caps, and other favorites.

There's rack of lamb as well as shrimp and a long list of pasta classics. Every week the chef comes up with a new and interesting special. Open daily for dinner except Monday. $$. (904) 471-9373.

Barnacle Bill's. 14 Castillo Drive, St. Augustine 32084. The fresh catch of the day can be served fried or broiled at this popular seafood center located across from the Visitor Information Center. Order gator tail, mahi-mahi, red-hot wings, oysters, scallops, catfish, or one of a half dozen shrimp concoctions. If you don't do seafood, there's steak, chicken, and ribs. The combination platters are fun and adventurous for big eaters. $-$$. Open daily 11:00 A.M. to 9:00 P.M. (904) 824-3663.

Basket Case. 9B King Street, St. Augustine 32084. Located in the heart of the historic district, this place will bring an order to you anywhere in that area—a godsend if you're staying in a B&B that serves only breakfast. Or call in a take-out order for a day at the beach. Boar's Head deli meats and cheese make up the long list of sandwiches. Order Cuban-style beans and rice or sandwiches, a Reuben, beer, wine, or one of the special coffees or lattes, espresso, frozen latte, or cappuccino. Gift baskets can be made for any occasion, so surprise your travel partner with a festive take-home picnic. Open every day at 10:00 A.M. $. (904) 810-2299.

Columbia Restaurant. 98 St. George Street, St. Augustine 32084. This is an outlet of the family-operated chain that was founded in Tampa in 1905. Don't miss the classic 1905 Salad. The paella takes some advance planning but is worth the wait. It can be ordered for a couple or a crowd. Try one of the fish dishes, meltingly tender beef and pork, or the chicken with yellow rice, all served traditionally with rice and beans and fried plantains. All the desserts are good, but the flan is irresistible. After you eat, don't miss the gift shop. Open daily for lunch and dinner and for Sunday brunch. Call for reservations, which are strongly recommended. $$-$$$. (904) 824-3341.

Conch House. 57 Comares Avenue, St. Augustine 32084. Dine in a Caribbean island resort where you can enjoy your meal in a grass shack right on the water. Start with a honeydew daiquiri or the goombay smash. Breakfast choices range from conventional waffles and omelettes to tangy *huevos rancheros*. At lunch, have a veggie burger, Caribbean chicken sandwich, shrimp and chorizo, or a specialty burger. Fried seafood, including cracked conch, is on both the lunch and dinner menus. So are a tempting list of salads and appetizers.

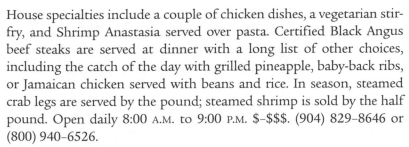

House specialties include a couple of chicken dishes, a vegetarian stir-fry, and Shrimp Anastasia served over pasta. Certified Black Angus beef steaks are served at dinner with a long list of other choices, including the catch of the day with grilled pineapple, baby-back ribs, or Jamaican chicken served with beans and rice. In season, steamed crab legs are served by the pound; steamed shrimp is sold by the half pound. Open daily 8:00 A.M. to 9:00 P.M. $-$$$. (904) 829–8646 or (800) 940–6526.

Cortessés Bistro. 172 San Marco Avenue, St. Augustine 32084. The bistro is also home to the Flamingo Room and some of the city's most sizzling nightlife. Come for cocktails and dinner, then stay for the jazz. The menu offers a huge choice ranging from soups and "light plates" to salads, hot and cold sandwiches, pasta specials, and a bistro menu (herb-crusted lamb chops, Minorcan fish stew, veal Oscar, and Black Angus beef) served from 5:00 P.M. on. The international wine list is impressive. Open daily for lunch and dinner. $$-$$$. (904) 825–6775.

Dairy Queen. 100 San Marco Avenue, St. Augustine 32084. Deliciously out of place in the midst of all this oldness, DQ is a beacon of familiarity where you can pick up a take-out meal or eat in cool comfort. The menu is pretty simple: hotdogs and hamburgers with fries. Kids like the Pick-Nic meals that include a sweet and a toy. The Blizzards, Smoothies, and Mud Slides are indescribably delicious on a hot day. $. Open daily 7:00 A.M. to 10:00 P.M., until 11:00 P.M. on Friday and Saturday. Lunch served from 10:00 A.M.

Gypsy Cab Company. 828 Anastasia Boulevard, St. Augustine 32084. In an ideal location between the historic district and the beach, this place serves what they call urban cuisine. It starts with a great soup from a choice that includes Bahamian clam chowder, cream of chicken tarragon, black bean, lentil, or gazpacho. Then come appetizers and salads. For lunch have the grouper, chicken with black beans and rice, Italian sausage sauté, or Seafood Santa Fe. Dinner entrees include chicken stuffed with Gorgonzola, veal in bacon-horseradish cream, braised lamb shank, and much more. The Florida peach cake and hazelnut icebox cakes are favorite desserts. Open every day for dinner from 5:30 P.M.; weekend brunch is served 10:30 A.M. to 3:00 P.M. The Gypsy Bar & Grill next door serves tapas, appetizers, and drinks. Live entertainment is offered Wednesday, Friday, and Saturday nights. $-$$. (904) 824–8244.

Harry's Seafood Bar & Grille. 46 Avenida Menendez, St. Augustine 32084. New Orleans lives in the Old City in a laidback restaurant that serves fried oyster po'boys, red beans and rice with smoked sausage, crawfish, gumbo, or Catfish Pontchartrain. The menu is as wide as Bourbon Street, offering burgers, fish, fried platters, soups, and just plain steaks or chicken for those who don't do Cajun. Have the bananas Foster for dessert. There's a children's menu, and kids get Mardi Gras beads to keep. $$. (904) 824-7765.

The Kings Head British Pub. 6460 U.S. 1 North, St. Augustine 32084. If you love all things English, come here for the pub ambience (darts, "draught" ales on tap), and pub grub such as fish-and-chips, steak and kidney pie, bangers and mash, pasties, and Scotch eggs. Vegetarian dishes are available, too. On Sunday make reservations for a traditional roast beef and Yorkshire pudding feast. On the first Sunday of the month, classic and antique cars gather here. Open daily except Monday. $$. (904) 823-9787.

La Pentola. 835 South Ponce de Leon Boulevard, St. Augustine 32084. Located in the Sebastian Harbor Marina Mall, La Pentola's gifted chef creates pastas, fresh seafood, and meats in the Mediterranean tradition. Start with escargot or Brie baked in crust, then choose one of the many pastas, including a vegetarian selection. Or order fresh fish, shrimp, lamb, steak, veal, pork or chicken, served with rosemary-garlic potatoes and all the trimmings. Wild game and other exotics are a house specialty, and there's an impressive list of wines and beers. Open for lunch and dinner daily except Sunday. Reservations are suggested. $$. (904) 824-3282.

La Strada. 4075 South Highway A1A, St. Augustine Beach 32080. This pleasant Italian bistro offers indoor or patio dining on classics (lasagna, veal Marsala) or inventive specialties (penne with cauliflower, raisins, and pine nuts or roasted duckling in cranberry and port wine sauce). Open daily for dinner; early birds are served 4:30 to 6:00 P.M. Reservations are suggested. (904) 471-0081.

Le Pavillon. 45 San Marco Avenue, St. Augustine 32084. Le Pavillon is a Continental restaurant in one of the city's fine old homes downtown. Luncheon main dishes include the quiche of the day, a choice of salads, an omelette, or an oyster platter, as well as any of the dinner entrees, which are available during lunch. Begin dinner with oysters, escargot, the soup of the day, or the pâté, then dine lightly on one of the half dozen crepes choices (Florentine, beef and mushroom,

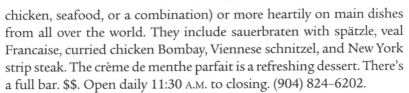

chicken, seafood, or a combination) or more heartily on main dishes from all over the world. They include sauerbraten with spätzle, veal Francaise, curried chicken Bombay, Viennese schnitzel, and New York strip steak. The crème de menthe parfait is a refreshing dessert. There's a full bar. $$. Open daily 11:30 A.M. to closing. (904) 824–6202.

95 Cordova. 95 Cordova Street (at King Street), St. Augustine 32084. Elegance has been reborn at this restaurant in the splendid Casa Monica Hotel, one of the great railroad hotels built at the turn of the twentieth century. Have a drink first in the Cobalt Lounge, then try the New World Eclectic cuisine in the dining room and return to the lounge for dancing to live music. Open breakfast through dinner; for lighter dining, pick up pastries and sandwiches in the Gourmet Deli ($) to take on a picnic or enjoy on the patio. $$$. (904) 810–6810.

O. C. White's. 118 Avenida Menendez, St. Augustine 32084. Dining is simple and basic in this old Spanish structure overlooking the marina, Bridge of Lions, and bay—good fish or meat with salad, vegetables, and freshly baked bread. Try the crab cakes, scallops, a steak or chicken specialty, or the shrimp. There's live entertainment for happy hour Monday through Friday. Open every day for dinner and for lunch in season. $$. (904) 824–0808.

Raintree. 102 San Marco Avenue, St. Augustine 32084. This restaurant is operated by a couple who sailed from England to America on their 45-foot yacht, bought a Victorian building that took them ten months to restore and turn into a restaurant, and lived happily ever after. The food is superb, the wine list one of the finest in the state, and the dessert bar a world in itself. Many people come here just for dessert, coffee, and a nightcap, but do treat yourself to dinner here sometime. Menu highlights include mahi-mahi and blue crab baked in puff pastry, beef Wellington, cashew-crusted pork tenderloin, Black Angus beef, and much more. $$$. (904) 824–7211.

South Beach Grill. 45 Cubbedge Road, Crescent Beach 34242. On the ocean a block south of State Road 206 on Highway A1A, this casual spot where you dine outdoors almost at the water's edge is a favorite with beachgoers. The catch of the day is served grilled, blackened, or sautéed, or have the fragrant cioppino made with half a dozen different seafood treats. Chicken fajitas are served in a wrap, or you can get a Black Angus sirloin steak, chicken jambalaya with andouille sausage, or the chargrilled chicken breast house specialty. Platters, burgers, and wraps are popular at lunch. Open for lunch and dinner daily; early-bird specials and happy hour from 4:30 to 6:00 P.M. $-$$. (904) 471-8700.

Verrazano Pizza & Sub. Publix Plaza, St. Augustine Beach 32084. Verrazano's is a New York–style pizza joint where you can't go wrong on the pizzas, poppers, hot and cold subs, or a spaghetti dinner. Delivery is free anywhere on the island. The menu is pretty standard, with anything you'd want in a pizza topping. There are also calzones and saucy meatball or chicken hot subs. Dinner choices are spaghetti with meatball, eggplant Parmesan with spaghetti, or chicken Parmesan with spaghetti, all served with bread and salad. $. (904) 461-9797.

Zaharia's Restaurant & Lounge. 3496 Highway A1A South, St. Augustine Beach 32084. Lamb, chicken, choice steaks, and fresh seafood are served with a Greek or Italian accent at this longtime, family-run favorite. Start with calamari, escargot, or oysters Rockefeller, then choose from the kebabs, prime rib, fresh fish, ribs, and much more. Children get their own menu. There's a full bar. Dinner dishes are available from 3:00 P.M., and early-bird specials run till 7:00 P.M. Open daily until 9:30 P.M. Reservations are accepted. $$. (904) 471-4799.

WHERE TO STAY

Note: St. Augustine has far more historic bed-and-breakfast inns than can be listed here. If you like the personal service and homey ambience of a B&B, book through www.Getaway4Lovers.com, or request a list of Superior Small Lodgings (hotels under fifty rooms that meet the program's standards) from (800) OLD-CITY. Decide if you want lodgings on the beach, handy to the interstate west of town, or in the old city, where almost everything is within walking distance. If your focus is on the restoration area, it's handiest to stay here, park the car at your lodgings, and walk everywhere.

Anastasia Inn. 218 Anastasia Boulevard, St. Augustine 32080. Just across the Bridge of Lions, this is an excellent location for getting to the beach, the old city, shopping, sight-seeing, and restaurants. It's a modern two-story motor hotel with refrigerator, microwave, and coffeemaker in every room, satellite TV with HBO,

heated swimming pool, and a whirlpool. City tours pick up free at the hotel. If you fly in, ask about the airport shuttle. Continental breakfast is included. $$–$$$. (904) 825–1879 or (888) 226–6181.

Beacher's Lodge. 6970 Highway A1A South, St. Augustine 32086. This condo-style hotel offers oceanfront suites with furnished kitchenettes, a guest laundry, and cable television. Swim off the beach or in the oceanfront pool. There is no restaurant on site. $$–$$$. (904) 471–8849 or (800) 527–8848.

Casa Monica Hotel. 95 Cordova Street, St. Augustine 32084. The Casa Monica is a splendid restoration of a grand hotel built in 1888 to lure affluent travelers to Florida on Henry Flagler's railroad. Flagler didn't spare the horses when it came to extravagance in design, furnishings, and service. With the restoration of the hotel, the golden age is back. Walk to attractions and restaurants in the old city. Swim in the second-story pool. Work out in the fitness center, and don't miss the fine dining in the hotel restaurant. Take a guest room or one of the romantic tower suites. $$–$$$. (904) 827–1888 or (800) 648 1888.

Centennial House. 26 Cordova Street, St. Augustine 32084. This property has been restored from rafters to roost to create romantic rooms with gas fireplaces, luxury baths with oversize whirlpool tubs, cable television, and VCRs (choose your program from the video library). The hotel's in the heart of the historic district, within walking distance of attractions and restaurants. Watch horse-drawn carriages pass on Cordova Street, or find privacy in the garden courtyard away from city sounds. Rates include full breakfast. $$$. (800) 611–2880 or (904) 810–2218; www.centennialhouse.com.

Clarion Inn Historic Downtown. 1300 Ponce de Leon Boulevard, St. Augustine 32084. This is a good choice for those who want to stay in the historic area and prefer the amenities of a motor inn. It's the home of a Denny's Restaurant and Riley's Pub and is handy to sight-seeing, shopping, other restaurants, and the historic area. Rooms have coffeemaker, hair dryer, 25-inch television with free HBO, and iron and ironing board. The big swimming pool is long enough for swimming serious laps. Ask about AAA and AARP discounts. $$–$$$. (904) 824–3383.

Comfort Inn. 901 Highway A1A South, St. Augustine Beach 32080. This property is a short walk from the beach. Suites have Jacuzzi tubs and kitchenettes. Ask if you want a microwave and refrigerator. Rooms have two doubles or a king and big TVs with cable channels including HBO. There's a big swimming pool and a heated whirlpool. Continental breakfast is included, but there is no on-site restaurant. $$–$$$. (904) 471-1472 or (800) 221-2222; www.comfortinnstaugbeach.com.

Comfort Suites at World Golf Village. 475 Commerce Lake Drive, St. Augustine 32095. If golf is your game, this place puts you in the center of s 6,300-acre resort that is devoted to world-class golf. Swim in the heated indoor or outdoor pool and work out in the fitness center. Each of the suites has a separate bedroom, living area with sofa sleeper and desk, and a wet bar with microwave, refrigerator, and coffeemaker. Two phones have dataports. Rates include continental breakfast. $$$. (800) 228-5150; www.hotelchoice.com.

Hampton Inn. 430 Highway A1A Beach Boulevard, St. Augustine 32080. This hotel is right on the snowy sands edging the Atlantic surf. Play beach volleyball, use the fitness center, swim in the pool, soak in the whirlpool, and enjoy a free continental breakfast each morning. Family and Jacuzzi suites are available. Ask about a microwave and refrigerator, and be sure to specify an ocean view. $$–$$$. (804) 471-4000 or (800) HAMPTON; www.elitehospitality.com/hampton. (*Note:* The 800 number can also be used to book Hampton Inns in the historic district, west of town near the outlet mall, and north of here on Vilano Beach.)

Holiday Inn. 860 Highway A1A Beach Boulevard, St. Augustine Beach 32080. Step out the door to the pool and, just beyond it, the Atlantic beach. This is the home of Crabbies Bar & Grill, open seasonally, and the year-round Beach Garden Restaurant. Room service is available. Shopping and additional restaurants are nearby. Kids stay and eat free. $$–$$$. (904) 471-2555 or (800) 626-7263.

Penny Farthing Inn. 83 Cedar Street, St. Augustine 32084. In this six-room inn on three floors, you can sleep in an elegant bedchamber with a private bath, fireplace, and whirlpool tub. Relax on the porch swing, or take a personalized bicycle tour. There's parking on site—a plus because you can walk to historic attractions without worrying about a parking place. Rates include a full breakfast. $$–$$$. (800) 395-1890 or (904) 824-2100; www.pennyfarthinginn.net.

St. Francis Inn. 279 St. George Street, St. Augustine 32084. One of the oldest structures in town, dating to 1791, the inn is as handy to everything today as it was centuries ago. There are sixteen guest rooms with plenty of choices in size, location, and decor. Some rooms have a private balcony, fireplace, and/or whirlpool. The inn has a Mediterranean-style garden courtyard, sometimes with live music, a swimming pool, in-room phones and cable television, bicycles for guest use, and private parking. Guests get free admission to the St. Augustine Lighthouse and Museum. Included in rates are the evening social and a buffet breakfast. $$–$$$. (800) 824–6062 or (904) 824–6068; www.stfrancisinn.com.

Sheraton Vistana Resort at World Golf Village. 100 Front Nine Drive, St. Augustine 32092. Nightly rentals are available at this one- and two-bedroom time share resort. Each villa has a private patio and full kitchen. Swim in the heated outdoor pool, play volleyball, or take to the lighted tennis courts; stroll out the door and you're on the golf course. Ask about golf packages and priority reservations at twenty-five area courses. $$$. (904) 940–2000 or (800) 477–3340; www.vistana.com

World Golf Village Renaissance Resort. 500 South Legacy Trail, St. Augustine 32092. A destination in itself, this plush resort is surrounded by 6,300 manicured acres dotted with two, eighteen-hole championship golf courses designed by Jack Nicklaus and Arnold Palmer. The resort is inland, so this isn't a beach vacation, but it has great swimming pools, grounds, and activities as well as the golf, so bring the family. Dine in a variety of restaurants, or order from room service. Enjoy the billiards room, cigar room, twenty-four-hour health club and sauna, and a big gift shop; enroll the children in the kids' club. All units have in-room coffee, wet bar, refrigerator, two TVs, two phones, and hair dryer. Suites have balconies and microwaves. $$$. (904) 940–8000 or (800) HOTELS–1; www.renaissancehotels.com.

PONTE VEDRA BEACH

Today this area just north of St. Augustine is one of the most affluent areas of northeast Florida, home to millionaires and tony resorts. It has a fascinating history. During World War I, when minerals were mined from local sands for the war effort, the place was called Mineral City. The first golf course was built here in 1922 for the use of miners. During World War II, four German soldiers came ashore here from a submarine, carrying explosives and intent on sabotage. (They were caught before they did any damage.) A marker on the beach shows their landing place. On the sands of Pablo Beach in 1922, Jimmy Doolittle took off for San Diego, breaking a transcontinental air speed record and earning the Distinguished Flying Cross. Since earliest explorations, the beauties of these beaches have attracted adventurers, hoteliers, and travelers in search of the solace of waved-washed sands. From St. Augustine, cross the bridge to Vilano Beach and follow scenic Highway A1A north to Ponte Vedra Beach.

WHERE TO GO

Bicycling is the ideal way to see Flagler and St. Johns Counties with their endless acres of conservation areas and parks, Washington Oaks State Gardens, beaches, and designated bicycle routes. For a map of the bicycle trails, contact the Northeast Florida Regional Planning Council, 9143 Phillips Highway, Suite 350, Jacksonville 32256; and request *Bike Ways of Northeast Florida.* (904) 363–6350.

Guana River State Park. 2690 South Ponte Vedra Boulevard, Ponte Vedra Beach 32082. The park comprises a vast expanse of golden marshes, pine flatwoods, coastal strand habitat, and miles of beaches as flat as a mirror. One account by a Spanish historian leads today's researchers to think that these lands may have been the site of Ponce de Leon's first explorations in the sixteenth century. Fish in fresh water or salt, boat on the Guana and Tolomoto Rivers, swim and surf in the Atlantic, and hike or bike 9 miles of unpaved service roads. Bring your binoculars for the nature watching and a picnic lunch to spread on a beach blanket. The park is open 8:00 A.M. to sundown every day. State park fees apply. (904) 825–5071.

WHERE TO STAY

Ponte Vedra Inn & Club. 200 Ponte Vedra Boulevard, Ponte Vedra Beach 32082. This property has been dispensing excellence in hospitality since 1928. Stay in an ocean-view room or suite that has an oversize bathroom, robes for him and her, designer toiletries, twenty-four-hour room service, and nightly turndown service. In the morning you'll find the newspaper outside your door. The inn does a lot of conference business, but it's also a favorite for families or romantic getaways. Children ages 4 to 12 have their own programs

June through August. The resort is best known for its two eighteen-hole golf courses, but there's also a sophisticated spa, a racquet club with fifteen Har-Tru courts, a business center with everything you'll need to stay in touch with the office, fishing, boating, a gym with individual Cybex stations, and four big oceanfront swimming pools. On the beach, kayaks, beach umbrellas, and beach chairs are available for rent. Dine in the elegant Florida Room, the rustic Outpost, or informally in the Golf Club or Surf Club. Have a drink in the Audubon Lounge, dance in the Seahorse Lounge, or have a frozen specialty drink at sundown in High Tides. $$$$. Ask about packages. (904) 285-1111 or (800) 234-7842; www.pvresorts.com.

Sawgrass Marriott Resort. 1000 PGA Tour Boulevard, Ponte Vedra Beach 32082. Famed for its golf courses, this is a luxury resort by any standards, even if you don't go near the links. Luxuriate in the spa or swimming pools, hike or bicycle the sprawling grounds, and dine in a choice of casual or formal restaurants. Hotel rooms or spacious apartments are available in a wide range of prices and packages. $$$-$$$$. (904) 286-7777; www.marriottsawgrass.com.

N

0 Miles 40

Jacksonville
Ponte Vedra Beach
10
301
1
St. Augustine
95
17
100
Palatka
A1A
Hawthorne
19
Palm Coast
1
Flagler Beach
Crescent
City
Bunnell
95
Lake
George
17
11
Ormond Beach
40
Ocala
Barberville
Daytona Beach
National
Aston
De Leon
Springs
Forest
40
441
19
De Land
4
New Smyrna Beach
Altoona
Orange City
Cassadaga
1
Canaveral
National
Seashore
Eustis
Sanford
46
Leesburg
Mt. Dora
17
Lake
Harris
92
46
Indian
Titusville
Merritt Island
National Wildlife Refuge
Bushnell
417
Kennedy
Space Center
Clermont
50
Christmas
River
Orlando
528
95
Cape Canaveral
BEE LINE EXPRESSWAY
Cocoa
27
4
417
Cocoa Beach
33
1
A1A
Kissimmee
98
92
17
St. Cloud
Satellite Beach
Polk City
Poinciana
192
Melbourne
Auburndale
Lakeland
441
95
Haines City
Winter
27
Lake Kissimmee
State Park
FLORIDA
Sebastian Inlet
St. Rec. Area
Haven
Lake
Kissimmee
1
60
Bartow
Lake
Wales
TURNPIKE
Alafia River
St. Rec. Area
98
17
60
Pelican Island National
Wildlife Refuge
39
37
Vero Beach
64
Avon Park
Wauchula
Sebring
441
68
Fort Pierce
64
Highlands Hammock
State Park
27
98
70
A1A
17
70
Lake Placid
70
Arcadia
95
1

Leesburg
Polk City
St. John's R.

ATLANTIC
OCEAN

Christmas · Cape Canaveral

Head east from Orlando on State Road 50 and you'll be out of the traffic maelstrom by Christmas. It's no joke. There really is a Christmas, Florida, once just a quaint post office where people had their cards postmarked. Today it's quickly becoming a part of the Orlando crush, a greenspace and historic attraction. We've combined the communities from Titusville south through Merritt Island as one day trip known as Cape Canaveral which is the home of Merritt Island National Wildlife Refuge, Kennedy Space Center, Cocoa Beach, and other close-clustered spots just east of Orlando via Route 50.

Before you go you should be aware that the best beaches in the area for launch watching are Klondike, Floridana Beach, Canaveral National Seashore, Playalinda, and Sebastian Inlet. The best for lively beach action are Cocoa Beach, Satellite Beach, Indian Harbor Beach, and Melbourne Beach.

CHRISTMAS

During the Christmas season in 1837, as the Second Seminole Indian War raged in Florida, a force of 2,000 U.S. Army troops and the Alabama Volunteers established a supply depot in the pinewoods near this spot, handy to the St. Johns River. Most of them marched away to fight the Battle of Okeechobee on Christmas Day, but about eighty soldiers remained encamped here. By March, the fighting had moved southward and the fort was no longer needed.

Although the fort was manned for less than four months, a small community grew up around it. Today centered on busy U.S. 50, Christmas has a Christmas tree that is lit all year, a manger scene, and a post office where you can mail letters and cards that are stamped with the Christmas postmark.

WHERE TO GO

CARE Foundation. No mail address. One-quarter mile past Fort Christmas on Fort Christmas Road is a shelter for exotic animals that need special care. It's open only on Sunday 11:00 A.M. to 2:00 P.M., but come here to see who's in residence and what you can do to help. (407) 482–4092.

Fort Christmas Historical Park. Orange County Parks and Recreation Division, 4801 West Colonial Drive, Orlando 32808. Located 2 miles north of State Road 50 on County Road 420, the park is free and fabulous—a real slice of history in a wooded setting where kids can run wild around the playground and adults can picnic and relax or play tennis or basketball. Tour the fort, which houses an excellent museum. Stroll the grounds, where old Cracker homes, a school, and other historic buildings have been moved to save them from demolition. Covered picnic pavilions are available for rent by advance reservation. Admission is free. The park opens daily at 8:00 A.M. and closes at 6:00 P.M. in winter and 8:00 P.M. in summer. The fort-museum is open 10:00 A.M. to 5:00 P.M. Tuesday through Saturday and 1:00 to 5:00 P.M. Sunday. (407) 836–6200.

Jungle Adventures. 26205 East Highway 50, Christmas 32709. Gators are raised for meat and hides on this working alligator farm. Take a jungle cruise for a look at gators in their natural environment, then stock up on frozen alligator meat in the gift shop. See exotic cats, walk the nature trail, see a replica of an early Spanish fort, take a guided tour of a sixteenth-century Seminole village, and see a wildlife show starring wolves, snakes, Florida panthers, and alligators. Adults $14.50, seniors $11.50, and $8.50 for children ages 3 to 11. Open daily 9:30 A.M. to 5:30 P.M. (407) 568–1354; www.jungleadventures.com.

Tosohatchee State Reserve. 3365 Taylor Creek Road, Christmas 32709. The reserve covers 28,000 acres of wilderness that has been sculpted by fire and flood along the St. Johns River. Hike, bicycle the rugged trails, hunt or camp by permit, bring a horse to ride the trails, fish, or sit quietly to watch for wading and shorebirds, bobcats, gray foxes, gopher tortoises, owls, and other wildlife. Call ahead. (407) 568–5893.

CAPE CANAVERAL

The communities of Cape Canaveral are lumped together because it's likely you'll stay in one community, shop and dine in many others, and sightsee in them all during the same trip(s). Melbourne is the chief city here, with a major airport. Cape Canaveral is the entire area, referring to the cape that juts out into the Atlantic Ocean. It is the home of Kennedy Space Center, Canaveral National Seashore, and Merritt Island National Wildlife Refuge. Port Canaveral has grown into the second-busiest cruise ship port in the nation.

To reach Cape Canaveral from Christmas, continue east on State Road 50 (known as Colonial Drive in town and as Cheney Highway as it proceeds eastward), then go north or south on U.S. 1 or I-95 to your destination. Canaveral National Seashore and Titusville are north; just about everything else in this Day Trip is south.

WHERE TO GO

Ace of Hearts Ranch. 7400 Bridal Path Lane, Cocoa 32927. The ranch is an ecotourist's paradise. Call to see what's on the menu today: horseback rides on the beach, pony parties for little ones, a marshmallow roast, a rail ride along the river, or a wild airboat ride in the wetlands. In the petting zoo, make friends with Babe, the pig, as well as chickens, ducks, and other critters. Prices are a la carte and vary according to the activity. (321) 638–0104.

Airboat rides in the marshy uplands of the St. Johns River are available by reservation from Airboat Ecotours. (321) 631–2990 or (321) 638–9565.

Canaveral National Seashore. 308 Julia Street, Titusville 32796. This preserve is a 24-mile stretch of pristine beaches plus acres of wetlands, lagoons, dunes, and hammocks. To reach the visitor center, take exit 84A off I-95, then take State Road 44 east to Highway A1A, then south for 10 miles. Playalinda, Klondike, and Apollo Beaches are part of this massive play land, which also has sites for hike-in or boat-in camping. Most people come here for a day at the beach, but there's much more for the angler, nature lover, bird-watcher, backpacker, kayaker, and hiker. Note that part of the Seashore is called Mosquito Lagoon for good reason. Bring plenty of bug dope. If a stiff wind is blowing, though, you may not need it, especially right on the beach. Some beaches are closed in turtle nesting season, and prohibitions are strictly enforced. Don't trespass. (321) 428-3384.

Cocoa Village. 430 Delannoy Avenue, Cocoa 32922. Located on State Road 520 along the Indian River, the village is the historic heart of a coastal community that has grown west to the subdivisions and malls. Stroll brick sidewalks past old shops and former mercantiles that have been turned into smart boutiques and restaurants. The streets of the old village often ring with festivals, but street entertainers might be here on ordinary days, too. Shop for jewelry, clothing, gifts, collectibles, beads, books, and arts galore. Dine in one of the restaurants, and visit the specialty shops for pastries and gourmet foods to take home. If you write ahead for maps and information, you'll receive discount coupons. (321) 631-9075; www.cocoafl.com. Make an entire day of it by adding a lunch, brunch, or dinner cruise aboard the *Cocoa Belle*. Reservations: (321) 632-6262.

Kennedy Space Center Visitor Complex. Mail code DNPS, Kennedy Space Center 32899. From Orlando, take State Road 528 east to State Road 407 North and then State Road 405 East. The route to the complex is well marked, so follow the signs. The moment you enter, look at the day's schedule so that you can make the best use of your time. There's more here than can be done in one day, especially if you're a serious space follower.

The Astronaut Encounter is usually held three times a day, depending on the season, and it's your chance to chat with a real astronaut. Take one of the bus tours to see where launches take place, view the IMAX and 3-D movies, photograph the Rocket Garden, walk through the full-size replica Space Shuttle, and watch assembly of the next batch of equipment slated for the International Space Station. If the children get restless, take them to the Play Dome for some high-voltage fun.

Have lunch in one of the restaurants, or reserve well ahead to participate in the "Dine with an Astronaut" program. It's not offered every day, but for about $30 for adults and $20 for children you get a big meal, a special dessert called Chocolate Liftoff (complete with a chocolate space shuttle), an autographed souvenir, and the company of an astronaut, who will tell about his or her adventures in space.

Shop the gift store for one of the best selections of space souvenirs and educational space material on the planet. Real mission briefings are given hourly at the Launch Status Center. This is a living, working space center, always different and always in the news. For $25 for adults and $15 for children ages 3 to 11, get a Maximum Access Badge that buys admission, unlimited bus transportation, and the IMAX movies. Premium tours with extra stops are $20 additional. Launch tickets cost $34.50 for adults and $15.50 for children ages 3 to 11 for a package that includes bus transportation to the viewing site and a Maximum Access Badge. Tickets for launches are available from the ticket plaza at the visitor complex. Call (321) 449-4444, or visit www.KennedySpaceCenter.com. Shipping and handling are extra.

Merritt Island National Wildlife Refuge. The visitor center is 4 miles east of Titusville on State Road 402. In the shadows and smoke of giant rockets, an 140,000-acre wilderness is habitat to one of the largest and most diverse communities of common, rare, endangered, and threatened species in the United States, plus myriad plant communities of the forests, dunes, and wetlands. Start with orientation at the visitor center, where rangers and volunteers steer you right. Then take a self-guided drive along the one-way, 7-mile Black Point Wildlife Drive before striking off on foot on the 5-mile trail, complete with boardwalks and observation platforms. The visitor center is open Monday through Friday 8:00 A.M. to 4:30 P.M. and weekends 9:00 A.M. to 5:00 P.M. For safety reasons, the refuge is sometimes off limits during space launches. Admission is free. (321) 861-0667; www.merrittisland.fws.gov.

Osprey Outfitters. Guided kayak excursions are offered in the refuge. (321-267-3535) To learn more about the waterways, known as the Indian River Lagoon National Estuary, call (800) 226-3747.

U.S. Astronaut Hall of Fame. 6225 Vectorspace Boulevard, Titusville 32780. This is as much a must-see for space groupies as the Space Center itself. The heroes of the space frontier are honored here in displays and photographs, and you'll get a taste of space flight in a simulator. Drive the Shuttle Lander, ride a Mission to

Mars, tour a full-size replica of the Space Shuttle, test your reflexes in a Mercury capsule, and see how many Gs you can take. Admission is $13.95 for adults and $9.95 for children ages 6 to 12. The gift shop has serious space souvenirs, gifts and books, and you can eat in the Cosmic Cafe. Hours are 9:00 A.M. to 5:00 P.M. daily, with no one admitted after 4:00 P.M. Hours may be extended in high season. (321) 269-6100; www.AstronautHallofFame.com.

This is also the home of U.S. Space Camp Florida, where children and young adults can experience a five-day camp or children and their parents can plug into a parent-child weekend. For information on aviation programs, visit www.dogfite.com; for space camp details go to www.spacecamp.com.

Warbird Air Museum. 6600 Tico Road, Titusville 32780. The museum showcases military aircraft from the two world wars, Korea, and Viet Nam. You'll see the Valiant Air Command's fine collection of aviation memorabilia, including uniforms, gear, and arts. Many of the museum volunteers actually flew or worked on these birds, so don't be afraid to ask questions. The gift shop is well stocked with aviation gifts and collectibles. Hours are 10:00 A.M. to 6:00 P.M. except Thanksgiving, Christmas, and New Year's Day. Admission is $9.00 for adults and $5.00 for children age 12 and under. Military and seniors get in for $8.00. (321) 268-1941; www.vacwarbirds.org.

WHERE TO SHOP

The Irish Shop. 811 North Atlantic Avenue, Cocoa Beach 32930. The shop is located in the Galleria. Ask the Irish staff here about your favorite collectibles, Irish gifts and arts, and keepsake jewelry. They can even book you on a trip to the Emerald Isle. Hours vary seasonally, but it's generally open daily except Sunday 10:00 A.M. to 5:00 P.M. (321) 784-9707.

Ron Jon Surf Shop. 3850 South Banana River Boulevard, Cocoa Beach 32931. Ron's is a Florida icon, a must-see place to stop and shop along Highway A1A. Located 12 miles east of well-marked exits off I-95, the shop complex spreads over two acres—a galaxy of goods for the beach or surf. Stock up on everything from floats to swim suits, clogs, sunblock, T-shirts, surf boards, and beach balls. While the original is in New Jersey and clones are spreading all over the world, including Orlando and Fort Lauderdale, this is still Florida's first. Like the beach, it's open twenty-four hours a day, seven days a week. (321) 799-8888; www.ronjons.com

WHERE TO EAT

Bernard's Surf. 2 South Atlantic Avenue (Highway A1A), Cocoa Beach 32931. Bernard's gives you three eateries for the price of one. The big complex also contains Fisher's Seafood Bar and Grill and Rusty's Seafood and Oyster Bar (a clone is located in Port Canaveral in a picturesque setting in the shadow of the cruise ships). Show up early for happy hour and early-bird specials, or linger late over a lobster feast, fresh fish cooked to order, chicken, or a steak. Lunch on weekdays is a boffo buffet. Bring the kids, who will get their own menu. Hours vary seasonally, so call ahead. $-$$$. (321) 783-2401.

Corky Bell's Seafood. 4885 North U.S. 1, Cocoa 32926. Located between Cocoa and Titusville, Corky's is an old Florida landmark, delightfully ramshackle, where the deep fryer reigns and vegetarians find slim pickings. Seafood platters are bigger than Neptune's chariot. The rib-eye steak dinner with baked potato, onion rings, hush puppies, and coleslaw is a belly buster. Waits can be long, especially on Friday and Saturday nights, and they don't take reservations. $$. (321) 636-1392.

The Cove. 1462 State Road A1A, Satellite Beach 32937. The Cove has been a local favorite for half a century. Bring the whole family for wholesome dining, dancing, and fun. The restaurant is best known for its ribs, crab legs, and prime rib, but there are also seafood dishes, steaks, chops, salads, chicken, and a kids' menu. Dine inside or outdoors on the patio. $$-$$$. (321) 777-2683.

The Dove. 1790 State Road A1A, Satellite Beach 32979. This local icon is south of Patrick Air Force Base, and getting here on the seaside highway is part of the fun. The menu has an Italian accent with forays into the French Riviera. Your meal starts with a surprise appetizer of *pasta e fagioli*, so prepare yourself for a filling feast. Order a main course, and a salad will soon appear. Enjoy one of the veal dishes, chicken, fresh seafood, or a steak. A tangy lemon liqueur appears between courses. Open for lunch and dinner daily except Sunday. Reservations are recommended. $$-$$$. (321) 777-5817.

Durango Oak Fire Steakhouse. 3455 Cheney Highway, Titusville 32780. Located in the Space Shuttle Inn, the Durango does seafood as well as it does Colorado prime steaks. The oak fire is always burning, so you can order a grilled quesadilla, strip steak, Porterhouse, top sirloin, bacon-wrapped shrimp, Campfire Chicken, and other fire-seared treats. There's also meat loaf, pasta, main-dish salads, and a list of side dishes for those who prefer to order a la carte. At lunch try one of the mammoth sandwiches with a mountain of seasoned fries. For dessert, tackle the Chocolate Avalanche or apple cobbler. Open daily for lunch and dinner. $-$$. (321) 269-9100.

Fat Boys Barbecue. 4280 South Washington Avenue, Titusville 32780. It doesn't get more down-home than this, y'all. Dig into the famous Bar-B-Q Feast—priced by the couple, trio, quartet, or platoon—with ribs, chicken, beans, slaw, garlic bread, and much more. Also available are smoky sandwiches, burger platters, a luncheon buffet, charbroiled steaks, shrimp or catfish, or Brunswick stew. Breakfasts are brawny and bargain priced. Buy homemade jams and jellies to take home, and ask at the desk about shipping the barbecue overnight to your friends nationwide. Open daily, breakfast through supper. $. (321) 267-3468.

Gregory's Steak & Seafood Grille. 900 North Atlantic Avenue, Cocoa Beach 32926. Certified Angus beef stars at this popular hangout, where Groucho's Comedy Club upstairs has 'em rolling in the aisles every Thursday at 9:00 P.M. Make an evening of it. Have a drink from the full bar, then dine on a big steak, cooked to order, or the best in fresh local and flown-in seafood. Select the right wine from a comprehensive list. Open daily 5:00 to 10:30 P.M. $$-$$$. (321) 799-2557.

Pig & Whistle. 801 North Atlantic Avenue, Cocoa Beach 32931. Located in the Galleria, this is a real English pub, complete with dart board, beer on tap, fish-and-chips, and all your favorite pub grub, as well as hearty meat-and-potatoes fare. Play video games or pool. There's a full bar. Open daily 11:00 A.M. to 2:00 A.M. $-$$. (321) 799-0724.

Punjab. 285 Cocoa Beach Causeway, White Rose Center, Cocoa Beach 32926. The Punjab serves Indian cuisine, including clay oven specialties. Dishes are cooked to taste, with as much heat as you like or no heat at all. Open Monday through Saturday 11:00 A.M. to

2:30 P.M. and for dinner nightly except Sunday from 5:00 P.M. $–$$. (321) 799–4696.

Roberto's Little Havana. 26 North Orlando Avenue, Cocoa Beach 32932. This spot specializes in authentic Cuban sandwiches, main dishes, desserts, and coffees; they even serve Hatvey Cuban beer. Open daily except Sunday for breakfast, lunch, and dinner. $–$$. (321) 784–1868.

Royal China. 1275 North A1A, Cocoa Beach 32931. This is where chefs from mainland China create luscious Mandarin, Hunan, Cantonese, and Szechwan specialties as well as live Maine lobster and fresh fish, cooked to order. Request low-fat, low-salt, or no MSG; they're happy to oblige. They also offer a separate children's menu. Orders of $20 and more can be delivered. Open daily for lunch, early birds, and dinner; the lounge stays open till 2:00 A.M. $. (321) 784–8008.

Rum Runners. 695 North Atlantic Avenue (A1A), Cocoa Beach 32931. This is a must for visitors who like to party hearty in a good-times setting. Start with one of the fifteen rip-roaring specialty rum drinks. The clam chowder is a house specialty. Order from a long list of seafood, including the catch of the day, fresh crab cakes, frog legs, conch fritters, and shrimp. There's also chicken, pasta, and baby-back ribs. Open every day 11:00 A.M. to 2:00 A.M. $–$$. (321) 868–2020.

WHERE TO STAY

Best Western Space Shuttle Inn. 3455 Cheney Highway, Titusville 32780. This property boasts a steakhouse and lounge, heated swimming pool, sauna, video game room, playground, free HBO, a fitness park with a fishing lake, picnic area with gazebo, guest laundry, and complimentary continental breakfast. Also offered are many creative packages that include nature tours, space attractions, or a casino cruise. Port Canaveral is only thirty minutes away, so it's also an affordable place to stay before or after a cruise. $$. (800) 523–7654 or (321) 269–9100; www.spaceshuttleinn.com.

Clarion Hotel. 260 East Merritt Island Causeway (State Road 520), Merritt Island 32952. This hotel is everything a visitor could want in a home base for exploring the Space Coast or for a pre-

or post-cruise stay near Port Canaveral. The courtyard is surrounded by tropical greenery and centered by a swimming pool. Rooms have a coffeemaker, and king rooms also have a microwave and refrigerator. The hotel has its own restaurant, lounge, tennis courts, and fitness center. $$–$$$. (321) 452-7711 or (800) 584-1482; ww.clarionspacecoast.com.

Doubletree Oceanfront Hotel. 2080 North Atlantic Avenue, Cocoa Beach 32931. The Doubletree is the perfect pied-à-terre for a stay along the Space Coast. Book an oceanfront room with a private balcony, or splurge on the concierge floor, where special perks include a lounge with free breakfast and snacks. A Doubletree trademark is the freshly baked chocolate chip cookies that everyone receives on check-in. The hotel has an oceanfront lounge and restaurant serving Mediterranean cuisine, brick-oven pizza, and fresh seafood. Take the Beeline Expressway to where it turns south and becomes Highway A1A; the hotel is 5 miles south, on your left. $$$. (321) 783-9222, (800) 222-TREE, or (800) 552-3224.

Radisson Hotel at the Port. 8701 Astronaut Boulevard, Cape Canaveral 32920. This is a good choice for space travelers, cruisers, a romantic weekend, or a business trip. It isn't on the ocean, but it's only a mile from the home port of the Disney ships and has a big outdoor heated swimming pool. Two-room whirlpool suites have one or two king-size beds with a queen-size sofa sleeper. Two-bedroom suites have microwave, refrigerator, wet bar, and 32-inch television. Eat in the restaurant or order from room service. $$–$$$. (321) 784-0000 or (800) 333-3333; www.radisson.com.

Ramada Oceanfront Resort. 1035 Highway A1A, Satellite Beach 32937. This AAA three-diamond resort fronts the Atlantic, with private balconies and see-forever views. Ask for a business-class room if you need a desk, dataports, and other business aids. Rooms have a coffeemaker and full cable television. Swim off the sandy beach or in the heated pool. Play tennis, have a drink in the lounge, and dine in the gourmet restaurant. Don't miss the Sunday brunch. $$–$$$. (321) 777-7200 or (800) 345-1782.

Royal Oak Resort & Golf Club. 2150 Country Club Drive, Titusville 32780. Stay in a country club setting and play the championship eighteen-hole Dick Wilson golf course. The club is the winter home of many golf professionals, and the course provides a lovely stroll through rolling hills past sparkling lakes. Every room has a coffeemaker and refrigerator. Get a package that includes accommodations, eighteen holes of golf including greens fee and cart, a second round for the cart fee only, advance tee time reservations, and daily club storage and cleaning. Meals are served in the Terrace Room; a snack bar is halfway around the course. The resort also has an Olympic-size pool, driving range, and practice greens. $$–$$$. (800) 884-2150 or (321) 269-4500.

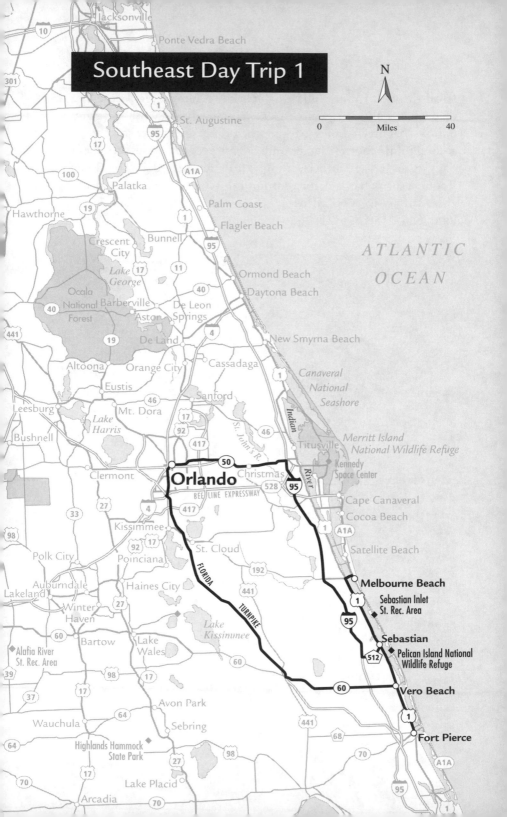

Sebastian Inlet · Vero Beach

SEBASTIAN INLET

Growth in Florida is spurting alarmingly, but developers and tourist hordes haven't yet overrun this stretch of the state. The community of Sebastian has parks, marinas, and yacht brokerages that lend a salty flavor and plenty of waterfront on the Intracoastal Waterway, the inlet, and the Atlantic. From Orlando, go east on State Road 50 or the Beeline to I–95, then south to the Sebastian exit.

WHERE TO GO

Mel Fisher's Treasure Museum. 1322 U.S. Highway 1, Sebastian 32951. The museum houses many of the treasures that illustrate why this is known as the Treasure Coast. Unknown numbers of Spanish galleons sank on reefs just offshore, and their bounty continues to wash ashore. View a movie on treasure hunting, take a guided tour, and shop for real treasures from real wrecks. Open daily 10:00 A.M. to 4:30 P.M. Admission is charged. (561) 589–9875.

Pelican Island National Wildlife Refuge. On the Indian River Lagoon between Sebastian and Wabasso. For information, write to addresses provided in the Regional Information section, or visit pelicanisland.fws.gov. The largest land network in the world dedicated to conservation of wildlife habitat and resources, this system spreads over ninety million acres and 500 geographically diverse refuges. Here you'll see loggerhead turtles, manatees, wood storks, green sea turtles, and bird life galore. This entire area is prime for birding, especially during spring and fall migrations. Call ahead to ask about boat tours. (561) 567–3520.

River Queen cruises. 1660 Indian River Drive, Sebastian 32951. Enjoy narrated sight-seeing and nature-watch trips on the Sebastian and Indian Rivers, usually at 10:00 A.M., noon, and 4:30 P.M. Bird spotting is excellent, and you may also see alligators, manatees, and bottlenose dolphin. Drinks and snacks are available on board. Dolphin-watch cruises last two and three hours; a sunset cruise that includes Pelican Island lasts about ninety minutes. Prices are $15.00 to $18.00 for adults, $10.00 for children ages 3 to 10; seniors get a $1.00 discount. Reservations are highly recommended. (888) 755–6161 or (561) 589–6161.

Sebastian Inlet State Park. 9700 South Highway A1A, Melbourne Beach 32951. This park is a favorite with surfers, offering some of the best combers in the East. It's also a great beach, park, and fishing area and the home to a museum housing real Spanish treasure. Arrive by car, or buzz over in your boat and dock at the marina. Bring a picnic lunch, everything you need for the beach, and your camera, and make a day of it.

In 1715 a Spanish treasure fleet wrecked off these shores, and a treasure museum, sparkling with booty, now stands on the site where the shipwreck survivors camped. Little could be salvaged at the time, but bits of treasure continued to wash ashore for centuries afterward. Three glorious miles of sands and dunes are set aside for swimming, surfing, snorkeling, and scuba diving (no spear fishing). Rent a canoe, runabout, or kayak. Take an ecotour of the Indian River aboard a forty-nine-passenger boat. In June and July take a ranger-led moonlight walk to watch turtles lay their eggs. A concession near the beach picnic area sells basic items and serves breakfast and lunch daily. Fees apply for tours and services, and there's a small park entry fee. The park is open during daylight hours. (321) 984–4852 for park information; (561) 589–9659 for camping reservations; (321) 724–5424 or (800) 952–1126 for the marina, boat rental, and boat tours.

Skydive Sebastian. 400 West Airport Road, Sebastian 32951. Everyone is welcome, from the merely curious to the experienced parachutist. If you're a novice but want to try a jump, you can be strapped to a seasoned diver and float to earth without a care. Skydive University is on site, training skydivers at all levels. Generally open during daylight hours; make an appointment for jumps. (800) 399-JUMP or (561) 388-5672.

WHERE TO EAT AND STAY

Key West Inn and Capt. Hiram's. 1580 U.S. 1, Sebastian 32958. Located on the Sebastian waterfront, Capt. Hiram's has indoor dining with weather control, or you can sit outdoors on the deck overlooking the river. There's live music after dark, so make an evening of cocktails, dinner, and dancing into the late hours. Seafood is cooked your way, including charcoal-grilled. Sumptuous sandwiches are popular at lunch. Peel-and-eat shrimp is available by the pound or half pound. Real Maryland crab soup shares the menu with crab cakes, shrimp, steaks, mussels, scallops, and chicken. The restaurant is open for lunch and dinner and has a delightful gift shop. The Bahamian Sandbar is right on the beach.

The inn offers rooms with balconies overlooking the water. Take a suite or efficiency apartment; rates include breakfast. From I-95, take exit 69; travel east on County Road 512 for 7.5 miles to U.S. 1, then left for another 0.5 mile. $$. (800) 833-0555 or (561) 388-8588; www.hirams.com.

VERO BEACH

According to one rating guide, little Vero Beach is one of the "Best Little Towns in America." It's also the winter home of the Los Angeles Dodgers. From Sebastian, follow U.S. 1 south to Vero Beach. (For a loop back to Orlando, take State Road 60 west to the Florida Turnpike and follow the pike north to Orlando. Just off the turnpike is a rest stop with picnic tables and a hiking path to Blue Cypress Lake.) Along the shore are end-of-the-world resorts. In town, find upscale shops and smart dining.

WHERE TO GO

Environmental Learning Center. 255 Live Oak Drive off Country Road 510, near the Wabasso Bridge. See a butterfly garden. Walk the boardwalk through a mangrove forest and look for coon oysters. Ask at the visitor center about canoe trips and workshops. The home of poet Laura Riding-Jackson is on the grounds. It's a fine example of practical, homespun Florida "Cracker" design. The center is open daily during daylight hours except Monday. The home is open Saturday 10:00 A.M. to 2:00 P.M. Admission is free. (561) 589–5050 for the center; (561) 589–6711 for the Riding-Jackson house.

Harbor Branch Oceanographic Tours. 5600 U.S. 1 North, Fort Pierce 34946. This is a serious research facility, not a tourist attraction, which makes for exciting discovery and participation. Tour the campus to observe whatever research is going on; visit a wildlife sanctuary and the aquaculture pavilion, and view a sculpture collection. Cruise Indian River Lagoon aboard a pontoon boat on the ninety-minute Lagoon Wildlife Boat Tour, while a kaleidoscope of birds swoop overhead; manatees or dolphins usually surface alongside. The gift shop offers marine novelties and 14-karat gold jewelry. Campus tours are $10.00 for adults and $6.00 for children ages 6 to 12; boat tours are $19.00 for adults and $12.00 for children. Both operate Monday through Saturday; call for tour times. (561) 465–2400, extension 688.

Indian River Citrus Museum. 2140 Fourteenth Avenue, Vero Beach 32960. This museum remembers the pioneers who made a living by planting the citrus groves that are still the backbone of this area's agriculture. The words "Indian River Fruit" will be more meaningful after you've seen early tools and memorabilia from a bygone era. Open Tuesday through Friday 10:00 A.M. to 4:00 P.M. Donations are appreciated. (561) 770–2263.

McKee Botanical Garden. 350 South U.S. 1, Vero Beach 32960. Located just south of Indian River Boulevard, the garden has been here since 1932, when a family established a "jungle garden" in a true tropical hammock. They planted exotics from all over the world, but interest faded when flashier attractions came to the Sunshine State. The garden was closed for almost twenty years before it was resurrected in 2001. Hurray for its comeback! Start with the fifteen-minute video, which includes some charming 1930s footage. Walk quiet trails to see vestiges of the Florida that used to be, on your own or with a guide, then stop in the cafe for lunch or a snack. Shop the gift shop for souvenirs, pottery, and unique gardening goodies. Hours are 10:00 A.M. to 5:00 P.M. Tuesday through Saturday and noon to 5:00 P.M.

Sunday. Admission is $6.00 for adults, $5.00 for seniors, and $3.59 for children ages 5 to 12. (561) 794–0601; www.mckeegarden.org.

Riverside Theatre. 3250 Riverside Park Drive, Vero Beach 32960. This is the only professional theater on the Treasure Coast. Two stages present more than 250 performances each year, so check ahead to see what will be playing during your visit. Musicals, drama, comedy, and children's theater are on the menu. (561) 231–6990 or (800) 445–6745; www.riversidetheatre.com.

WHERE TO SHOP

Blue Dog. 1966 Commerce Avenue, Vero Beach 32960. This shop features one-of-a-kind accessories for the home and garden. Shop for paintings, furniture, planters, sculpture, and much more. Hours vary seasonally, so call ahead. (561) 562–1919.

Prime Outlets. State Road 60 at I-95, Vero Beach. This is one of a chain of outlet malls known for big bargains on brand-name goods. Featured are Oneida, Springmaid Wamsutta, BOSE, Book Warehouse, Remington, Dooney & Bourke, Zales, Hush Puppies, Dexter, Bass, Polo Ralph Lauren, Versace, Liz Claiborne, and many more, plus a sumptuous food court. Hours are 10:00 A.M. to 8:00 P.M. Monday through Saturday and 11 A.M. to 6:00 P.M. Sunday. Closed Easter, Thanksgiving, and Christmas. (561) 770–6171 or (877) GO-OUTLETS; www.primeoutlets.com.

WHERE TO STAY

Disney's Vero Beach Resort. County Road 510 at Highway A1A, Vero Beach 32960. This is pure Disney magic, set on a brown sugar-sand beach. Have breakfast with Goofy any Saturday morning. Swim in the big pool. Take part in planned activities. Dine in the Green Cabin Room, where you can order from the regular or appetizer menu 3:00 to 10:00 P.M. Live entertainment is offered seven nights a week, so linger over drinks and coffee. Elegant dinners are also served at Sonya's Restaurant; the casual Shutters serves breakfast, lunch, and dinner. Suites are actually time-shares, available for rent by the night. $$$. (561) 234–2180; www.dvcresorts.com.

Dodgertown. 3901 Twenty-sixth Street, Vero Beach 32960. This is the spring training home of the Los Angeles Dodgers as well as an eighty-nine-villa complex where guests can play tennis and golf, work out in the fitness center, and swim in an Olympic-size pool. Villas have full kitchens and separate bedrooms with plenty of room for couples or families. $$$. (561) 569-4900; www.dodgertownverobeach.com.

Holiday Inn. 3385 Ocean Drive, Vero Beach 32963. Take an oceanfront suite with wet bar, microwave, toaster, and refrigerator or a king room facing the ocean or pool. Dine in the prestigious Treasure Coast Grill or informally on the pool deck. Enjoy live music in the Treasure Coast Pub. All rooms have refrigerators, coffeemakers, and a free copy of USA Today every weekday. $$-$$$. (800) HOLIDAY or (561) 231-8069.

Palm Court Resort Hotel. 3244 Ocean Drive, Vero Beach 32963. This hotel sits on its own 300-foot ocean beach, offering a long list of water-related fun from kayaking to surfing and snorkeling. It's a good base for exploring the Environmental Learning Center on Wabasso Island. Golf or tennis can be arranged nearby. $$-$$$. (800) 245-3297 or (561) 231-2800; www.palmcourtvero.com.

Vero Beach Inn Resort on the Beach. 4700 North Highway A1A, Vero Beach 32963. This is a good choice for "doing" Vero because it's on the pristine sand beach as well as handy to golf courses, tennis, water sports, and scuba diving. Book a double or king room, junior suite, or two-bedroom suite. Boogie boards, ironing boards, microwaves, and refrigerators are available to rent. There's no charge for the coffeemaker, hair dryer, pool towels, and iron. Swim in the spacious free-form pool, bubble in the hot tub, or run barefoot into the surf. The inn's restaurant serves breakfast, lunch, and dinner overlooking the ocean. $-$$$. (800) 277-8615 or (561) 231-1600.

St. Cloud · Melbourne

ST. CLOUD

Beginning in the 1870s, soldiers who had served in the Civil War drifted into central Florida to settle down on ranches or to cluster in small towns. St. Cloud retains some of the "cow town" flavor of those early years. Kissimmee and St. Cloud share one convention and visitor bureau, but it's rare to find St. Cloud mentioned in travel guides. That's because Walt Disney bought 50 square miles of land just west of Kissimmee, and most growth sprawled in that direction. St. Cloud, well to the east, plays a distant second fiddle, but that is just fine with most folks there.

At St. Cloud you can still find the Florida your grandparents saw when they came South in a pre-Disney era. Stroll the old downtown area to peek into boutiques, antiques shops, and cozy eateries. From Orlando, take the St. Cloud exit off the Florida Turnpike South and head east on U.S. 192. Stroll or drive the area from Tenth to Twelfth Streets on New York and Pennsylvania Avenues to find the best antiques shopping and offbeat dining.

WHERE TO GO AND EAT

Forever Florida and the Crescent J Ranch. 4755 North Kenansville Road, St. Cloud 34773. This massive 4,700-acre working cattle ranch and nature preserve honors the memory of the founder's son, who died of Hodgkin's disease when he was a teenager. While in the hospital, he shared his dream of preserving the area next to the ranch

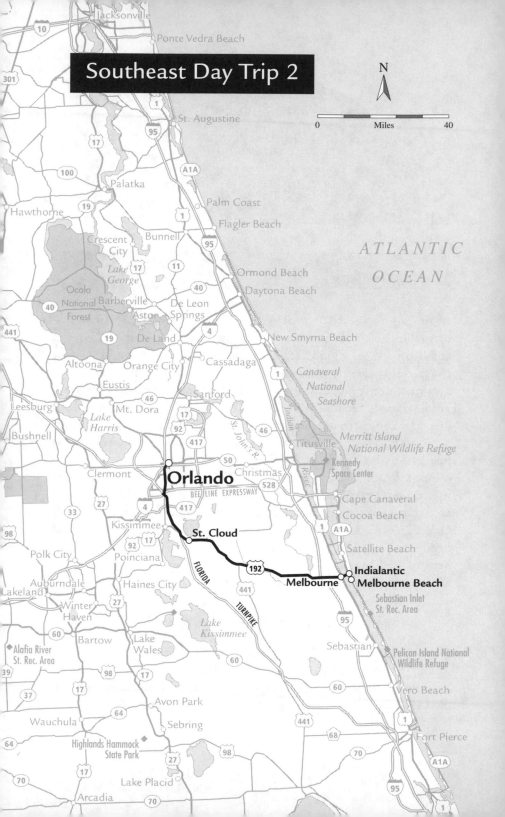

Southeast Day Trip 2

N

0   Miles   40

as a nature refuge, and his father, Dr. William Broussard, has made that dream a reality. Take a nature tour. See ranch and farm animals up close. Take a bicycle or horseback tour. Eat native Florida foods in the Cypress Restaurant, then relax in a rocker on the veranda or, if the day is cool, warm up next to the stone fireplace. Shop for gifts and souvenirs, or book a coach or covered-wagon tour. In the Bio Park, nature species including the red wolf, otter, and Florida panther have a refuge. Activities are priced a la carte. Call for reservations and information. (407) 957–9794 or (888) 957–9794.

MELBOURNE

Even though it's part of the Space Coast tourism orbit, Melbourne is much more than rockets. It's the site of an international airport that is a good alternative to flying into Orlando and is a major community with its own identity. To reach Melbourne from St. Cloud, go southeast on U.S. 192.

WHERE TO GO

Archie Carr National Wildlife Refuge. 1300 Highway A1A, Melbourne Beach 32951. This refuge protects one of the best places in the Western Hemisphere for loggerhead turtles to nest. Call to see if any ranger-led excursions are planned during your visit. The refuge also offers spectacular bird-watching. It's open every day during daylight hours. No admission charge. (321) 861–0667.

Brevard Zoo. 8225 North Wickham Road, Melbourne 32940. The zoo is home to more than 400 animals representing 109 species from around the world. In the free-flight aviary you'll see cockatoos, lorikeets, and a laughing kookaburra. In natural-appearing habitats see a dingoes, red kangaroos, wallabies, llamas, and giant anteaters. Weather permitting, take a guided kayak tour of the zoo's wetlands area for $10 additional. Also extra is a ride on the train, and you'll need a few dollars to buy nectar to hand-feed the birds. Kids love the Paws-On learning center. Bring a picnic lunch (tables are provided), or eat in the snack bar. Admission is $7.00 for adults, $6.00 for seniors, and $5.00 for children ages 2 to

12. Open daily 10:00 A.M. to 5:00 P.M. Closed some holidays, so call ahead. (321) 254–WILD.

Brevard Museum of Art & Science. 1463 Highland Avenue, Melbourne 32935. The museum has both live and static displays. Create music, witness a jazz performance, explore the art galleries, and let the kids linger among the hands-on exhibits. The museum shop is a good place to find science toys and projects. Admission for adults is $5.00, $3.00 for seniors, and $2.00 for children and students. Open Tuesday through Saturday 10:00 A.M. to 5:00 P.M. and Sunday 1:00 to 5:00 P.M. Closed Monday and major holidays. (321) 242–0737.

Dream Believer. Sea Pirate River Cruises, 705 South Harbor City Boulevard (U.S. 1), Melbourne 32901. You'll find it behind the Coral Bay Restaurant between the Eau Gallie and Melbourne Causeways. Take a dinner cruise, complete with a hot buffet dinner, live entertainment, and a cash bar. Stand on deck to enjoy the harbor lights and a starlit sky, or enjoy the nightlife scene with music and dancing. Reservations are essential. Fare including dinner is $30.50 for adults and $22.00 for children ages 3 to 12. A luncheon cruise with nature views of the Indian River costs $22 for adults and $16 for children. (321) 724–0024; www.seapirate.com.

WHERE TO SHOP

Catherine's Corner. 841 East New Haven, Melbourne 32901. This shop carries sunny and smart beach wear, casual resort togs, and cool, comfortable cottons for everyday wear. Open daily except Sunday 9:00 A.M. to 5:00 P.M. (321) 724–9335.

Super Flea and Farmers' Market. Located off I-95 at exit 72 in Melbourne, more than 900 booths sell fresh produce and everything else under the sun, from shoes to sunbonnets. Choose from a variety of vendors in the food court, where beer and wine are also sold. There's plenty of parking in the ten-acre lot. Open Friday through Sunday, rain or shine, 9:00 A.M. to 4:00 P.M. (321) 242–9124.

WHERE TO EAT

Barnhill's. 800 South Babcock Street, Melbourne 32901. Barnhill's is one of a Southeast chain, a sure thing if you love a big buffet feed with a lot for your money. Sirloin steak is in the lineup nightly, and there are also fried chicken, farm-raised catfish, plenty of other meats and vegetables, shrimp three nights a week, and a seafood buffet on Friday. For a list of other locations within two hours of Orlando (including Ocala, Orange City, Lakeland, and Leesburg), visit www.barnhills.com. Open daily for lunch and dinner. $-$$, with special pricing for children. (321) 728-8813.

Bonefish Willy's Riverfront Grille. 2459 Pineapple Avenue, Melbourne 32901. This spot offers a great view of the river, whether you're indoors or outside on the deck. Seafood is the star of the culinary show here, but landlubbers can choose beef or chicken. The beer is cold and the fritters crusty. Dress in casual resort duds, and enjoy the laid-back atmosphere. Open Tuesday through Thursday 4:00 to 10:00 P.M., Friday and Saturday 11:30 A.M. to 10:00 P.M., and Sunday noon to 9:00 P.M. $$. (321) 253-8888.

Conchy Joe's. 1477 Pineapple Avenue, Melbourne 32901. Conchy Joe's is on the river at the Eau Gallie Causeway. Stop in for Florida seafood with a Bahamian accent. Live reggae plays at the chickee bar, which is famous for its tropical drinks and rum punch. Snack at the raw bar, or dine on steak, seafood, chicken, ribs, or chops. Open daily for lunch and dinner. Happy Hour drink specials are served 3:00 to 6:00 P.M., and early-bird bargains are served every day 4:00 to 6:00 P.M. Waits can be long, especially on Friday evening. Reservations aren't accepted, so call ahead and ask the best time to show up. $$-$$$. (321) 253-3131.

WHERE TO STAY

Hilton Melbourne Airport. 200 Rialto Place, Melbourne 32901. This is the best place to stay before an early flight, but it's also a good pied-à-terre for touring the southern Space Coast, with all the hospitality bells and whistles to make up a carefree getaway they call a Hilton Bounceback Vacation. A full breakfast is included with room rates. The hotel is handy to the city's high-tech corridor and has business traveler–friendly desks, dataports, and on-site car rental. The lobby, lush with greenery and waterfalls, is a good place to see and be seen. The hotel has a swimming pool, hot tub, restaurant, lounge, fitness center, and lighted tennis courts. $$-$$$. (800) 437-8010.

Ocean Reef Club. 1333 South Miramar Avenue (Highway A1A), Indialantic by the Sea 32903. The club is a collection of oceanfront villas, so take your choice of a three- or four-room apartments with two baths, complete kitchen, private patio, cable television, and VCR. Two-bedroom units have one bathroom, living room, and kitchen. Largest units sleep up to seven. Rates are by the night, week, or month. $$–$$$. (321) 723-2951 or (800) 552-5848.

Windemere Inn by the Sea. 815 South Miramar Avenue, Indialantic by the Sea 32903. This dream of a bed-and-breakfast inn on the beach is elegantly styled and warmly traditional. Visit the Web site, look over the three Victorian-style rooms, and make your choice. Or just call for reservations and discuss the choices with the innkeeper. A gourmet breakfast comes with the deal. (321) 728-9334 or (800) 224-6853; www.windemereinn.com.

Poinciana · Lake Wales

POINCIANA

Poinciana isn't found on all road maps, but follow our directions and you'll find a sprawling wilderness untouched by time—and just south of Orlando. Begin by taking U.S. 17-92 south toward Haines City and turn east on Cypress Creek Parkway, State Road 580.

WHERE TO GO

Disney Wilderness Preserve. 6075 Scrub Jay Trail, Kissimmee 34759. Follow State Road 580 to Dover Plum, then right to the Conservation Learning Center. Off Pleasant Hill Road, Poinciana sets aside 12,000 acres at the headwaters of the Florida Everglades ecosystem to host rare scrub jays, bald eagles and their nests, bobcats, sandhill cranes, gopher tortoises, and lakes filled with large-mouth bass. Walk the self-guided trail for a look at Florida wilderness with all of its beauties and surprises. Bring binoculars and walk the 2.5- or 4.5-mile hiking trail. Take a trail walk with an interpretive guide on Saturday at 9:30 A.M. On Sunday at 1:30 P.M. take a buggy ride to observe longleaf pines and wetlands. Open daily 9:00 A.M. to 5:00 P.M. Call to confirm times for guides and rides. Hiking costs $2.00 for adults and children ages 6 to 17. Buggy rides are $7.00 and $5.00, respectively. (407) 935-0002.

LAKE WALES

One of the loveliest hamlets of central Florida's hilly lake country, Lake Wales suffers growing pains but still retains much of the charm that brought tourists here generations ago. The community is the home of time-honored Chalet Suzanne, and cattle graze miles of pastures in the surrounding countryside. From Poinciana, retrace your route west on State Road 580 to U.S. 27, then south to Lake Wales.

WHERE TO GO

Bok Tower Gardens. 1151 Tower Boulevard, Lake Wales 33853. The gardens have been here for generations of tourists and loyal locals, who love the ever-changing gardens and the song of the sixty-bell carillon. Gardens are spectacular in February and March when the azaleas bloom, but something is alight here year-round, even on the most bleak winter day. Sit in the shadow of the tower, or explore woodland paths. Bring a picnic or eat in the cafe. Save time for the gift shop and ice cream parlor. A half-mile trail leads through the Pine Ridge Preserve, a habitat of longleaf pine and turkey oak. Sometimes open to the public is the ravishing Pinewood House and Gardens, a textbook Mediterranean Revival home built in 1931 as the winter home of a steel magnate. Most furnishings are original to the house, which is a showplace when decorated for Christmas. Bok Tower Gardens admission is $6.00 for adults, $2.00 for children. Open daily 8:00 A.M. to 6:00 P.M., later when moonlight concerts are held. Additional charges may apply for Pinewood. (863) 676–1408; www.boktower.org.

    Lake Kissimmee State Park. 14248 Camp Mack Road, Lake Wales 33853. This is more than a great state park for hiking, fishing, camping, picnicking, boating, and wildlife watching. It's also the home of one of the most unusual living history performances in the South. Held only on weekends, Cow Camp re-creates the way Florida wranglers lived in the mid-nineteenth century. They weren't called cowboys, because the term "boy" was considered an insult in the old South. They were "cow hunters" who used long braided whips to "pop" cattle out of the scrub. Western-style cattle drives were impossible in Florida, where cattle hid in thickets and swamps. As you walk down the path from the parking lot, a century slips away and you're in a time warp. Ulysses S. Grant is president, and these cow hunters can't discuss anything that isn't known in the times in which they live. Authentic Florida scrub cattle and stout marshtackie horses, both introduced by the Spanish to survive in the hot, buggy swamps of Florida, are usually seen in the camp. The park is open every day 8:00 A.M. to sunset. (863) 696–1112; www.dep.state.fl.us/parks.

WHERE TO EAT

Gift Mill. 823 U.S. Highway South, Lake Hamilton 33851. Located north of Lake Wales, just south of Haines City, the Gift Mill is a general store with an old-time soda fountain, a place to browse as well as dine or snack. Bread bowls are a specialty of the house, filled with your choice of salads or hot combinations such as Oozing Italian Meatballs, Sissy's Chicken Stew, or the Wot-Ever Daily Special. Children can get a Teenie Beanie Wienie bread bowl filled with beans and wieners or their choice from the grown-up menu. Have a hearty whole-meal salad or a sandwich platter. Desserts focus on homemade fruit pies, including an apple pie with no added sugar. Or you can have homemade ice cream in a dip, sundae, waffle cone, or Chocolate Volcano. Open Monday through Saturday 9:00 A.M. to 8:00 P.M. and Sunday 10:00 A.M. to 6:00 P.M. $. (863) 439–5075.

Vinton's Grille. 229 East Stuart Avenue, Lake Wales 33853. Vinton's is the place for a relaxed night out, especially on Friday and Saturday nights, when there's live music. The extensive, eclectic menu begins with smart starters such as black bean and cheese spring rolls served with homemade salsa, baked French onion soup, or a tangy smoked-fish spread served with French bread. Make a meal of appetizers, or move on to the salads, especially the famous spinach salad, or a Cajun burger, blackened-fish sandwich, or a New Orleans–style mufuletta. If you want a hot dish, choose from the special of the day, seafood jambalaya, or the fish of the day served with rice and vegetables. Desserts are sumptuous, from the bourbon pecan pie to the homemade Key lime pie, and there are half a dozen fancy after-dinner coffees. Open Tuesday through Saturday 5:00 to 11:00 P.M. $$. (863) 676–8242.

WHERE TO STAY

Chalet Suzanne Restaurant and Inn. 3800 Chalet Suzanne Drive, Lake Wales 33853. This golden nugget of Florida history has a heartwarming story. During the Depression, Bertha Hinshaw was widowed with two children. She had a fine education for a woman of her times, had traveled abroad when her husband was alive, and was a sophisticated hostess and chef. So she hung out a shingle on U.S. 27, offering meals. One of her early drop-ins was famous food writer Duncan Hines. He praised her in his column, and soon Chalet Suzanne became one of Florida's most sought-after dining rooms. Four generations later, it is still family operated and still showered with awards, yet it hasn't lost the small-town friendliness that launched it. You've seen canned Chalet Suzanne soups in gourmet shops; buy them here by the case. Shop for antiques and visit the pottery. The traditional menu starts with the famous romaine soup and marches on through multiple courses. The wine cellar is outstanding. Open daily for breakfast, lunch, and dinner. Reservations are highly recommended. Each room in the inn is different. Guests can use the swimming pool, fish in the lake, and land their airplanes on the private airstrip. $$$–$$$$. (863) 676-6011 or (800) 433-6011; www.chaletsuzanne.com.

G. V. Tillman House. 301 East Sessoms Avenue, Lake Wales 33853. This property was a grand mansion in another century. Today it offers five guest rooms, four with private bath, to overnight guests. Walk to the city park, public library, and tennis and racquetball courts, or drive to Bok Tower Gardens in five minutes. At day's end, sit on the wraparound veranda with a cup of coffee and some good reading, or ask the hosts for a tub of popcorn to enjoy while you watch TV in the library. Ask about the bass fishing package, which includes your own fishing guide. A bountiful breakfast is served 8:00 to 9:00 A.M. in the parlor overlooking Crystal Lake. $$. (800) 488-3315; www.tillmanbb.com.

Green Gables Inn. 1747 North U.S. 27, Lake Wales 33853. This is an old-fashioned "tourist court" motel, handy to the highway and smartly updated with a fitness center, guest laundry, in-room coffee, cable television, and phones with dataports. There's a swimming pool, tennis courts, hot tub, and on-site restaurant and lounge—and a private fishing dock just outside the door. $–$$. (863) 676-2511.

Noah's Ark. 312 Ridge Manor Drive, Lake Wales 33853. This bed-and-breakfast inn is housed in a Mediterranean-style building dating to 1922. During Prohibition it served as a speakeasy. Today you'll get an antiques-furnished guest room with private bath, air-conditioning, and color TV. Guests are welcome to use the sitting room, drawing room, and terraces. Breakfast is included in rates. $$. (800) 346–1613 or (863) 676–1613.

Avon Park · Sebring · Lake Placid

AVON PARK

This sleepy village deep in Florida's belly hasn't changed much in decades, which makes it a tempting day trip away from the din of the city. Take I–4 southwest from Orlando to the U.S. 27 exit, then turn south onto this historic artery that is still a pretty, interesting drive through cattle country past sparkling lakes and through unspoiled hamlets along the spine of a prehistoric ridge. U.S. 98 and other roads running east and west through this area, was part of the original route used by Florida cow hunters to take cattle to Punta Rassa on the Gulf of Mexico for shipment to Cuba. Today it's known as the Florida Cracker Trail.

In a quest for snakes, alligators, and other swamp denizens to study, Connecticut native Oliver Martin Crosby came to this area in 1884, followed by others in search of winter warmth. An early British settler suggested the name Avon because the town reminded her of Shakespeare's birthplace on England's Avon River. Today's residents call it the City of Charm, a land of thirty lakes and enough outdoors to attract 30,000 hikers each year.

WHERE TO GO

The Mile-Long Mall, a nickname for Avon Park's Main Street, is a swath of specialty shops and restaurants. Browse from one to the next, with a stop at the Hotel Jacaranda for lunch.

South Day Trip 2

WHERE TO EAT

El Zarape. 10 North Central Avenue, Avon Park 33825. This restaurant serves up a Mexican buffet *el grande* with familiar favorites, including tacos and tons of fillings, just like Mamacita used to make. Open every day 11:00 A.M. to 9:00 P.M. $. (863) 452–1945.

WHERE TO STAY

Fernach Bed & Breakfast. 902 West Main Street, Avon Park 33825. This peaceful oasis in charming downtown is hosted by pleasant folks who will serve you a continental breakfast before you leave. $$. (863) 453–3104.

Hotel Jacaranda. 10 East Main Street, Avon Park 33825. This grand old hotel has been restored to its Flapper Era look. It's owned by a hospitality school, which means affordable rates, great meals, and high service and housekeeping standards set by demanding teachers. The heated swimming pool is enclosed, and each room has individual climate control, television, and telephone. Master suites have bedroom, living room, and bath. Grand Suites have two bedrooms, living room, and two baths. The Sunday Grand Buffet is a stunner, prepared by culinary students who are learning all the latest techniques and tastes, and the everyday lunch buffet is boffo. $$. (863) 453–2211.

Lake Brentwood Motel. 2060 U.S. 27 North, Avon Park 33825. This property is rustic and plain, just the perch for anglers who like a lakefront location, a private dock, horseshoes, croquet, free use of boats and canoes, and picnic tables with grills. Take a room or an efficiency with cooking facilities. Golf, tennis, and restaurants aren't far away. $–$$. (863) 453–4358.

SEBRING

South of Avon Park is Sebring, a planned paradise laid out around a central circle with spokes/streets fanning out all around. It has been internationally famous for years as the home of the twelve-hour

Sebring Grand Prix of Endurance auto race, but there's much ado here all year. For a really offbeat side trip from Orlando, come here by Amtrak and get a glimpse of Florida's vast cattle ranches and orange groves along the way. If you're a race fan, book early. If you're not, come at other times, when it's easier to get a room and restaurant reservations.

WHERE TO GO

Chamber of Commerce. 309 South Circle, Sebring 33870. Located downtown, this is a good place to stop for information and maps. Open Monday through Friday 9:00 A.M. to 5:00 P.M. (863) 385–8448 or (877) 844–6007.

Highland Hammock State Park, west of Sebring off Highway 634, is more than an awesome 3,800-acre wildlife sanctuary buzzing with birds and bugs. It's also Florida's first state park and home of the largest oak tree in Florida, the tallest sable palm in the country, some 1,000-year-old hardwoods, and a sweeping expanse of some of the last remaining hammock in the state. Walk eight nature trails, camp, picnic, take the catwalk across the swamps to watch for alligators, or take the tram tour for a modest fee. A horseback-riding trail is available to those who bring their own horses. (Horses must have a recent negative Coggins test.) Campground sites accommodate tents or RVs. Ask at the ranger station for a birder's list and perform your own survey. A museum honors Civilian Conservation Corps workers who created the park in the 1930s and 1940s. It's so lush and gentle a jungle, kids will see Fern Gully and grownups will see Bali Hai here. Admission is $3.25 per car. Camping is extra. Open 8:00 A.M. to sunset daily. (942) 386–6094.

Panoz Racing School. Sebring International Raceway, 113 Midway Drive, Sebring 33870. This is a serious training ground for future race drivers, but anyone is welcome to take a one-, three-, or four-day course to improve his or her driving skills. If you meet SCCA requirements after your course, you'll be certified to drive in real races. Training is in cars designed specifically for high-speed race training. Courses are taught by top competitors in such leading series as Formula 1, NASCAR, SCCA, and British Formula 3. The one-day course, for those who just want a taste of the action, begins with classroom work, then an afternoon on the track. Longer courses provide classroom work, plenty of track time, lapping days, GT races, and other programs. Ask about packages that include accommodations. $$$. (888) 282-GTRA; www.panozracingschool.com.

Lake Jackson. An 11-mile trail circles this natural lake. Take your bicycle, baby stroller, in-line skates, or walking shoes. A good place to start is downtown at The Circle. (863) 471-5100.

WHERE TO EAT

Foons Garden. 1775 U.S. 27 South, Sebring 33870. Foons' serves traditional Asian favorites as well as a great Mongolian grill. Order hot and spicy or mild from a long list of appetizers, soups, fried rice, sweet and sour, egg foo young, lo mein, chow mein, chop suey, beef combinations, seafood, poultry, pork, and vegetarian. Open daily from 11:00 A.M., with a lunch buffet served 11:00 A.M. to 3:30 P.M. daily except Sunday. $. (863) 386-0502.

Idyl Our II Tea Room. 747 Southeast Lakeview Drive, Sebring 33873. This tearoom is just off the circle in an old boardinghouse that is said to be haunted. Fresh bread is delivered daily to order, and it's made into sandwiches to be served with homemade soup and a sinful dessert, such as apricot cream-cheese bars, raspberry chocolate fingers, or chocolate cloud cheesecake. There's live music during dinner most weekends. Thursday 4:00 to 6:00 P.M., it's a coffeehouse serving specialty coffees, fruit drinks, and hot chocolates. In season, high tea is served twice weekly by reservation only. Bed-and-breakfast rooms are also available. $. (863) 385-8101.

The Tea Room in **Sebring Lakeside Golf Resort Inn.** 500 Lake Sebring Drive, Sebring 33870. This is one of those charming lakefront places where you feel like an old friend, even if this is your first visit. The tearoom is open for lunch only, and reservations are suggested. $. (863) 385-7113. The inn has rooms, suites, golf, and much more. $$–$$$. For inn reservations, call (888) 2SEBRING.

WHERE TO STAY

Chateau Élan. 150 Midway Drive, Sebring 33870. This is a smart, modern boutique hotel in a patch of Florida outback that, until the hotel was built, sprang to life only during the famous twenty-four-hour Sebring auto races. It adjoins the track, so bookings are hard to get during race events. Accommodations are splendid, with coffeemakers in each room, satellite television, phone with dataport, hair dryer, and iron and ironing board. Work out in the fitness room, play golf, attend auto-racing school, and pamper yourself in the European-style spa, where massages, facials, restorative body treatments, and hydrotherapy are on the menu. The restaurant is stellar and offers room service as well as breakfast, lunch, and dinner. The lounge and outdoor swimming pool overlook the track's famous hairpin turn. You can also drive into historic Sebring for dining and shopping. Ask about race school packages, golf getaways, and a day package that includes lunch and a tour of the track. $$–$$$. (863) 655-6252; www.chateauelansebring.com.

Inn on the Lakes. 3100 Golfview Road at U.S. 27 South, Sebring 33870. The inn is a modern lakefront resort offering water ski and jet ski rentals, tennis, workout rooms, a lakeside restaurant with lounge, a coin laundry, swimming pool, and tempting golf packages. Suites have wet bars. $$–$$$. (863) 461-9400 or (800) 531-5253.

Kenilworth Lodge. 836 Southeast Lakeview Drive, Sebring 33870. This eye-arresting Mediterranean Revival–style lodge opened in 1916 overlooking Lake Jackson. Centered by a massive lobby with a grand staircase, it offers efficiencies, apartments, villas, and rooms with a refrigerator in each unit. The swimming pool is 80 feet long, and there's a golf course with a choice of seven golf packages. Water-ski, play tennis, bicycle, and catalog the bird life. Pull up a rocker on the veranda to read the morning paper, and plan to come back to this spot in time for sunset over the lake. Dine in the lodge's restaurant; rates include breakfast. Weekly rates give you one night free. $–$$$. (800) 423-5939 or (863) 385-0111; www.kenlodge.com.

Quality Inn. 6525 U.S. 27 North, Sebring 33870. This property is part of a reliable chain with an Olympic-size swimming pool, a tiki bar outdoors, and a lively lounge as well as a full-service restaurant. Ask about golf packages. Rooms have free premium movie channels, in-room coffee service, free local calls, pay-per-view movies, iron and ironing board, and a daily *USA Today* left at your door. Room service is available, and pets are welcome in some rooms. $$–$$$. (863) 385-4500.

LAKE PLACID

Continuing south on U.S. 27 from Sebring soon brings you to Lake Placid. The city claims to have been the largest town (in area) in the nation at one time, when it was a community named Lake Stearns after the U.S. Surveyor General at the time. Dr. Melvil Dewey, inventor of the Dewey Decimal System arrived in the 1920s and got behind efforts to promote the area as a winter resort with a new name. Growth has been slow but steady, allowing the area to retain its small-town flavor.

WHERE TO GO

Historical Museum. 19 Park Avenue West, Lake Placid 33852. The museum is housed in the city's old rail depot. In addition to interesting antiques and local memorabilia, the museum contains an old caboose and the entire old jailhouse. Hours are 1:00 to 3:30 P.M. Monday through Friday; admission is free. No phone, but you can call the Chamber of Commerce: (863) 465–4331 or (800) LK–PLACID.

Murals are Lake Placid's claim to fame. It has more than two dozen eye-popping, masterfully done outdoor paintings that depict area history and culture in what is called "uptown." Bring a wide-angle lens, a tripod, and a time-delay camera so that you can put yourself in the picture with a cattle drive that comes complete with sound effects, an airboat, the caladium field, or one of the historic scenes. See the murals anytime on a self-guided tour, allowing plenty of time to shop uptown's interesting boutiques and crafts shops. A mural map can be picked up during business hours at the Chamber of Commerce, 18 North Oak Street, Lake Placid 33852, or at most area merchants.

Arriving in town on U.S. 27, note the 360-foot-high **Placid Tower.** Take the elevator or climb the stairs for a view of the area's twenty-seven lakes (fifteen with boat camps) and color-drenched caladium fields. Admission is $3.00 for adults and $1.50 for children. Open 7:00 A.M. to 9:00 P.M. daily. Allow time to enjoy the shops and restaurants at the base of the tower. (863) 465–3310.

WHERE TO EAT

Caddy Shack. 240 East Interlake Boulevard, Lake Placid 33852. This is the best place in town for a breakfast of blueberry pancakes with a side of bacon or ham. The cook offers a new luncheon special every day plus soup, salads, sandwiches, and burgers. Open every day for breakfast and lunch only. $. (863) 699-5575.

Heron's Garden. 2200 Highway 27 South, Lake Placid 33852. Heron's is famous for its Greek salad and shish kebob. Choose from a menu of steaks, chicken, fresh seafood, and a selection of pasta dishes. There's a lounge with full bar. $$. Open from 11:00 A.M. every day. (863) 699-6550.

WHERE TO STAY

Best Western Lake Placid Inn. 2165 U.S. 27 South, Lake Placid 33852. This property is modern and comfortable with full hotel facilities, including a swimming pool, plenty of parking, a full-service restaurant, and lounge with dancing. Breakfast is on the house. $$. (800) 771-4013 or (863) 465-3133.

Lake Grassy Motel. 1865 U.S. 27 South, Lake Placid 33852. This homey place has one-bedroom suites. Kitchens are fully furnished, so bring supplies; there is no restaurant on site. Rent by the night, week, weekend, or month, and bring your trailerable boat to launch from the motel's own ramp. $-$$. (863) 465-9200.

Tower Restaurant. 461 U.S. 27 North, Lake Placid 33852. The Tower is revered for its massive and mixed menu. At lunch, see mile-high sandwiches served with a choice of coleslaw, applesauce, or baked beans; or have the soup of the day, chicken and grape salad, or an old-fashioned hot meat loaf, turkey, or roast beef sandwich with real mashed potatoes and gravy. At dinner, comfort foods such as meat loaf, corned beef and cabbage, and liver and onions share the menu with grouper, charbroiled ham, T-bone steak, pastas, and hot sandwich platters. Try the Greek salad, or have a main-dish salad such as chicken Caesar. Don't miss the corn muffins and homemade pies. Early birds save on dinners and drinks. Open daily for lunch and dinner. $-$$. (863) 699-9996.

I-4 wanders southwest from Orlando toward Tampa. Just barely past Orlando's attractions area, you'll find a cluster of small communities that offer a Mayberry-like atmosphere. Don't blink as you go past it on I-4, or you'll miss the Polk City exit. It's the off-ramp to another world—a world of small towns with village squares surrounded by storefronts, once hardware stores and grocers, that are now boutiques and tearooms.

POLK CITY

Venturing into the community itself, you'll find a charming village square surrounded by shops. However, Polk City's most impressive attraction is right at an interstate exit, well worth a stop on your way to somewhere else.

WHERE TO GO

Fantasy of Flight. 1400 Broadway Boulevard, Southeast Polk City 33868. Watch for the exit off I-4 to find one of the world's greatest aircraft collections as well as an attraction with plenty of punch. Start by going through a time tunnel into the history of aviation. Experience a jump into occupied France, see a World War I bunker, and visit an English airfield. Then come into the twenty-first century to fly a simulator and tour the restoration area, where inter-

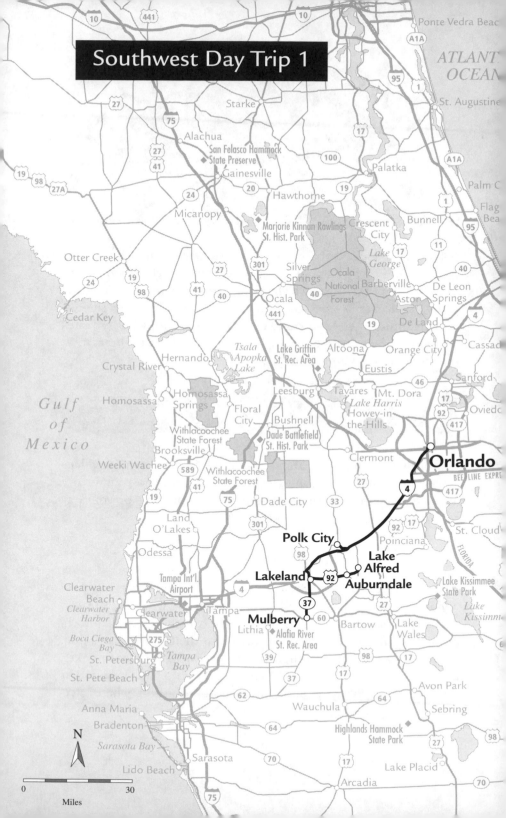

Southwest Day Trip 1

esting planes are always being worked on. See the back lot where movie props and bits and pieces are stored, and spend time in a hangar filled with a fortune in antique airplanes. Many are one of a kind; most are flyable. No admission is required to eat at the Compass Rose, a delightful diner like those found in airports in the 1950s. The attraction is handy to I-4, with easy-off, easy-on access, so stop for breakfast or lunch and a look at the gift shop—even if you aren't staying to tour the attraction. Hours are 9:00 A.M. to 5:00 P.M. daily except Christmas and Thanksgiving. Fees are $24.95 for adults, $13.95 for children, and $22.95 for seniors. (863) 984-3500; www.fantasyofflight.com.

LAKELAND

Each April, Lakeland is abuzz with small planes as it hosts Sun 'n Fun, one of general aviation's most important annual events. Aircraft of all sizes and colors zero in on the airport here for contests, camping, and the kind of tale swapping known as "hangar flying." Even if you're not an aviation buff, you'll love the color and verve of it all. The community's other chief claim to fame is the Florida Southern College campus, the largest collection of Frank Lloyd Wright buildings in the world. Lakeland, located just off I-4 halfway between Orlando and Tampa, makes a good headquarters for exploring the surrounding small towns, including Auburndale and Lake Alfred, along Highway 600.

WHERE TO GO

Florida Southern College. 111 Lake Hollingsworth Drive, Lakeland 33801. This active college is also the home of a dazzling collection of buildings designed by Frank Lloyd Wright. If you're a fan of this quirky architect, whose disciples forgive his leaky roofs and high-maintenance designs, a free walking tour of the campus is one of the state's great bargains. Stop first at the visitor center for information and to shop the gift shop. The visitor center is open Tuesday through Friday 11:00 A.M. to 4:00 P.M., Saturday 10:00 A.M. to 2:00 P.M., and Sunday 2:00 to 4:00 P.M. The campus is open year-round, even when classes aren't in session, but not all buildings are open. It's best to phone ahead. (863) 680–4110.

ISAM (International Sport Aviation Museum). 4175 Medulla Road, Lakeland 33802. The museum is filled with sport airplanes and memorabilia, a must for aviation buffs—especially those who follow aviation as a competitive sport. You'll need up to three hours to see it all. Hours vary, so call ahead. A modest admission is charged. (863) 644–0741.

Mulberry Phosphate Museum. Route 60 at Route 37, Mulberry 33860. Located just south of Lakeland, this is a surprise find. Florida is an archaeological treasure trove from stem to stern, and here is living proof. Thousands of creatures died here in the Cenozoic Era and were preserved in lands that were later mined for phosphates. See more than 3,000 specimens, including a whale vertebra with a shark's tooth imbedded in it, a prehistoric *equus* horse, and a five-million-year-old skeleton of a dugong, ancestor of the modern manatee. Admission is free, and special digs are arranged for kids. Open Tuesday through Saturday 10:00 A.M. to 4:30 P.M. (863) 425–2823.

Polk Museum of Art. 800 East Palmetto Street, Lakeland 33801. At this small but important art museum, view changing exhibitions plus a sculpture garden, galleries filled with contemporary American works, an impressive collection of pre-Columbian artifacts, Asian arts, and a collection of European arts with a fine showing of Georgian silver and antique ceramics. From here you can walk to the Florida Southern campus or the city's antiques district. Open Monday and Saturday 10:00 A.M. to 5:00 P.M., Tuesday through Friday 9:00 A.M. to 5:00 P.M., and Sunday 1:00 to 5:00 P.M. Closed major holidays. Free. (863) 688–7743; www.PolkMuseumofArt.org.

WHERE TO SHOP

The Attic Gallery. 205 Main Street, Auburndale 33823. The Attic is stocked with fine antiques and collectibles, a place for serious browsing for gifts, accessories, and additions to your own collection. Open daily except Sunday, with a 2:00 P.M. closing on Saturday. The Dirkes family will also open the gallery by appointment. (863) 967–2267.

The Barn Antiques; The Stable Gifts; The Back Porch Restaurant. Route 557, Lake Alfred 33850. Located 4 miles north of Lake Alfred, this is a cheery, family-operated place where lunch is served in its own picnic basket. Shop for antiques, silk flowers, seasonal accessories, and gifts galore. Hours vary seasonally, so call ahead. The restaurant is rated $-$$. (863) 956-2227.

Biggar Antiques. 140 West Haines Boulevard, Lake Alfred 33850. Biggar's has been family-run here for more than forty years. Their specialty is country store antiques and memorabilia for private buyers as well as for decorators who furnish restaurants. Buy a poster, tin sign, or country furniture. Hours are Tuesday through Saturday 10:00 A.M. to 4:00 P.M. (863) 956-4853.

Curiosity & Collectibles. 121 Main Street, Auburndale 33823. This shop brings browsers to Polk County to look for that perfect accent piece or a whimsical souvenir. Open daily except Sunday and Monday. (863) 965-9237.

Hometown Christmas & Gifts. 212 East Park Street, Auburndale 33823. This is really six shops in one. Shop for Christmas decor, bath and body, cards and stationery, or gifts and collectibles, then have a cup of comfort in the Park Street Cafe. Open daily except Sunday and Monday. (863) 965-7291.

International Market World. 1052 Highway 92, Auburndale 33823. This big flea market lures visitors who are speeding by on the highway. See its 1909 carousel, shelves filled with crafts and art supplies, new and used oddments, and food concessions. Open Friday through Sunday 8:00 A.M. to 4:00 P.M. (863) 665-0062.

Lake Alfred Antique Mall. 155 East Haines Boulevard, Lake Alfred 33850. The "mall" houses only six vendors, so it's small enough to be intimate and personal yet large enough to offer a good selection of antiques in many interest areas. Each booth has its own specialties. Open Tuesday through Saturday 10:00 A.M. to 4:00 P.M. (863) 956-2488.

The Old Angler's Antiques Mall. 380 South Lakeshore Way, Lake Alfred 33850. This complex carries antique fishing tackle and lures, military and sports memorabilia, and other rare collectibles in addition to antique furniture, glassware, pottery, linens, and carvings. Open daily except Sunday 9:00 A.M. to 6:00 P.M. (863) 956-2525.

The Peacock. 212 Howard Street, Auburndale 33823. Pass a pleasant afternoon looking for antiques and collectibles and chatting over a steaming cup of good tea at this fine gift shop and tearoom. Open Tuesday through Saturday 10:00 A.M. to 5:00 P.M. and until 7:00 P.M. on Tuesday and Thursday. (863) 965–1684.

Something Special. 113 Easter Lake Avenue, Auburndale 33823. This shop specializes in Seraphim angels, bone-china tea sets, Beanie Babies, and Lefton lighthouses. Shop for gifts; they'll be boxed free. Open daily except Sunday. (863) 965–7815.

This Olde House. 1070 South Lake Shore Way, Lake Alfred 33850. This six-room house is filled with gifts and antiques plus a selection of unfinished furniture. Shop for stuffed animals, unusual candles, frames, and furniture Tuesday through Saturday 10:00 A.M. to 4:00 P.M. (863) 956–9433.

WHERE TO EAT

Crispers. 217 North Kentucky Avenue, Lakeland 33801 (downtown), or 3615 South Florida Avenue, Lakeland 33803 (Merchants Walk). This is a popular lunch place as well as a favorite for takeout. Homemade soups are made fresh daily and available to eat in or take out by the bowl, pint, or quart. There's also a good choice of sandwiches, including a crunchy vegetarian selection on grainy bread, a hot Reuben, and breast of chicken with bacon. Sandwiches are available by the whole or half, and there are a dozen salads with a variety of dressings to make a meal or a side dish. In addition to punch, iced tea, and juices, there are frozen specialties such as Chocolate Monkey, Coconut Fantasy, and Caramel Chiller. Ice cream, cake, cheesecake, and cookies round out the desserts. Check out their menu at www.crispersonline.net, then phone in your take-out order. Open daily except Sunday 10:30 A.M. to 7:30 P.M. $. (863) 682–8636 (downtown); (863) 646–2299 (Merchants Walk).

Terrace Grille. 329 East Main Street, Lakeland 33801. It's worth a visit just to see this swank 1920s hotel, and the food keeps pace with your high expectations. Start with the soup of the day or spinach and artichoke fondue, macadamia-crusted Brie, or fried oysters in a Creole remoulade. Main dishes include the chef's vegetarian plate, jumbo lump crab cakes, an oak-grilled pork chop with whiskey

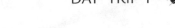

butter, grouper seared with wild mushrooms and topped with oyster stew, wood-grilled steaks or rack of lamb, mahi-mahi, and much more. Open daily for breakfast, lunch, and dinner. Reservations are recommended. $$–$$$$. (863) 688-0800 or (888) 644-8400.

Lavender & Lace Tearoom & Gift Shop. 430 North Lake Shore Way, Lake Alfred 33850. This combination Victorian tearoom and a shop sells everything you need to do a proper English tea at home. Sit down to an authentic English tea with little sandwiches or sweets, then shop for gifts for your Anglophile friends. Open daily except Sunday 11:00 A.M. to 3:30 P.M.

Ye Olde Curiosity Shoppe & Tea Room. 733 East Palmetto Street, Lakeland 33801. Here's another place to have a proper English tea, served on the best English china with all the right accompaniments. Shop for antiques, English foods, accessories, and collectibles while you're here. Open daily except Sunday 10:00 A.M. to 4:00 P.M. $. (863) 802-0064.

Also see **The Back Porch** (Where to Shop).

WHERE TO STAY

Best Western Diplomat Inn. 3311 U.S. 98 North, Lakeland 33805. This property is a favorite with golfers, who headquarter here while sampling the forty-odd courses in the area. The inn is the home of a lounge with a comedy club and is less than 2 miles from Tiger Stadium, where the Detroit Tigers play in winter. A hot buffet breakfast is included in rates. All rooms have a coffeemaker, iron and ironing board, hair dryer, 25-inch color cable television, and dataports. $$$. (863) 688-7972 or (800) 237-4699.

Lakeland Terrace Hotel. 329 East Main Street, Lakeland 33801. The hotel opened its doors in 1924, one of the finest in something new to Florida—a year-round hotel. The boom was on, and this handsome high-rise went up in the heart of downtown, overlooking Lake Mirror. Today you can walk to the courthouse and Amtrak station. Dine in the Terrace Grille, or have a drink in the Terrace Bar. It's restful and refined, newly renovated to take you back to another age. Choose one of the seventy-three guest rooms or one of the fifteen suites with separate bedroom plus a sleeper sofa. All units have in-room coffee, a working desk with dataports, table television, individual climate control, and iron and ironing board. $$–$$$. (863) 688–0800 or (888) 644–8400; www.terracehotel.com.

Lake Morton Bed & Breakfast. 817 South Boulevard, Lakeland 33801. Continental breakfast is included in rates at this four-room inn located in a handy downtown location. Choose a room or a suite. $$. (863) 688–6788.

WINTER HAVEN

Water skiing was not invented here, but the sport owes much of its popularity to warm Florida waters, where it became a year-round passion. It's still one of the most important reasons to come to this hotbed of water ski shows, schools, competitions, and even a water ski hall of fame and museum. From Orlando, go west on I-4 then south on U.S. 27 and west on U.S. 17–92 into Winter Haven.

WHERE TO GO

Cypress Gardens. 2641 South Lake Summit Drive, Winter Haven 33884. This spot has been an evergreen oasis since the 1930s, when a swamp was transformed into a garden showplace on the shores of Lake Eloise. Take an electric boat tour past a floral spectacular that changes with the seasons. The cypress trees have been here since time began, and the show begins with them, followed by more trees, shrubs, topiaries, and waterfalls and climaxing in oceans of bright annuals that are changed each season. It's not too much to come here every week to soak up the beauty, sunshine, and sweet breezes off the lake. Bring plenty of film; Southern belles in hoopskirts will gladly pose for your shots.

The gardens alone can occupy tranquil hours, but the park also offers breathtaking ski shows, a flashy ice show, a butterfly conservatory, wildlife on display, a petting zoo, a radio museum, a paddle-

Southwest Day Trip 2

wheel boat with lunch and dinner cruises, plenty of shops and snackeries, and a very good sit-down restaurant. Plan to spend all day and, during special events, into the evening. Special events include big-name concerts, Christmas lights, the annual Mum Festival, and much more. Admission is $32.95 for adults and $16.95 for children ages six to twelve plus $6.00 to park a car, $8.00 for preferred parking, and $8.00 for RVs. Ask about multiday, combination, and annual passes. Hours are 9:30 A.M. to 5:00 P.M. every day, later during light festivals. (863) 324–2111 or (800) 282–2123; www.cypressgardens.com.

WHERE TO EAT

Bread Bowl. 823 U.S. Highway 27 South, Lake Hamilton 33851. A pleasant drive east from Winter Haven on the shores of one of the area's prettiest lakes, this homey place welcomes shoppers as well as diners, so make an afternoon of it. Dine on a bread bowl filled with a selection of hot delights (meatballs, chicken stew, chili, broccoli beef, the daily special) or a cold salad (crab and shrimp, Waldorf chicken, tuna). Dare the Dagwood Salad, a battleship-size bounty of meats, cheeses, and greens served with hot, buttered buns. Sandwich platters are a hearty meal. Kids like the Teenie Beanie Weenie Bread Bowl. For dessert, order from the old-fashioned soda fountain, which has a full menu of sundaes, sodas, dips, and floats; or have one of the homemade pies, including no-sugar-added apple. Finish with one of the gourmet coffees or teas. Ask about take-out picnics, whole meals, and whole pies. Open Monday through Saturday 9:00 A.M. to 8:00 P.M. and Sunday 10:00 A.M. to 6:00 P.M. $–$$ (863) 439–5075.

WHERE TO STAY

Cypress Motel. 5651 Cypress Gardens Road, Winter Haven 33884. This AAA two-diamond inn is handy to Cypress Gardens, a good headquarters for visiting the gardens and local sight-seeing. There's a choice of rooms, including some with kitchenette. The motel is set back from the noise of the highway and has a heated pool, laundry for guest use, and cable TV. Rooms have coffeemakers with coffee service, and a continental breakfast is included in the tab. Pets are welcome. If you're a member of AAA or AARP, ask about discounts. $$. (800) 729–6706 or (863) 324–5867; www.cypressmotel.com.

Holiday Inn. 1150 Third Street Southwest (U.S. 17), Winter Haven 33880. This property has kept pace by renovating its 228 rooms and parlor suites. All have two queen-size or one king-size bed, 27-inch television, coffeemaker, hair dryer, iron and ironing board, refrigerator, dataports, and voice mail. Swim in the outdoor pool while the kids splash in their own wading pool. Have a drink in the Club House Lounge, then dinner in the Country Kitchen, which can also provide room service if you prefer. The hotel is 3 miles from Cypress Gardens. $-$$. (883) 294-4451; www.holiday-inn.com.

Scottish Inns. 1901 Cypress Gardens Boulevard, Winter Haven 33880. This clean, green, economical inn offers a refrigerator in each room, free HBO, a coin laundry, and a nearby restaurant. The location is handy for visiting Cypress Gardens, Walt Disney World Resort, and everything between. For a few dollars more, get an efficiency and do your own cooking. $-$$. (863) 324-3954.

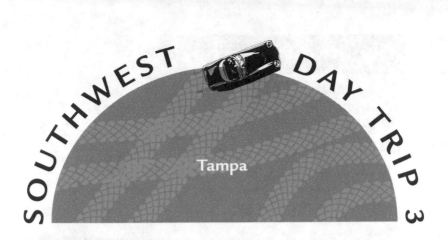

TAMPA

Save this trip for a two- or three-day weekend because each of the theme parks, Busch Gardens Tampa Bay and Adventure Island, is worth more than one day. In fact, season passes are a good value if you live close enough to come here more than twice. Kids never tire of the water park, and adults love the ever-changing scene of birds, flowers, animals, and shows at Busch Gardens.

Tampa itself is one of Florida's most beguiling cities, from its Latin tempo to its fresh, youthful bustle. It's a major cruise port, has fine museums and shopping, hosts blockbuster events and festivals, and is the home of world-class resorts and spas. For Orlando residents, it's a second home where dining and shopping are world class, big-name artists play in concert, and an international airport sometimes provides better connections or rates than can be found at Orlando International Airport.

Early Native Americans called the area "Tanpa," or Sticks of Fire, but somewhere along the way the spelling was changed. Ponce de Leon was here in 1521, and Hernando de Soto sailed into Tampa Bay in 1539. But it wasn't until 1772 that Dutch mapmaker Bernard Romans recorded the Hillsborough River and gave it a name. Today's downtown was history's Fort Brooke.

Development began when Henry B. Plant arrived with his railroad, a steamship line ran to Havana, and a flamboyant $3 million hotel was raised to house rich tourists. In 1885 a tract of land east of

Tampa was opened by Cuban exile and cigar manufacturer Don Vincente Martinez Ybor. Soon the city swarmed with expatriate Spaniards, Cubans, Germans, and Italians, who made it the cigar capital of the world. To begin this Day Trip, head west from Orlando on I-4 to I-275 south into Tampa.

WHERE TO GO

Adventure Island. 10001 McKinley Drive, Tampa 33612. Adjacent to Busch Gardens, this is the place to spend a torrid day splashing in cool waters. The thrill rides are as scary and exciting as the placid pools are relaxing and renewing. This thirty-acre tropic paradise has something for every age. Ride five-person rafts on Wahoo Run through one tunnel and four waterfalls. Dare the Splash Attack, where you'll be soaked. Ride through tubes and down slides. Float the wave pool and play volleyball. Eat at Mango Joe's Cafe, Surfside, or Gulfscream, or bring your own picnic. Lockers, showers, and changing facilities are here for your use. Admission is $26.63 for adults, $24.49 for children, and $23.96 for seniors, plus $4.00 parking for a car or RV. Ask about combination tickets to Adventure Island and Busch Gardens. Hours vary seasonally, so call ahead. (813) 987-5000; www.adventureisland.com.

Alafia River State Recreation Area. Mail address: c/o Hillsborough River State Park, 15402 U.S. 301 North, Thonotosassa 33592. Located in Lithia, 10 miles southeast of Tampa on Country Road 39, this 6,000-acre reclaimed phosphate mine is now a picnic place and playground. Bring your fishing tackle. The area has no phone or admission charge.

Busch Gardens Tampa Bay. 3000 East Busch Boulevard, Tampa 33612. This complex is more than a one-day wonder. In fact, every day is different. Plantings change, entertainers and shows are added or changed, and the wildlife never fails to delight and surprise. With the luxury of time, sit on a park bench and watch the passing Africa scene from the Casbah to the veldt. Browse shops for safari wear. Stalk a flamingo or a giraffe—with your camera, of course. Have lunch in old Africa. Schedule your time to see all the shows. Visit the nursery to watch newborn animals being fed. Sign up for a behind-the-scenes tour. Ride the roller coasters: Montu, Kumba, Gwazi, Python, and Scorpion. Admission is $48.76 for adults, $39.22 for children, and $45.56 for seniors. Parking is $6.00 for a car, $7.00 for an RV. Admission includes all attractions except the Serengeti Safari. Ask about multiday passes and combination tickets that include Adventure Island. Open daily; hours vary seasonally, so call ahead. (813) 987-5082; www.buschgardens.com.

Canoe Escape Inc. 9335 East Fowler Avenue, Tampa 33687. This company outfits you to explore the Hillsborough River through 16,000 acres of natural wilderness right at the doorstep of this pulsing city. Sign on for tours lasting from two hours to all day, and float downstream past a wildlife panorama starring turtles, alligators, and a world of birds. Canoes rent for $32. Open daily 9:00 A.M. to 5:00 P.M., earlier on weekends. (813) 986-2067; www.canoeescape.com. Kayak tours and rentals can also be arranged at various times and places through **Kayak Tampa Bay,** P.O. Box 292396, Tampa 33687. (813) 986-2067; www.kayaktampabay.com.

Channelside. Channelside Drive, Tampa 33601. This $35 million festival shopping and dining center is located at the waterfront, adjacent to the Florida Aquarium. Come early and stay on for supper and the evening.

Cruise out of the Port of Tampa, home to luxury cruise ships including Holland America's *Noordham,* Celebrity Cruises' *Zenith,* and Royal Caribbean Cruise Lines' *Rhapsody of the Seas.* Schedules, ships, and itineraries change throughout the year. Check with a travel agent who specializes in cruises; for information about Garrison Seaport Center, call (813) 905-5131.

Dinosaur World. 5145 Harvey Tew Road, Plant City 33565. This place is a must if you have middle-schoolers. Walk through a jungle inhabited by one hundred life-size dinosaurs, each with a plaque explaining its life and times. It takes about two hours to see them all. Bring a picnic and spend the day. A playground, gift shop, and museum round out the experience. Open daily 9:00 A.M. to dusk. Admission is $9.75 for adults, $7.75 for children, $8.95 for seniors. (813) 717-9865; www.dinoworld.net.

Duck Tours of Tampa. Mail address: P.O. Box 274108, Tampa 33688. Catch the Duck at 514 Channelside Drive in Tampa or at 800 Second Avenue Southeast in downtown St. Petersburg at The Pier. These are authentic World War II DUKWs—a vehicle that is half boat, half truck, and all fun. You'll drive city streets for a narrated tour, then launch for a waterfront jaunt. You'll spend eighty minutes getting your bearings, so this is the tour to take *before* you take off on your own explorations. Adults tour for $18.50; ducklings ages 3 to 12, $9.95. Tours depart hourly, rain or shine, every day; reservations are recommended because weather or traffic conditions could affect the schedule. (813) 310–DUCK for Tampa; (727) 432–DUCK for St. Petersburg.

Florida Aquarium. 701 Channelside Drive, Tampa 33601. Located downtown, this is one of the South's finest aquariums, a place to follow a drop of water from where it falls on upland Florida all the way to where it meets the sea. See creatures that live in fresh, brackish, and ocean waters; from shy manatees to sharks and rays in areas representing wetlands, bays and beaches, coral reefs, and offshore. Hands-on exhibits include a touch tank that delights children. This is just one of the attractions in the port area, so arrive early and spend the day here and in the area's shops and restaurants. Open daily 9:30 A.M. to 5:00 P.M. Adult admission is $12.95, $7.95 for children, and $11.95 for seniors. Parking is $4.00. (813) 273–4000; www.flaquarium.org.

J. B. Starkey's Flatwoods Adventure. 12959 State Road 54, Odessa 33556. This honest-to-goodness family ranch rambles along the Anclote River north of Tampa. Take a range-buggy ride through unspoiled flatlands, pine ridges, and pastures. Walk the boardwalk that spans the swamps, giving you a bird's-eye view of native plants, critters, and bird life. Hear from real ranch hands the story of Florida's centuries-long importance as a cattle ranching center. Adults $14.75, children $7.75, seniors $13.75. Tours vary seasonally, so call ahead. (813) 926–1133; www.flatwoodsadventures.com.

Kid City, The Children's Museum of Tampa. 7500 North Boulevard, Tampa 33604. As the name implies, this is a kid-sized, hands-on fun and learning center for active children. Let them be firefighters, drive a car, shop for groceries, and learn to cross streets safely in a village of more than a dozen buildings. Admission is $4.00. Open Monday through Friday 9:00 A.M. to 5:30 P.M., Saturday from 10:00 A.M., and Sunday from noon. (813) 935–8441.

MOSI. 4801 East Fowler Avenue, Tampa 33601. MOSI is short for the Museum of Science and Industry, and everyone calls it by its nickname. Its IMAX Dome Theater shows awesome movies that put you right in the action, so fasten your seatbelt. Out of 450 hands-on activities, kids will find enough here to stay happy and involved all day. Interactive and interpretive exhibits are for every age from young adults to seniors. Don't miss the hurricane exhibit, the Back Woods with its native plants and animals, space shuttle exhibits, and the chance to ride a virtual bicycle over the longest high-wire bicycle adventure in any museum in the nation. Outdoors, stroll the butterfly garden. Adult admission is $13.00, children $9.00, seniors $11.00. Open daily at 9:00 A.M.; closings vary seasonally. (813) 387–6100; www.mosi.org.

Ybor City State Museum. 1818 East Ninth Avenue, Tampa 33601. This museum is housed in an old bakery, capturing completely the Spanish-Italian flavor of the old city, which was the cigar capital of the United States by 1900. See complete "shotgun" houses that were built for cigar makers, as well as memorabilia from throughout the area's history. The old Ybor City trolley line, stilled in 1946, runs again on a 2.3-mile track that is gradually being extended. Open Tuesday through Saturday 9:00 A.M. to 5:00 P.M. Admission is $5.00 for adults and $3.00 for children. (813) 247–6323.

WHERE TO SHOP

International Plaza. West Shore at Boy Scout Boulevard (next to the airport). New in late 2001, this is the largest and most fashionable shopping mall west of Tampa. Neiman-Marcus, Nordstrom, Lord & Taylor, and Dillard's are the anchor stores, and more than 200 other shops and restaurants offer hours of shopping, dining, and people-watching pleasure. There's parking for 6,000 cars. Hours vary, but stores are all open by 10:00 A.M. and some restaurants stay open late. (813) 342–3780.

Old Hyde Park Village. Located south of downtown at Swann and Dakota Avenues, this is a strolling village where you can browse among sixty upscale shops, stopping here for a glass of wine and there for dinner or coffee. Sidewalk cafes are fun for people-watching. (813) 251–3500.

WHERE TO EAT

Ashley Street Grille. 200 North Ashley Drive, Tampa 33602. Located in the Radisson, this restaurant has won accolades for its dashing cuisine, which starts with a surprise *amuse bouche* pre-appetizer as a gift from the chef. The house salad is greens in port wine vinaigrette with goat cheese, pears, and sun-dried cherries. Have the lobster ravioli in Fra Diavolo sauce, pan-roasted mahi-mahi, herb-marinated chicken, or a hearty mixed grill. For lighter dining (and pocketbooks), the chef offers grilled chicken Caesar salad; grilled chicken salad with goat cheese, pears, and port vinaigrette; or a Black Angus beefburger with bacon. The wine list is massive, with many fine vintages available by the glass as well as the bottle. Desserts are a triumph—from apple crumble torte with honey and vanilla ice cream to a trio of chocolate confections. Open nightly for dinner. Reservations are essential. $$–$$$. (813) 223–2222.

Bern's. 1208 South Howard Avenue, Tampa 33602. Bern's has been a local institution forever, a dining experience like no other. It's best known for its homegrown vegetables and butter-tender steaks, hand-cut to the ounce and cooked to your taste—bloody, black, or anything in between. An elaborate chart on the menu helps you through the choices, from a small filet mignon at under $20 to a sixty-ounce strip sirloin priced at $156. Entrees come with French onion soup, baked potato, garlic toast, garlic butter, onion rings, and a sampling of fresh vegetables. Or order vegetables and side dishes a la carte: baked potato with sour cream and bacon, mushrooms, steak fries, Canadian wild rice, and much more. To order dessert, you leave your table and are reseated upstairs in a private booth with closed-circuit TV. By the time you make the change, your appetite is rekindled for tackling one of the house's memorable sweets. The wine cellar is one of the largest and most comprehensive in the South. Call for hours and reservations, which are essential. $$$–$$$$ plus 12 percent service charge. (352) 254–3355.

Capdevila's at La Teresita. 3248 West Columbus Drive, Tampa 33602. This is a mouthful of a name for a simple hometown Cuban restaurant where a feast is made from black beans, white rice, and crusty Cuban bread. The roast pork is pull-apart tender; other Cuban classics include breaded steak, chicken with yellow rice, and fried plantains. $. (813) 879–4909.

Columbia. 2117 South Seventh Avenue, Tampa 33601. This eatery is in the old section of town known as Ybor City, the place where Rough Riders mustered for the attack on San Juan Hill and where this restaurant was founded in 1912. The food takes you back to turn-of-the-twentieth-century Tampa, Havana, or Madrid. Desserts, with flamenco dancing, are worth a special evening Monday through Saturday. Call ahead if you want the world-famous paella, which takes awhile. Although other Columbia restaurants in Florida serve much the same menu, this one demands a special visit to see the original tiles and decor. Call for hours and reservations. $$$. (813) 248–4961.

Hungry Harry's. 3116 Land O' Lakes Boulevard, Land O' Lakes 34639. Harry's is north of Tampa, a half mile north of State Road 54 and Highway 41. Take a ride in the country to find real wood-fired barbecue that has been famous in these parts since 1981, when Harry started his barbecue pit to make food for his friends. Order a slab of ribs, chicken by the whole or part, and trimmings such as garlic bread, corn on the cob, coleslaw, baked beans, and potato salad. Burgers and meatball and vegetarian subs are also good. Order your barbecue sauce mild, sweet and smoky, or what Harry calls hellacious hot. Open for lunch and dinner every day. $–$$. (813) 949–2025.

Lakeside Grill & Lounge. 4422 Land O' Lakes Boulevard, Land O' Lakes 34639. This restaurant is a short drive north of Tampa into scenic lake country. Start with the shrimp and sausage gumbo, fried pickles, portobello mushroom pie, or the smoked-fish dip. There's a long choice of steaks from the grill, seafood selections, pastas, and old-fashioned comfort foods plus the veggie brochette for vegetarians. The kids' menu features all their favorites at tiny prices. $$. (813) 996–9999.

Mise en Place. 2616 South MacDill Avenue, Tampa 33608. This smart, sophisticated, locally popular bistro is best reserved for an unhurried dinner with a choice from the commendable wine list. Start with onion quiche with goat cheese or mussels in a tomato sauce scented with fennel. Your server can steer you to a fresh fish dish, succulent chicken, a comforting ragout, or a veal concoction. Call for hours. Reservations are accepted only for parties of six or more, so get up a group—or be prepared for a long wait. $$–$$$$. (813) 839–3939.

Primadonna. 915 South Howard Avenue, Tampa 33602. Primadonna is Italian to the core. The owner is from near Venice, and he knows his pastas and pancettas. You can't go wrong with the pasta of the day. Open daily except Sunday for lunch and dinner. Reservations are recommended. $$–$$$. (813) 258–3358.

SideBern's. 2208 West Morrison Avenue, Tampa 33602. This place is kin to the famous Bern's Steak House next door. The menu is wildly eclectic, ranging from dim sum to pastas, curries, and whole-meal salads. If it's meat and potatoes you're after, go to Bern's. Both sites excel at desserts—they share a pastry chef. Call for hours; reservations are highly recommended. $$$. (813) 258-2233.

StarShip **Dining Yacht.** Channelside, downtown Tampa, no mail address. It's a yacht, not a cruise liner, which means an intimate setting for cruise-ship-style dining and entertainment. Lunch and dinner cruises leave port every day; meals are three courses. Bird-watching is great by day, but night cruises take in the breathtaking sparkle of the city's lights on the water. Reservations are essential. $$$. (877) 744-7999 or (813) 223-7999.

WHERE TO STAY

Chase Suite Hotel by Woodfin. 3075 North Rocky Point Drive, Tampa 33607. This property offers one- and two-bedroom suites for the price of an ordinary room, with continental breakfast included. Suites have separate bedroom(s), full kitchen, dining area, televisions, fireplace, hair dryer, ironing board, and all the comforts of home. It's on Rocky Point overlooking the bay, handy to shopping and attractions and not too far from the beaches. Swim in the heated pool, and soak your cares away in the hot tub. $$-$$$. (877) 433-9644; www.woodfinsuitehotels.com.

Days Inn Fairgrounds. 9942 Adamo Drive, Tampa 33619. This is a good choice if you want to stay on the east side of town, handy to I-75. The hotel has a pool, and continental breakfast is included in the modest prices. It can be hard to get a room here during special events at the state fairgrounds, so book early. $$. (813) 623-5121 or (800) 222-8733.

Hyatt Regency Westshore. 6200 West Courtney Campbell Causeway, Tampa 33607. This is a full-service high-rise hotel with everything the leisure or business traveler could ask for in the heart of Tampa, yet it's on a spit of land that offers some of the best bird-watching in the county. Choose elegant or informal dining or room service, swim in the heated pool, and work out in the fitness center. The concierge can arrange any activity from downtown dining to golf to offshore fishing. $$$. (813) 225-1234 or (800) 233-1234; www.westshore.hyatt.com.

Radisson Riverwalk Hotel Tampa. 200 North Ashley Drive, Tampa 33602. The hotel offers 284 splendid rooms and suites overlooking the Hillsborough River in the heart of downtown. Walk to the Convention Center, Ice Palace, art museum, and the dazzling Performing Arts Center to see big-name concerts and Broadway shows. The big swimming pool overlooks the river; the Riverwalk is a 7-mile-long ribbon you can stroll, jog, bike, or in-line skate. The location is perfect for day trips, equally handy to Busch Gardens to the east and beaches to the west. Dine elegantly in the hotel's Ashley Street Grille or more casually in its Boulanger Deli/Bakery. $$$-$$$$. (813) 223-2222; www.radisson.com/tampafl_riverwalk.

Safety Harbor Resort and Spa. 105 North Bayshore Drive, Safety Harbor 34695. This is one of the best spas in the state, providing a full menu of sophisticated spa and salon services as well as spa cuisine, golf, tennis, unlimited use of bicycles, and twenty supervised fitness classes daily. Rooms have coffeemakers, cotton robes and slippers, unlimited local calls and free access to long-distance services, and a daily paper. Valet parking is complimentary. Ask about singles, romance, and mother-daughter packages. $$$-$$$$. (727) 726-1161 or (888) 237-8772; www.safetyharborspa.com.

ST. PETERSBURG–CLEARWATER

In the early days, the trip from Tampa all the way to St. Petersburg–Clearwater took an extra half a day after passengers got off the train because they had to go all around Tampa Bay. They kept streaming westward, however, toward the Gulf of Mexico and its incomparable sunsets. For today's traveler, it means an extra forty-five to sixty minutes on the interstates to get here. It's fun to vary the trip by taking I-4/I-275 over the Sunshine Skyway Bridge southward, follow State Road 699 down the coast then head north from St. Petersburg on I-75 to connect with I-4 and the return to Orlando. Whatever route you decide to follow, you're sure to enjoy your day at the beaches.

WHERE TO GO

Anclote Key State Preserve. Mail address: c/o Caladesi Island State Park, 1 Causeway Boulevard, Dunedin 34698. Located off Tarpon Springs, this cluster of sand spits in the Gulf of Mexico was chosen as the site of a lighthouse during the Grover Cleveland administration. Now a full-size key, it's protected from development by its remoteness—3 miles off the coast. Arrive in your own boat or rent a boat on the mainland. Bring everything you need, including food and drinking water. The beaches are superb for swimming and shelling. Watch for forty-three species of wildlife, including bald eagles and ospreys. Hike the island's diverse habitats, which include

Southwest Day Trip 4

tidal marsh, maritime hammock, dunes, and swamps. There aren't any planned trails, so walk lightly with as little impact on the terrain as possible. Primitive camping is permitted in an area that has tables, grills, and pit toilets. The preserve is open 8:00 A.M. until sundown every day. Call ahead for information. (727) 469–5918.

Caladesi Island State Park and Honeymoon Island State Recreation Area. 1 Causeway Boulevard, Dunedin 34698. The sands are rearranged every decade or so by hurricanes, making them a new discovery with each visit. A scheduled passenger ferry runs to the islands from Clearwater, so advance planning is needed. A wonderland of wildlife, the islands are home to a long list of birds, marine life, small mammals, grasses, seashells, and vines. Stay at the marina on board your boat, anchor off, or bring your backpack and take a primitive campsite. Trout, redfish, snook, tarpon and kingfish are caught in season; cast-netting for mullet is popular. Overnight visitors must register before sundown and bring all their needs with them. Picnic tables, a snack bar, and showers are available. Small fees are charged for day use or camping. (727) 469–5918 or (727) 469–5942.

Captain Nemo's Pirate Cruise. Clearwater Marina, Clearwater Beach 33767. Go a-pirating on a playful ship where everyone gets to shoot water pistols, brandish cutlasses, and hunt doubloons. It's a family favorite. Sailings are four times daily, weather permitting. Fares are $28 for adults, $22 for children 13 to 17 and seniors, and $18 for children 3 to 12. Call for reservations. (727) 446–2587.

Clearwater Marine Aquarium. 249 Windward Passage, Clearwater 33767. This aquarium is less flashy than some others because it's also a rehabilitation and study center. That makes it all the more authentic and endearing. With reservations, join Marine Life Adventures, an interactive experience that takes you into the waters of Clearwater Bay. Admission is $8.75 for adults, $6.25 for children. Open Monday through Friday 9:00 A.M. to 5:00 P.M., Saturday to 4:00 P.M., and Sunday 11:00 A.M. to 4:00 P.M. (727) 441–1790; www.CMaquarium.org.

WHERE TO EAT

Flying Bridge. 5500 Gulf Boulevard, St. Pete Beach 33706. Located in the Trade Winds Resort, this is a good place to take the kids, who can watch paddleboats go by as they eat. Dine poolside on extra-large burgers or fish sandwiches, salads, and light bites. Open for breakfast, lunch, and dinner. $–$$. (727) 562–1240.

Frenchy's Rockaway Grill. 7 Rockaway Street, Clearwater Beach 33767. Frenchy's is so informal, all you need is a bathing suit cover-up and flip-flops to meet the dress code for dining on the wooden deck. Play volleyball on the beach to work up an appetite for jerk chicken or fish, quesadillas, calamari, Cajun specialties, or a perky she-crab soup. Hours change with the seasons, so call ahead. $–$$. (727) 446–4844.

Hurricane Seafood. 809 Gulf Way, St. Pete Beach 33706. This eatery is upstairs on a rooftop deck, with unbeatable views of the sunset. Start with the grouper chowder, then have shrimp stuffed with crab, wrapped in bacon, and broiled. There's also snow crab, chicken, burgers, and steaks. Have a drink first in the cabana bar. Hours vary seasonally, so call ahead. $$. (727) 360–9558.

Johnny Leverock's Seafood House. 10 Corey Avenue, St. Pete Beach 33706. Seafood is king at this rock-solid local favorite. Shrimp is the house specialty, served in a dozen ways from simply steamed to shrimp diavolo to crusty, coconut-battered nuggets. The menu also features chicken, steaks, and plenty of fish choices with all the trimmings. Arrive early enough to enjoy the view of Boca Ceiga Bay. Call for hours and reservations. $$. (727) 367–4588.

Salt Rock Grill. 19325 Gulf Boulevard, Indian Shores 33785. The grill is between Indian Rocks Beach and Redington Shores. Porous limestone "salt" rocks are heated in an open wood fire and used to quick-sear tuna, steaks, mahi-mahi, pork tenderloin, and vegetables, imparting an incomparable juiciness and flavor. Sunsets reflect beautifully in the Intracoastal Waterway, so arrive in time for cocktails at sundown followed by a leisurely dinner. $$–$$$. (727) 593–7625.

WHERE TO STAY

Adam's Mark Clearwater Beach Resort. 430 South Gulfview Boulevard, Clearwater Beach 33767. The resort is right on the white sands of the beach, offering 217 rooms overlooking the bay or the Gulf. Swim in the sea or the big pool. The resort rents equipment for water sports and offers a good choice of dining options. $$$–$$$$. (727) 443–5714 or (800) 444–ADAM; www.adamsmark.com.

Don CeSar Beach Resort & Spa. 3400 Gulf Boulevard, St. Pete

Beach 33706. For generations this has been the Pink Palace, an apparition that rises out of the white sand and glows like pink coals in the setting sun. In the Gatsby era, it was a hangout for the famous and infamous, including Lou Gehrig, Clarence Darrow, and Al Capone. The years caught up with "The Don" after World War II, when it saw service as a convalescent center, but relentless renovations have made it a showplace once again. Now a AAA four-diamond hotel, it's filled with luxuries, from the elegantly appointed guest rooms (Sealy 700 Posturepedic mattresses, goose down pillows and comforters, 220-thread Egyptian cotton sheets) to facilities such as in-room massage, an old-fashioned ice cream parlor, world-class salon and spa, twenty-four-hour room service, an impressive lobby bar, and a variety of dining venues. Sup in grand style at the Maritana Grille or the King Charles Sunday Brunch, or go barefoot at the Beachcomber Bar. For casual dining, there's the Sea Porch Cafe.

Take afternoon tea, play golf or tennis nearby, swim in the heated plunge pool, relax in a whirlpool, parasail, snorkel, join in aerobics or aqua aerobics, and spoil yourself with a sea scrub or body masque. Water toys can be rented on the beach. Put the kids in the children's program where they'll have fun while you shop the hotel's boutiques. $$$$. A room fee applies per person, per night to pay for shoeshines, turndown, free local calls, long-distance access, parking, a choice of weekday newspapers, morning coffee in the lobby, and gratuities for housekeepers. (727) 360–1881 or (800) 282–1116; www.doncesar.com.

Gulfside Resort. 565 Seventieth Avenue, St. Pete Beach 33706. The Gulfside is a family-owned find, the kind of small, comfy place that people come back to every year. Units rent by the week and have cable TV, telephone with free local calls, and full kitchen with microwave. It's 200 yards from the Gulf beach, or you can swim in the heated pool. This is an affordable home base for anglers, golfers, water skiers, or baseball fans who follow spring training (fifteen minutes away) as well as for those who simply want to stay beachside while they explore the area. It's a member of Small Superior Lodgings, a group that must meet its group's standards for facilities and cleanliness. Drive to nearby shopping and restaurants. $. (800) 823–9552 or (828) 360–7640; www.gulfsideresort.com.

Radisson Resort on Sand Key. 1201 Gulf Boulevard, Clearwater

Beach 33767. The Radisson is an all-suite resort across the street from the beach. Choose among five restaurants. Swim under a waterfall in the heated pool. Sign up for a spa service or work out in the fitness center. Enroll the children in supervised activities every day. Shop the boardwalk, or relax in one of the lounges. $$$–$$$$. (727) 596–1100 or (800) 333–3333; www.radissonsandkey.com.

Renaissance Vinoy Resort and Golf Club. 501 5th N.E. Street, St. Petersburg 33701. In the halcyon days between the World Wars, a palace of a hotel was built here in the Mediterranean style that was so popular then in Florida. Now resorted to its Gatsby-era splendor, the Vinoy is not just a plush place to stay, it's the handiest location for travelers who want to be in the heart of town. Visit the Pier, home of museums, shops, and restaurants and known for its spectacular, rooftop views of the sunset. Walk to museums and churches. Book a boating or fishing trip at the marina across the street. Shop, dine, and stroll peaceful parks and neighborhoods. The Sunday brunch at the hotel's Marchand's Grill is one of Florida's best, but anytime is a right time to dine in this handsome room. The resort also offers dining in the Terrace Room, Alfresco, the exclusive Fred's Bar (open only to members and guests) or in the Clubhouse at the 18-hole golf course. The hotel's standard rooms are spacious and pleasant, its suites are showplaces and its patio suites have private hot tubs. Don't miss the gift shop. Ask about packages and special events. $$$–$$$$. (727) 894–1000 or (800) HOTELS-1; www.renaissancehotels.com.

Tampa Bay Hilton. 17120 Gulf Beach Boulevard, North Redington Beach 33708. This property has a band of pure white beach where you can watch a Gulf sunset at the tiki bar before the torches are lit and the evening's pleasures begin. Each of the rooms has its own balcony. Dine on Florida-Caribbean cuisine in Mangos, then dance to live music. Swim in the ocean, rent one of the water toys, or float in the azure pool. $$$. (727) 391–4000; www.HiltonRedingtonBeach.com.

Sarasota · Bradenton

SARASOTA

Long known as one of Florida's cultural capitals, little Sarasota shines. It has its own theaters, cabaret, dance companies, film festival, symphony, chamber music group, dinner theaters, chorale, jazz club, opera, ballet, dinner theater, and much more. Among its world-class attractions are the John and Mable Ringling Museum of Art, housing a host of masters, and the Asolo Theater, where you can see living productions in a thirteenth-century theater that was brought from Europe and reassembled here, piece by piece. See Regional Information for contacts, then plan an entire trip around the cultural offerings.

From Orlando, head west on I–4 and then south on I–75 to exits for Bradenton and Sarasota. You can work this day trip as a loop before heading back to Orlando.

WHERE TO GO

Golden Apple Dinner Theater. 25 North Pineapple Avenue, Sarasota 34236. The Golden Apple is a longtime local fixture offering cocktails, a prime rib dinner, then a popular Broadway show. Plan ahead to assure getting tickets for a show you want to see, then make it the focus of your day trip from Orlando. Tickets are $24.50 to $35.00. Reservations are essential. (941) 366–5454 or (800) 652–0920.

John and Mable Ringling Museum of Art. 5401 Bayshore Road, Sarasota 34243. The museum attracts visitors from all over the world

to see one of the most impressive collections of baroque paintings on the planet. Painted between 1550 and 1775, the massive paintings were collected by Ringling in the 1920s and 1930s. They'd fallen out of fashion with wealthy Europeans, and he was able to amass a priceless collection at a fraction of what the paintings are worth today. See works by Franz Hals, Peter Paul Rubens, and other masters. The courtyard is filled with fine sculpture. Other collections take you through the entire world of fine art. Give the museum several hours, and all day if you're an art connoisseur. There's a restaurant and gift shop, and the newly renovated Ringling mansion, Ca d'Zan. Open every day 10:00 A.M. to 5:30 P.M. Admission is $9.00 for adult, $8.00 for seniors, and free for children age 12 and under. (941) 355–5101.

Marie Selby Botanical Gardens. 811 South Palm Avenue, Sarasota 34236. The gardens are best known for their orchids, more than 6,000 of them, which are showcased, studied, and propagated. Other rare plants, collected in the wild on research expeditions, are on view for the public and scholars alike. Once a private estate, the Selby home is surrounded by eight and a half acres of the bay, with sparkling water views to ponder while you relax on a comfortable bench in the breezes. See the butterfly garden, Bamboo Pavilion, koi pond, and special collections of succulents, banyans, bromeliads, and palms. The museum is devoted to botany of the eighteenth, nineteenth, and twentieth centuries. Adult admission is $8.00, $4.00 for children ages 6 to 11. Open daily except Christmas 10:00 A.M. to 5:00 P.M. (941) 366–5731; www.selby.org.

Mote Aquarium. 1600 Ken Thompson Parkway, Sarasota 34236. This is a working research facility, staffed by top professionals as well as dedicated volunteers who are glad to answer your questions about all the sea creatures you'll see, including a moray eel, manatees, sharks, rays, and huge turtles. Pet a stingray and a horseshoe crab. Ask about the boat tour schedule and reservations. The gift shop is the perfect place to buy fishy souvenirs and educational materials based on the sea. Admission is $10.00 for adults and $7.00 students ages 4 to 17. Open daily 10:00 A.M. to 5:00 P.M. (941) 388–2451; www.mote.org.

Regal Cruises. Mail address: P.O. Box 1329, Palmetto 34220. This little-known cruise line sails out of a little-known port to provide one of the best mini-getaways within the Orlando orbit. Sarasota's Port Manatee is so small and uncrowded that you can drop off your luggage, park the car, and be hoisting a cold drink aboard ship in less time than it takes to get through the first line at larger ports. Cruises are seasonal, with itineraries ranging from four to seven nights. Ports of call include Key West, one or two Bahamian islands, or Mexico. *Regal Empress* has Las Vegas–style shows, fine dining to order, a swimming pool, Internet cafe, and a full casino. Book well in advance. (800) 270–7245; www.regalcruises.com.

Sarasota Jungle Gardens. 3710 Bayshore Road, Sarasota 34223. This botanical wonderland is also home to seventy species of reptiles, birds, and animals. See five educational shows, have a snack, shop for souvenirs, stroll the shaded paths, or just pick a park bench and watch nature's show unfold as it has here for more than half a century. Stay as long as you like for one admission price. Open every day 9:00 A.M. to 5:00 P.M. Adult admission is $9.00, $5.00 for children. (888) 861–6547.

WHERE TO SHOP

St. Armands Key. From I–75 take Sarasota exit 39, then west on State Road 780; or take U.S. 41 to State Road 780 west to St. Armands Key. It's on the road to popular barrier islands, but don't rush through this planned shopping area with its smart shops, galleries, restaurants, sidewalk cafes, snacks, and services. You can easily spend days browsing, noshing, people-watching, and seriously shopping for fashions, unique souvenirs and gifts, books, travel, beauty services, shoes, artworks, and everyday needs from medications to sunglasses. Hours vary. Follow signs to free parking. (941) 388–1554.

Towles Court is an old neighborhood that has been transformed into a community of artist studios, art galleries, and art schools where the art lover can browse, tour galleries, and have lunch at the Continental Cafe. Call ahead (941–362–0960 or 941–955–0050) for tours that include lunch. Most of the galleries and studios are open Tuesday through Saturday 10:00 A.M. to 4:00 P.M. The art colony is bounded by Highway 301, Adams Lane, Links Avenue, and Morrill Street, 3 blocks south of downtown Sarasota. For more information, visit www.towlescourt.com.

WHERE TO EAT

Barnacle Bill's. This is one of the area's favorite seafood chains, with locations in Sarasota at 3634 Webber Street (941–923–5800);

1526 Main Street (941-365-6800), and 5050 North Tamiami Trail (941-355-7700). You get all the ambience and great, fresh seafood tastes of the beach restaurants but without the long drive to the beach. Stop in for the catch of the day done to order, a steak, shrimp, chicken, or a combination platter. It's casual enough for the family, but the food is also good enough to bring a date or a client. $$. www.barnaclebillsseafood.com.

Columbia Restaurant. 411 St. Armand's Circle, Sarasota 34223. This a clone of the original Columbia, established in 1905 in Ybor City. Generations have loved this family-run chain for its enduring, endearing traditional recipes. They hark back to the old Cuba that had just won its independence from Spain. The paella takes extra time but can be the focus of a celebration evening. Or order one of the fish dishes, pork, chicken, steak, or meltingly tender beef done in "old clothes" style. Don't miss the special house salad or flan for dessert. Dine indoors or on the patio. Open daily for lunch and dinner. Reservations are recommended. $$-$$$. (941) 388-3987.

Ruth's Chris Steak House. 6700 South Tamiami Trail, Sarasota 34231. This is one of Florida's favorite chains, known for succulent steaks done to perfection and brought to you sizzling hot from the oven that Ruth herself invented. There's also chicken, chops, and seafood, including fresh Maine lobster. For the ultimate feast, have surf and turf. There is an impressive wine list and valet parking. Call for hours, which vary seasonally, and reservations. $$$. (941) 924-9442 or (800) 544-0808.

Sugar and Spice Family Restaurant. 4000 Cattlemen Road, Sarasota 34233. This eatery is one of Sarasota's delicious little secrets. You wouldn't expect to find an Amish restaurant in a Florida resort city, but long ago a colony of "Pennsylvania Dutch" settled here and spawned this and other great restaurants. Meals are hearty and homestyle, such as meat loaf and mashed potatoes, roasted turkey with all the trimmings, golden fried chicken, and liver and onions. The desserts, especially the pies, are sinfully good. The decor is rich in the crafts and symbols of the "plain people." Open daily except Sunday for lunch and dinner. $-$$. (941) 342-1649.

Yoder's Amish Restaurant. 3434 Bahia Vista Street, Sarasota 34239. Yoder's has been here long enough to be thoroughly Floridian, but the Yoders haven't forgotten their Amish roots. Everything is down-home delicious, brimming with old-fashioned flavor. Have crispy fried chicken with mashed potatoes, gravy, and fresh vegetables; or enjoy the juicy meat loaf. Save room for pie, especially one of the fruit pies made season by season as the harvests ripen. Open daily except Sunday for lunch and dinner. $–$$. (941) 955-7771.

WHERE TO STAY

Colony Beach & Tennis Resort. 1620 Gulf of Mexico Drive, Longboat Key 34228. This family-run resort enjoys a long list of loyal repeaters. It's best known for its fine tennis program, with play and instruction for all ages and all skill levels. Stroll the wave-washed Gulf beach, swim in the pool, take a fitness session with a trainer who can help you with your tennis game, or arrange a round of golf. Units have sleeping room for two to eight persons and full kitchens, but you can also call room service. Have at least one meal a day in one of the resort's outstanding, award-winning restaurants. The Colony is the home of the annual Hacker's Open for tennis buffs and an annual seafood and wine festival that brings in celebrity chefs. Children love the Kidding Around program for ages 7 to 12 and Kinder Kamp for ages 3 to 6. In addition to fun and creative activities, they'll be introduced to tennis at an early age. $$$–$$$$. (941) 383-6464 or (800) 4-COLONY; www.colonybeachresort.com.

    Coquina on the Beach. 1008 Ben Franklin Drive, Lido Beach 34236. The Coquina is just around the corner from chic, European-style St. Armands Circle. Beachfront and beach-view studios have two double beds and a full kitchen. Swim in the big pool or off the snow-white beach. Coffee is complimentary, but there's no restaurant on site. Ask about senior rates. $–$$. (941) 388-2141 or (800) 833-2141; www.coquinaonthebeach.com.

    Half Moon Beach Club. 2050 Ben Franklin Drive, Lido Beach 34236. This property is on one of the whitest, scrunchiest sand beaches on the Gulf of Mexico, with a smart Art Deco design and swank but barefoot ambience that brings in a high repeat rate. Seagrapes, the hotel's restaurant, is open every day for breakfast, lunch, and dinner. At dinner, they're renowned for seafood but also offer steak and pastas. Swim in the pool or the sea; stay in a hotel room or a suite with kitchenette. All units have a refrigerator, coffeemaker, daily newspaper, and beach towels. Cabanas, bicycles, beach umbrellas, and VCRs with movies can be rented. $$$. (941) 388-3694 or (800) 358-3245; www.halfmoon-lidokey.com.

Hilton Longboat Key Beachfront Resort. 4711 Gulf of Mexico Drive, Longboat Key 34228. This resort is a white vision rising from a white sand Gulf beach. Every room has a private patio or balcony; ask for a Gulf-view room or suite so that you won't miss any of the famous sunsets. Every unit has nightly turndown, minibar, and in-room safe. Dine in the Sunset Grill, or have lunch or a frozen drink outdoors at the pool bar. Swim off the private beach or in the heated pool. Shop for sundries and beach wear in the Beach Hut. Rent cabanas and equipment for water sports. A free shuttle takes shoppers to St. Armands Circle. $$$. (941) 383-2451 or (800) 282-3046; www.longboatkey.hilton.com.

Helmsley Sandcastle Hotel. 1540 Ben Franklin Drive, Lido Beach 34236. The Helmsley sits on a long stretch of snowy beach on the Gulf of Mexico, offering panoramic views of the water and everything you could ask for in resort activities. Sail, fish, play beach volleyball, or just sun on the beach. Rooms have safes, complimentary morning paper, and a small refrigerator. Dine in one of the two restaurants or order from room service, then relax after dinner in the lounge to live music. $$$-$$$$. (941) 388-2181 or (800) 225-2181; www.helmsleyhotels.com.

Holiday Inn Lido Beach. 233 Ben Franklin Drive, Lido Beach 34236. This property brings you the allure of pristine Lido Beach and all the hotel amenities of a major, modestly priced chain. Spacious rooms are done in sea tones. Ask for a Gulf-front room with a balcony, where you'll have a private view of the sunsets with their legendary green flash. Rooms have a coffeemaker, TV, phone with voice mail and dataport, ironing board and iron, and hair dryer. The hotel has a rooftop restaurant and pool bar, heated outdoor pool, fitness room, bicycle rental, gift and sundries shop, and a free airport shuttle. $$$. (941) 388-5555 or (800) 892-9174; www.lidobeach.net.

Hyatt Sarasota. 1000 Boulevard of the Arts, Sarasota 34243. This sleekly modern downtown hotel has everything the business or leisure traveler could ask for, plus a yachty ambience thanks to its Boathouse restaurant overlooking the marina. Even if you're not staying here, it's worth a visit to sample the innovative New American cuisine. The Sunday brunch is dazzling. Walk to the concert hall and other city sights and parks. The hotel has a swimming pool, fitness equipment, cable television, and an airport shuttle. The concierge can arrange fishing, boating, sight-seeing, golf, or a tennis match. $$–$$$. (941) 953–1234 or (800) 233–1234; www.sarasota.hyatt.com.

The Resort at Longboat Key Club. 301 Gulf of Mexico Drive, Longboat Key 34228. This AAA four-diamond resort sits on a wave-washed beach, with two championship golf courses, driving ranges, pro shop, clubhouse facilities including lockers and steam rooms, tennis courts, a children's program, a fitness center, swimming pool with Jacuzzi, captained sailing charters, charter fishing boats, and a choice of restaurants and lounges with live entertainment. Room service is also available. All the spacious, lavishly furnished guest rooms have a private balcony and refrigerator with icemaker. Also available are suites with up to two bedrooms. A 9.5-mile jogging path starts here and runs the length of the key. In-line skate rentals are available nearby. $$$–$$$$. (800) 237–8821 or (941) 383–8821; www.longboatkeyclub.com.

Riviera Beach Resort. 5451 Gulf of Mexico Drive, Longboat Key 34228. This homey little place is right on the beach and surrounded by lush green, with a full kitchen in each one- or two-bedroom apartment. It's one of a handful of spots in this tony area that fit our "$" rating. Pets are permitted, and there's a swimming pool. $. (941) 383–2552; www.rivierabeachresort.com.

Ritz-Carlton Sarasota. 1111 Ritz-Carlton Drive, Sarasota 34236. This property has been exciting news in downtown Sarasota since it opened late in 2001, looking right at home in this high-toned community. Walk to cultural attractions, shopping, and dining. All rooms have a view of the bay, marina, or skyline. Book a superior room, suite, or Club Level accommodations that have a separate lounge, concierge, and complimentary food and beverage presentations. Rooms have private balconies, housekeeping twice a day with evening turndown, twenty-four-hour room service, multiple telephone lines, high-speed Internet access, and marble baths. Use of terry robes and a free daily newspaper are provided. Play tennis day or night, or have the concierge arrange a tee time at one of the nearby golf courses. The big full-service adjacent spa incorporates native Florida botanicals into its full menu of soothing treatments. Dine elegantly in the Vernona for Mediterranean fare or more casually in the Bay View Bar & Grill. The bar, which has a cigar bar and single malts, is called Ca d'Zan after the historic Ringling property. Take a wellness, training, or fitness program, or just be lazy at the Beach Club on Lido Key's powder-white beach. It's reached by a free shuttle and has information, a tiki bar, restaurant, beachside pool with hot tub, and programs for children. $$$–$$$$. (800) 241-3333 or (941) 309-2000; www.ritzcarlton.com.

Silver Sands Gulf Beach Resort. 5841 Gulf of Mexico Drive, Longboat Key 34228. This property puts you on the beach in a resort room, apartment, or villa with up to three bedrooms. Daily maid service is provided. Swim in the heated beachside pool, use complimentary chaises and beach umbrellas, take to the putting green, or play tennis or shuffleboard. Kitchens are furnished with everything you'll need to cook every meal, or you can drive to a good selection of restaurants nearby. $$–$$$. (941) 383-3731 or (800) 245-3731; www.silverresorts.com.

Turtle Beach Resort. 9049 Midnight Pass Road, Siesta Key 34242. Each quiet, secluded cottage at this romantic hideaway has its own hot tub. Massages are just a phone call away. Watch turtles nest on Turtle Beach, listen to the wild parrots, watch for dolphins and manatees, and dine in the area's best seafood restaurants just footsteps away. Children and pets are welcome. You can bring up to two pets for a 10 percent additional fee. Add $150 for a romance package that includes champagne, dinner for two, and a sunset cruise. Most units have a full kitchen. One- and two-bedroom cottages and studios are available. Use the resort's bicycles, kayaks, rowboat, paddleboat, canoe, and fishing poles. The spacious swimming pool is heated. $$$ plus maid service. (942) 349-4554.

BRADENTON

The most direct route from Sarasota to Bradenton is I-75 North. Let's sort out the nomenclature. Bradenton Area beaches are Anna Maria, Holmes Beach, and Bradenton Beach—reached from the mainland at Cortez. The entire island is Anna Maria Island, bordered by the Gulf of Mexico to the west and Tampa Bay to the east. The island cities are Anna Maria, Holmes Beach, and Bradenton Beach. The beach road is State Road 789, known variously as Midnight Pass Road, Gulf of Mexico Drive, and Casey Key Road as it passes from island to island. Refer to a good map to decide what bridge is best for where you're going. One goes to Holmes Beach, one to Bradenton Beach, and then there isn't another until the U.S. 41 bridge from Sarasota to Lido Key.

Calusa and Timucuan Indians inhabited these sands long before recorded history, feasting on the bountiful seafood and shellfish. Homesteaders began arriving in 1892 by boat, and by 1921 the island was hitched to the mainland by a wooden bridge. Today there's a better highway and bridge, but the old span is still used as a fishing pier. State Road 84 enters the island at Holmes Beach, south of the city of Anna Maria. To reach Bradenton Beach, take State Road 684 from the mainland.

WHERE TO GO

Anna Maria Island Historic Museum. 402 Pine Street, Anna Maria Island 34217. This small effort is worth visiting to see relics and records of the people and events that shaped this lonely barrier island. The museum's home was once an icehouse where sawdust-packed ice, sailed down from the frozen north, was sold through the summer until it was gone. Hours vary seasonally. Donations are appreciated. (942) 778-0495.

Around the Bend Nature Tours. 1815 Palma Sola Boulevard, Bradenton 34209. Naturalist Karen Fraley will take you on walking tours, sunset cruises, a venturer's visit with a picnic, or a Backwaters History Cruise to Cortez Village, a working fishing village since 1889. There's a lot of variety and spontaneity here because it's the work of one dedicated woman, so call ahead to see what's on the schedule. Modest prices start at $10 and go to $35, including transportation and lunch. (941) 794-8773; www.aroundbend.com.

Gamble Plantation State Historic Site. 3708 Patten Avenue, Ellenton 34222. The plantation lies on the mainland just west of I-75 off U.S. 301. Established along the Manatee River in the 1840s, this successful sugar plantation once covered 3,500 acres. The home of Major Robert Gamble here is the only antebellum plantation house that survives in south Florida. Tour the mansion, furnished in the style of the mid-nineteenth century, and note the Judah P. Benjamin Confederate Memorial, dedicated to the secretary of state for the South. When the Confederacy fell, Benjamin took refuge here until a boat could be found to take him across Sarasota Bay. Fleeing Union soldiers, he escaped via the Caribbean to England, where he became a leading member of the English bar. The site is open Thursday through Monday 9:00 A.M. to 5:00 P.M. The house is open to tours only, given on the hour until 4:00 P.M. except at noon. Bring lunch; a shaded picnic area is provided. (941) 722-1017.

WHERE TO SHOP

Everything Under the Sun. 5704 Marina Drive, Anna Maria 34217. Visit this farmers' market to stock your condo or picnic basket, order citrus to send to friends back home, sip a citrus drink, or select gifts and souvenirs. Hours vary seasonally, so call (942) 778-4441.

Islander Antiques Mall. 9807 Gulf Drive, Anna Maria 34217. The island's biggest antiques center features stalls of dozens of dealers. Hours vary seasonally, so call ahead. Not all dealers are open all days, even when the mall is open. (942) 779-2501.

The Sea Hagg. 12304 Cortez Road West, Cortez 34215. This is a good place to stop on your way to or from Anna Marina Island. Buy nautical collectibles, antiques, art, and souvenirs as remembrances of your trip. Hours vary seasonally. Call (941) 795-5756.

WHERE TO EAT

Beach Bistro. 6600 Gulf Drive, Holmes Beach 34217. This is one of the island's smartest spots. Wear your best resort casual duds for an evening of fine Mediterranean cuisine with a good wine. Fresh seafood plays an important role, but you can also order a steak, rack of lamb, or a vegetarian dish. Reservations are essential in season. This is an award-winning restaurant, one of *Florida Trend*'s Top 200 and a consistent favorite with Zagat voters. Open daily for dinner. $-$$$. (942) 778-6444.

Bridge Street Pier & Cafe. 200 Bridge Street, Bradenton Beach 34217. The cafe is on the pier overlooking endless water. The most popular meal is all the grouper you can eat served grilled, blackened, or fried with all the trimmings. Dine indoors or outside under cover. There's a bait-and-tackle shop on the premises, so pick up your fishing needs and proceed onto the pier. Open daily 7:00 A.M. to 10:00 P.M. $-$$. (942) 778-1706.

Gulf Drive Cafe. 900 Gulf Drive, Bradenton Beach 34217. This laid-back and comfortable eatery enjoys a waterfront setting. Its famous breakfasts (Belgian waffles, fancy omelettes) are served anytime, but you can also choose from a generous menu of sandwiches, salads, seafood, pastas, and daily chef's specials. Dine indoors or outside. Open daily 7:00 A.M. to 9:30 P.M. $-$$. (942) 778-1919.

Island Gourmet Pizza. 5604 Marina Drive, Holmes Beach 34217. This place isn't kidding when it claims to be gourmet. In addition to sumptuous pizzas made to order with a big choice of toppings, they serve prime rib, duckling with raspberry sauce, pork Marsala, and other unusual items. They'll deliver pizza, hot or cold subs, sandwiches, salads, and beverages. Open Monday through Saturday 10:30 A.M. to 8:00 P.M. $-$$. (941) 378-3252.

Mr. Bones BBQ. 3007 Gulf Drive, Holmes Beach 34217. Mr. Bones has an eclectic selection that includes baby-back ribs, Indian specialties, vegetarian dishes, and whole-meal salads. End the meal with espresso or cappuccino. On weekends Mr. Bones opens for breakfast at 7:00 A.M. Other days, come for breakfast, lunch, or dinner after 8:00 A.M. $-$$. (942) 778-6614.

Rotten Ralph's. 902 Bay Boulevard South, Anna Maria 34217. Located south of the pier at the Galati Marina, this restaurant specializes in British-style fish-and-chips, but there is also a big choice of other seafood as well as sandwiches, steaks, burgers, and pub grub in a salty, waterfront setting. Ralph is renowned for his escargot and Key lime pie. Open every day for lunch and dinner 11:00 A.M. to 9:00 P.M. $-$$. (941) 778-3953.

Shells. 3200 East Bay Drive, Holmes Beach 34217. Shells is one of a small, popular, consistently good Florida chain. Fresh seafood is served with a California-Caribbean chic. Have one of the pastas, the catch of the day, or a terrific salad. Open for happy hour daily 4:00

to 7:00 P.M., dinner after 4:00 P.M., and Sunday noon to 10:00 P.M. $$. (941) 778–5997.

The Waterfront Restaurant. 111 South Bay Boulevard, Anna Maria 34217. This lands'-end location offers great views of the bay at any time, but it's spectacular at sundown. Watch for the legendary green flash, then order dinner featuring fish fresh from the fleet. Open daily from 11:00 A.M. $–$$. (941) 778–1515.

WHERE TO STAY

BridgeWalk. 100 Bridge Street, Bradenton Beach, Anna Maria Island 34217. This property has Key West style and all the comforts of home. Choose a room, studio, or one- or two-bedroom suite with full kitchen, fireplaces, whirlpool bath in the master bedroom, and spacious screened veranda. Views are of the beach and Intracoastal Waterway. Swim in the heated pool, dine on site, and walk to nearby shops, restaurants, and nightlife. $$$. (941) 779–2545 or (866) 779–2545; www.silverresorts.com.

Harrington House Bed & Breakfast. 5626 Gulf Drive, Holmes Beach 34271. This B&B pampers guests with personal service delivered by caring owner-hosts. It's on a private Gulf beach and has a heated swimming pool. $$. (888) 828–5566 or (941) 778–5444; www.harringtonhouse.com.

Sand Pebble Apartments. 2218 Gulf Drive North, Bradenton Beach 34217. This is a tropical treat on the edge of the Gulf. Comb 7 miles of salt-white sand. Self-catering studios and one- and two-bedroom apartments are equipped for housekeeping in style. Splurge on a unit with private pool or private whirlpool, or use the complex's own pool. Rentals are by the week or month. $$. (800) 500–7263 or (941) 778–3053; www.sandpebble.com.

Silver Surf Gulf Beach Resort. 1301 Gulf Drive North, Bradenton Beach, Anna Maria Island 34217. The resort sits on a private white-sand beach. Get a room, studio, or suite—all with daily maid service. Suites have a full kitchen; and studios have a microwave, coffeemaker, and minirefrigerator. Walk to restaurants, swim in the heated swimming pool, or book a sportfishing charter. Parasailing and bridge fishing are nearby. $$–$$$. (941) 778–6626 or (800) 441–7873; www.silverresorts.com.

Tradewinds Resort. 1603 Gulf Drive North, Bradenton Beach, Anna Maria Island 34217. The Tradewinds offers island living in laid-back style. It's on the bay side of the island, across the street from a private beach. Small and intimate, it has a Superior Small Lodging rating and three diamonds from AAA. Rentals are by the day, week, or month. $$. (941) 779–0010 or (888) 686–6716; www.tradewinds-resort.com.

Clermont · Bushnell · Dade City

CLERMONT

As the sprawling shadow of Orlando spreads over it, Clermont, just west of Orlando on State Road 50, is quickly losing its identity as a separate community. Still, Clermont is in pretty lake country, with open spaces that call for a special visit. Because it's an old crossroads dating back to long before the turnpike or interstates were built, you'll see vestiges of the old, pre-Disney Florida. Roadside stands sell oranges, grapefruit, goat milk fudge, and orange blossom honey. You'll see motor courts that were forerunners of modern motels and cornball attractions that continue to rope in road-weary visitors.

WHERE TO GO

CFT Sommer Sports. 838 West DeSoto Street, Clermont 34711. This company organizes bicycle rides within Lake County, including a triathlon. Call to see what's scheduled and when. (352) 396–1320; www.triflorida.com

Citrus Tower. 141 North U.S. 27, Clermont 33937. The tower is one of the tourist attractions your grandparents visited on their trips to central Florida, and somehow it has survived into the interstate era. U.S. 27 is no longer the main artery through the heart of Florida, but it continues to pump tourists into an area that still has the tower, but little citrus. Today's view from the twenty-two-story tower is of increasing urban sprawl, but the tower is worth

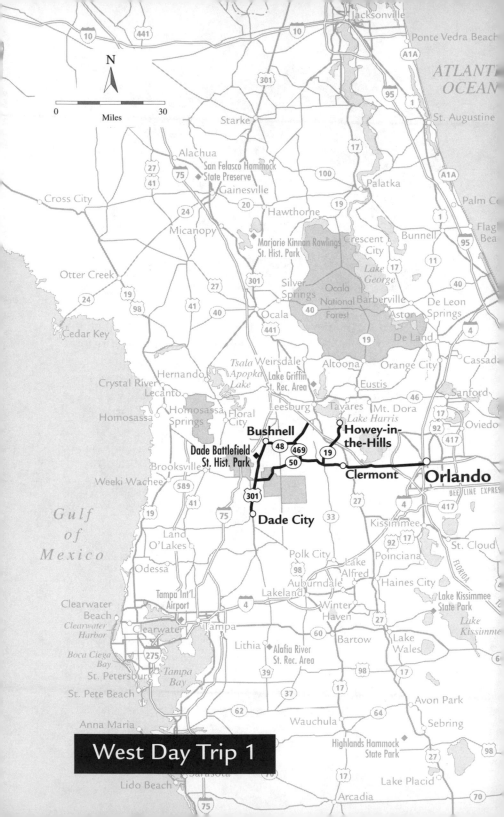

Gulf
of
Mexico

ATLANTIC
OCEAN

West Day Trip 1

Bushnell
Dade Battlefield
St. Hist. Park
Howey-in-
the-Hills
Clermont
Orlando
Dade City

visiting for its nostalgic exhibits as well as for the 225-foot elevator ride. Except Christmas and Thanksgiving, hours are 8:00 A.M. to 5:00 P.M. Monday through Saturday and 11:00 A.M. to 6:00 P.M. Sunday. (352) 394–4061; www.citrustower.com.

Lake Louisa State Park. 12549 State Park Drive, Clermont 34711. The park is 10 miles south of State Road 50 off County 561. This 4,372-acre park is on the shores of Lake Louisa, one of a chain of lakes formed by the Palatlakaha River. Come here to fish, swim, picnic, canoe, exercise your horse on miles of equestrian trails, or train your binoculars on red foxes, bobcats, white-tailed deer, pocket gophers, marsh rabbits, and a swirl of bird life. Open 8:00 A.M. to an hour before sundown. State park fees apply. (352) 394–3969.

Lakeridge Winery. 19239 U.S. 27 North, Clermont 33937. Lakeridge is a beautiful botanical site where sixty-seven acres of vineyards grow hybrid grapes that were developed especially for the hot, humid, grape-hostile Florida climate. Varieties including Blanc de Blanc have come a long way from the syrup-sweet muscadine and scuppernong wines that the South was once known for. Take the one-hour tour anytime, but the winery is especially lively at harvest times, mid-June and late August, with live jazz entertainment. The winery is open daily; free except during concerts and special events. (800) 768–9463; www.lakeridgewinery.com.

WHERE TO EAT

Cypress Tree. 11834 Lakeshore Drive, Clermont 34711. Located in the Lake Susan Lodge, this is a popular restaurant where locals come for shrimp, grouper, scallops, and live music on weekends. $$. (352) 394–3964.

French Corner. 915 Montrose Street, Clermont 33937. Located in the Mulberry Inn Bed & Breakfast, this restaurant is operated by a couple from Limoges, France, and their gifted chef, Dominique Laene. Main courses are spectacular, but what sets the meals apart is that each entree comes with five vegetables chosen from almost two dozen fresh, succulent varieties the chef prepares each day. Have the duck with maple syrup and pear, rabbit, the fresh catch of the day, frog legs, or the lamb stew, swimming in delectable sauce. Enjoy one of the flaky, fruit-filled pastries for dessert. There's no bar, but beer and a selection of excellent wines are available. The restaurant is open for lunch and dinner Tuesday through Thursday. Reservations are recommended. $$-$$$. (352) 242-0670.

WHERE TO STAY

Howard Johnson Express Inn. 1810 South U.S. 27, Clermont 34711. This sixty-five-room roadside motel is near everything and priced to please. There's a swimming pool and guest laundry, but otherwise this is a plain-Jane place for overnighting in a basic motel room. Parking is plentiful. Restaurants aren't far away. $. (352) 429-9033.

Lake Susan Lodge. 11834 Lakeshore Drive, Clermont 34711. This place takes you back to postwar Florida. Sleep in a lakefront cabin and fish in your choice of fifteen spring-fed lakes. The lodge has a bait-and-tackle shop, boat rentals, a store, docks, a launch ramp if you bring your own boat, and a popular restaurant, the Cypress Tree. $$. (352) 394-3964.

Mission Inn Golf & Tennis Resort, 10400 County Road 48M, Howey-in-the-Hills 34737. This resort is a groomed, green oasis halfway between Clermont and Tavares. Built in Spanish Mission style with red-tile roofs and graceful archways that frame views of the golf courses, the resort has courtyards with fountains; winding pathways to its 187 rooms, resorts, and villas; twenty-four-hour room service; two eighteen-hole golf courses; tennis; and boating out of a full-service marina, croquet, bicycling, jogging, and fishing. Shop in the arcade and dine in El Conquistador. $$$. (352) 324-2350; www.missioninnresort.com.

Motel 8. 135 North U.S. Highway 27, Clermont 34711. This basic motel has twenty-two cookie-cutter rooms, one of them with a kitchen. It's nothing fancy, one of the typical roadside motels that were built when U.S. 27 was a main route for snowbirds, but it's next to Citrus Tower and handy to the area's sight-seeing, shopping, and restaurants. $. (352) 394-6316.

Mulberry Inn Bed & Breakfast. 915 Montrose Street, Clermont 33937. Located on the corner of West Street, this B&B is more than a charming turn-of-the-century Florida Cracker house with comfortable rooms. It's also the home of the gourmet French Corner restaurant . The inn is open every day for bed-and-breakfast. $$-$$$. (352) 242-0670.

Summer Bay Resort. 17805 U.S. Highway 192, Clermont 34711. This is a popular destination for tourists because it's centrally located to sight-seeing in the Tampa and Orlando areas and has all the resort bells and whistles—swimming pool, a children's program, fitness center, and boat dock. Every unit has a kitchen. Restaurants are nearby. $$-$$$. (352) 242-1100.

BUSHNELL

From Clermont, stay with Route 50 through Mascotte, watching for a right turn (north) onto Route 469. This becomes Route 48 as you go through the community of Central Hill. Stay with Route U.S. 301 toward Dade Battlefield State Historic Site.

Although this day trip goes only as far as the Dade Battlefield south of Bushnell, the town itself has motels, a campground, and places to eat.

WHERE TO GO

Dade Battlefield State Historic Site. Mail address: P.O. Box 938, Bushnell 33513. The battlefield is just southwest of Bushnell off State Road 476 (Seminole Avenue).

One of the most poignant battles in American history took place in the lonely pinewoods here in 1835 during the Seminole Wars. Major Francis Dade and his force of 108 marching men were suddenly attacked by Indians, who had shadowed them for five days. Because the most suspect ambush points were behind them, Dade hadn't posted scouts. Worse still, it was raining, so the men's muskets and ammunition were covered with their coats. Half were killed or wounded with the first volley. With no shelter, the soldiers quickly felled a few pines to create meager breastworks, but still they died one by one. Two wounded soldiers made it to Fort Brooke to tell the tale, but it was almost two months before a party arrived at the scene of the massacre to bury the dead.

The scene is reenacted each year on the weekend closest to Christmas, but the site is worth visiting anytime. Bring a picnic, walk the trail, and see exhibits in the visitor center, which has rest rooms. Open Thursday through Monday 9:00 A.M. to 5:00 P.M. (352) 793–4781.

DADE CITY

Dade City was named for the major who, with 108 men, was ambushed north of here during the Seminole Wars. The community thrived in old Florida, but the interstates stole its thunder and downtown faded—only to be reborn as a chic center for antiques shops, boutiques, and trendy restaurants. Write ahead for a map (see Regional Information) showing historic homes, and take your own walking or driving tour to see more than sixty historic sites, including the old hospital, Victorian homes, and the stately court-house with its charming band shell. Ask, too, for the *Historic Down-town Dade City Shopping* guide, showing the locations of more than sixty antiques and specialty shops, galleries, and restaurants, most of them on or just off U.S. 301. From Bushnell follow U.S. 301 south to Dade City. After your visit, hop back on U.S. 301, this time heading north, back to Route 50 and Orlando.

WHERE TO GO

Pioneer Florida Museum. Mail address: P.O. Box 335, Dade City 33526. Located north of Dade City off U.S. 301, this is an entire village of buildings, including a shoe shop, a house dating to the mid-1860s, a 1913 depot with steam engine, a restored one-room schoolhouse, and much more. A variety of collections are shown in the main museum building and barn. Special events held here throughout the year include a quilt show and sale, magnolia show, pioneer craft days, and more. Hours are Tuesday through Sunday 1:00 to 5:00 P.M. Admission is charged. (352) 567–0262.

WHERE TO EAT

A Matter of Taste. 14121 Seventh Street, Dade City 33525. The restaurant is upstairs, with a nice view of the passing scene below. Choose from a tempting list of soups, salads, quiches, cold plates, and sandwiches or hot dishes, including a country skillet of vegetables, béarnaise sauce, and rice. The Tarpon Springs Greek salad is made with Greek potato salad and a homemade Greek dressing. The building dates to the early 1920s, when it was the headquarters of the city's telephone company. Call ahead for takeout. $. (352) 567-5100 phone or fax.

Kafe Kokopelli. 37940 Live Oak Avenue, Dade City 33525. This building was the original Ford agency, built to sell and service Model T's and all the cars that came later. Its tools were served by a pulley system that's now in the Smithsonian, but the remains can still be seen in the rafters. Burgers are served all day, and there are also hot and cold sandwiches, quesadillas, fried fish, vegetarian selections, snacks such as wings and nachos, and a killer raspberry–Key lime cheesecake. House wines, sangria, and specialty coffees finish the meal. Open for lunch and dinner Tuesday through Saturday. $. (352) 523-0055.

Lunch on Limoges. 14139 Seventh Street, Dade City 33525. Located on the old courthouse square, this eatery actually serves your lunch on Limoges china. A chalkboard shows daily specials, such as pecan grouper, chicken salad on a croissant, shrimp salad with fresh fruit, or poached salmon. Open Tuesday through Saturday 11:00 A.M. to 3:00 P.M. $–$$. (352) 567-5685.

WHERE TO STAY

Azalea House. 37719 Meridian Avenue, Dade City 33525. This home was built in 1906 nestled among bamboo, azaleas, and Spanish moss–hung oaks. Walk to antiques shops and restaurants downtown. Stay in the honeymoon suite, the Rose Room, or the Burgundy Suite, which has twin beds. A cold breakfast is served in the formal dining room, which has a fireplace, or on the veranda. $$–$$$. (352) 523-1773.

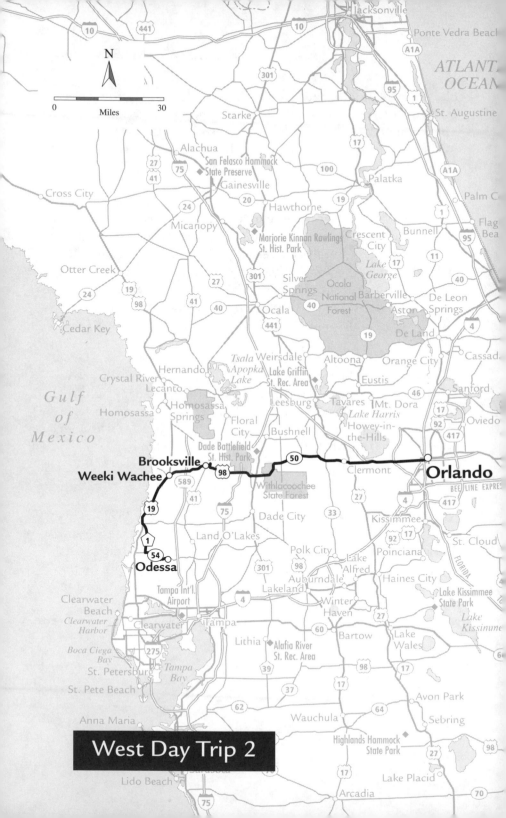

West Day Trip 2

Brooksville · Weeki Wachee

BROOKSVILLE

Brooksville was a hotbed of blockade-runner activity during the Civil War, when Confederate troops counted on it to supply them with beef, pork, and salt. Each year in January, the Brooksville Raid Civil War reenactment is one of the city's biggest tourism events. The historic hamlet is a good place to headquarter while you explore the springs, coasts, and forests of this area. Take State Road 50 west from Orlando; it joins U.S. 98 and takes you into Brooksville.

WHERE TO GO

Hernando Heritage Museum. 601 Museum Court, Brooksville 34601. The museum houses one of the state's best collections of Civil War relics, including a complete doctor's office and 6,000 antiques dating to the mid-nineteenth century. Admission is $2.00 for adults and 50 cents for children. Hours are noon to 3:00 P.M. Tuesday through Friday. (352) 799–0129. Ask about the Brooksville Raid, which is organized by the museum.

WHERE TO SHOP

Rogers' Christmas House and Village. 103 South Saxon Avenue, Brooksville 34601. The complex of shops is housed in five quaint old houses from the early 1900s. Shop all year for Christmas gifts and decorations in one of the Sunshine State's oldest and most popular Christmas stores. Open every day but Christmas 9:30 A.M. to 5:00 P.M. (352) 796–2415.

WHERE TO EAT

Blueberry Patch Restaurant and Tea Room. 414 East Liberty Street, Brooksville 34601. The Patch is filled with antiques to look over (and perhaps purchase) while you dine on soufflé, salad, or quiche, followed by homemade pie. Hours vary seasonally, so call ahead. $–$$. (352) 797–0084.

Mykonos II. 1740 East Jefferson Street, Brooksville 34601. This place specializes in a Greek combination dinner, but Italian and Cuban dishes are also available The Cuban sandwich makes a great lunch, but go Greek with the baklava for dessert. Call ahead for hours. $–$$. (352) 799–3154.

Ye Olde Fireside Inn. 1175 Broad Street, Brooksville 34601. This spot is as cozy as the name implies, serving a crusty beef Wellington that will take you back to old England. Seafood, chicken, and beef dishes are all good, and there's Key lime pie for dessert. Call for hours and reservations. $$–$$$. (352) 796–0293.

WHERE TO STAY

Claflin House Bed & Breakfast. 33 South Brooksville Avenue, Brooksville 34601. Claflin House is a Greek Revival–style mansion offering three guest rooms. Mornings begin with freshly baked pastries and coffee, and you're welcome to join your hosts on the veranda for lemonade in the afternoon. The house sits on an acre of pretty grounds in the center of the city's historic district. $$. (877) 799–7299; innformation.com/fl/claflin

Mary A. Coogler Cottage. 114 South Brooksville Avenue, Brooksville 34601. Located downtown, this two-bedroom guest house is named for an artist who once lived here. $$. (352) 796–6857. Through the same number, you can arrange to stay at the **Amapola Guest House** (238 North Lemon Avenue, Brooksville 34601), a fifty-year-old duplex. $$.

Verona House Bed & Breakfast. 201 South Main Street, Brooksville 34601. The Verona House was built in 1925 from a Sears and Roebuck kit delivered in rail cars. It's listed on the National Register of Historic Places. Stay in your choice of four bedchambers or the guest cottage, which has a full kitchen. A full hot breakfast is included. $$. (800) 355–6717; www.bbhost.com/veronabb/.

WEEKI WACHEE

The ancients gathered here for the sweet, healing waters, and it has been a landmark since before European settlement. To reach Weeki Wachee from Brooksville, head west on State Road 50.

WHERE TO GO

J. B. Starkey's Flatwoods Adventures. 12959 State Road 54, Odessa 33556. This is a real family ranch, rambling along the Anclote River north of Tampa and east of Tarpon Springs, about 25 miles south-southeast of Weeki Wachee. On your way to or from Weeki Wachee, plan to stop here on Route 54, a good east-west road running between U.S. 19 and U.S. 41 south of New Port Richey.

Take a range-buggy ride through unspoiled flatlands, pine ridges, and pastures. Walk the boardwalk that spans the swamps, giving you a bird's-eye view of native plants, critters, and bird life. Hear from real ranch hands the story of Florida's centuries-long importance as a cattle ranching center. Adult admission is $14.75, $7.75 for children, and $13.75 for seniors. Tours vary seasonally, so call ahead. (813) 926–1133; www.flatwoodsadventures.com.

Weeki Wachee Springs. 6131 Commercial Way, Weeki Wachee 34606. This is one of Florida's oldest attractions, still quaint, unique, and bubbling with charm. Real "mermaids" swim a lithe ballet, staying underwater for the entire show because they take discreet breaths of air through tubes. Two shows are given every day, but call ahead because times vary. One admission price covers the mermaid show and all-day fun at Buccaneer Bay water park, even though the water park is open only seasonally. Admission is $14.95 per person; yearly passes are an excellent value. Restaurants and snack bars serve a good choice of menus, but you're also welcome to bring a cooler (but no glass, please).

WHERE TO STAY

Best Western Weeki Wachee. 6172 Commercial Way, Weeki Wachee 34606. Located across the street from the springs, this property has a swimming pool, playground, and lounge. Lodgings are basic but comfortable. Spend a weekend at the water park and fishing in the Gulf of Mexico. Ask about fisherman's rates. $$. (352) 596-2007 or (800) 490-8268.

Inverness

This area is bordered to the west by the Withlacoochee State Forest and to the east by sprawling Tsala Apopka Lake. Ten thousand years ago, Paleoindians thrived along the warm, life-giving waters of the Withlacoochee River. Later, Seminoles settled in, and by 1836 white settlers began eyeing these moist woodlands north of Tampa. After the Civil War, settlement began in earnest. From Orlando, go northwest on the Florida Turnpike to where it joins I-75 at Wildwood. At the next exit, go west on State Road 44 to Inverness. From Inverness you can go north on Route 45 to Hernando. Or head 9 miles west to Lecanto. From there, head south on Highway 491, east on Highway 480, and north on U.S. 41 to reach the Withlacoochee State Forest and then into Floral City.

INVERNESS

The earliest burials in Magnolia Cemetery date to 1869, when settlers streamed into Florida to make new lives after the War Between the States. In time, the stagecoach route was replaced by a railroad, which in turn gave way to highways—and the motorcar changed everything. The original county seat, Mannfield, became a ghost town after the government moved to Inverness. Today, historic sites and the outdoors are still drawing visitors to this quiet, less-discovered part of Florida.

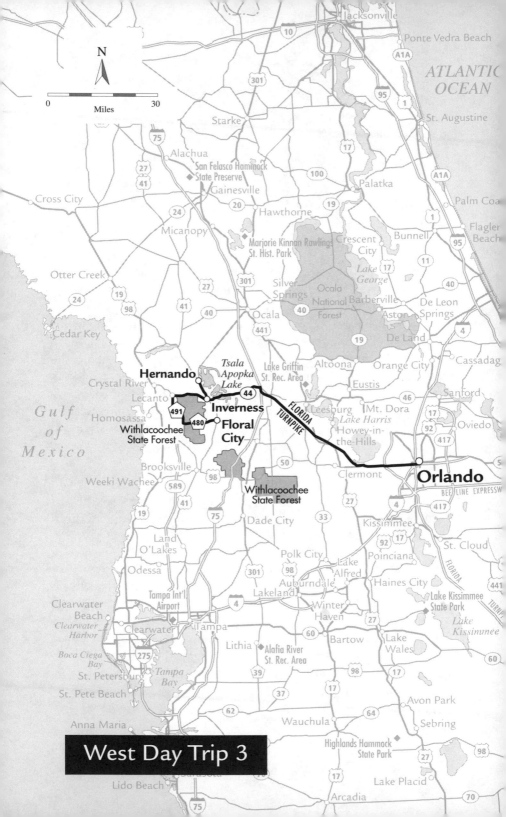

N

0 Miles 30

West Day Trip 3

WHERE TO GO

Citrus County Heritage Tour. Write for information (see Regional Information) on the historic highlights of the county and set out to see them on a series of pleasant, country drives through Crystal River, Inverness, Lecanto, Ozello, Homosassa, and Floral City. The Old Courthouse on the square in Inverness dates to 1911 and is one of only twenty-five historic courthouses remaining in the state. It's now a museum open weekdays and on Saturday morning. Shop the museum store for educational toys and unusual gifts. The Neoclassical Revival Masonic Temple dates to 1910, the Crown Hotel to the 1920s, and the Kelley House to 1903. The Atlantic Coast Line Railroad Depot was built in 1910 in the Prairie style introduced by Frank Lloyd Wright. In Florida City, see Pleasant Hill Baptist Church, founded in 1895 by Negroes who came to the area to work the phosphate mines. Follow the history of Florida architecture from the years before World War I through the Colonial Revival craze of the 1920s and the ever-present practicality of Florida Vernacular, with its wide verandas.

Fort Cooper State Park. 3100 South Old Floral City Road, Inverness 32650. Located 2 miles southeast of town, this park is home to Lake Holathikaha, the spring-fed waters that hosted battle-weary soldiers of the First Georgia Battalion of Volunteers in 1836 during the Second Seminole War. General Winfield Scott had marched to Tampa, leaving his sick and wounded behind to drink the healing waters and hold off the Seminoles as best they could. They held their own for sixteen days until Scott returned with supplies and reinforcements.

The remains of the old fort weren't excavated until the 1970s. Now the fort is the scene of reenactments featuring volunteers from all over the South. Walk 5 miles of nature trails looking for deer, fox, rabbits, owls, and herons. Swim, rent a canoe, or fish in the clear lake. Break out a picnic. Play volleyball or horseshoes. There's a primitive camping area, rest rooms, parking, and picnic tables. The park is open during daylight hours. State park fees apply. (352) 726–0315.

Old Courthouse Heritage Museum. One Courthouse Square, Inverness 32650. Once the courthouse for Citrus County, this museum houses a courtroom as it looked in 1912, rotating exhibits, galleries for local history and prehistory, and a museum store.

There's plenty of parking east of the museum and room for a picnic on the grassy grounds. Wallace Brooks Park, 0.75 mile northeast of the museum at Dampier Street and Martin Luther King Drive, has picnic tables and a playground. The museum is open weekdays 10:00 A.M. to 4:00 P.M. and Saturday 10:00 A.M. to 2:00 P.M. Admission is free, but donations are appreciated. (352) 341-6428.

Ted Williams Museum and Hitters Hall of Fame. 2455 North Citrus Hills Boulevard, Hernando 34442. This museum is a must-see for baseball fans and nostalgia buffs. Take U.S. 41 north out of Inverness. Sit in an eighty-seat theater to watch continuous videos of the Splendid Splinter and relive Ted's twenty-two-year-long career through displays that show his baseball career as well as his service as a Marine Corps pilot in World War II and the Korean Conflict. The great sluggers of all time are honored here, too: Babe Ruth, Lou Gehrig, Ty Cobb, Mel Ott, Ralph Kiner, and many more. Open Tuesday through Sunday 10:00 A.M. to 4:00 P.M. except major holidays. Admission is $9.00 for adults, $1.00 for children. (352) 527-6566.

Withlacoochee State Trail. Mail address: 12549 State Park Drive, Clermont 34711. The trail runs from Trilby to just below Dunellon along an old railway. It's paved in asphalt for 46 miles, a trail to hike, bike, or—if you stay off the paving—ride horseback. Write ahead for a map, then leave the car at one of the parking areas, such as the Inverness Depot listed above, and plan an excursion of a few hours or an entire day; or stay with the path, which is part of the Florida Trail and Croom Mountain Bike Trails, and end up miles away. The trail has a number of points of interest, access points, parks, and picnic areas, including one in Fort Cooper State Park. (352) 394-2280.

WHERE TO SHOP

Accents by Grace and Friends. 106 North Pine Avenue, Inverness 33450. Accents is a collection of delightful shops selling custom crafts, clothing, bears, old linen, sculpture, hand-blown glass, baubles, and bangles. Everything is imaginative and fun, and Grace will be glad to turn your purchases into a gift basket for any occasion. Hours vary, so call ahead. (352) 860-1990.

Connors Gifts. 218 Tompkins Street, Inverness 34450. This shop is perfectly placed across from the Crown Hotel, handy for shopping for collectibles and just the right gifts to take home with you.

Among the specialties are Lladro porcelains and Zingle-Berrys figurines.

Country at Home. 119 North Pine Avenue, Inverness 34450. This place is all about country and quaint, so shop here for candles, fragrances, frills, and fripperies. In stock is what proprietors claim is the largest collection of Boyds Bears in the South, so add to your collection of the bears and their pals. Hours vary seasonally, so call ahead. (352) 637–6621.

Ferris Groves. U.S. 41, Floral City 34436. This is the kind of highway stop our grandparents looked for as they drove the country roads of Florida. Buy for yourself or have citrus shipped for you. There's a luscious array of strawberries and tomatoes in season; freshly squeezed juice; seasonal citrus including red grapefruit, oranges, and short-season Honeybells; homemade pies; and a selection of jams and candies with or without sugar. Open daily except Sunday 9:00 A.M. to 6:00 P.M. (352) 860–0366.

Winnie's Lavender & Lace. 508 West Main Street, Inverness 33450. Located one-quarter mile west of the courthouse, Winnie's is a Victorian home turned into a two-story shopping paradise for those who love romantic accessories and gifts. Shop for framed art, decorator items, and unusual greeting cards. Hours vary, so call ahead. (352) 726–0068.

WHERE TO EAT

Churchill's. 109 North Seminole Avenue, Inverness 34450. Located in the Crown Hotel (see Where to Stay), Churchill's offers fine dining in the British tradition, with a good roast of beef, Yorkshire pudding, lobster, a regal filet mignon, candlelight, crisp napery, and Gershwin playing in the background. Come here for a very special evening, or dine more informally in the **Fox & Hound Pub**, which is also a good place for a drink before dinner at Churchill's. It's casual and friendly and "veddy" British, with a menu of such pub grub as steak and kidney pie washed down with a glass of shandy (beer and lemonade) or fish-and-chips accompanied by a dark ale. Call for hours and reservations. (352) 344–5555.

Jim's Cafe. 727 North U.S. 41, Inverness 34450. Jim's is a night-out, special-occasion place. Start with drinks from the full bar, then an evening of feasting and good live music. Have a steak, roasted chicken, or the catch of the day—and something chocolate for dessert. Linger over an after-dinner drink. Open Friday and Saturday until 3:00 A.M. Call for hours, which vary seasonally, and reservations, which are recommended. $$-$$$. (352) 341-5894.

Fishermans Restaurant. 12311 East Gulf to Lake Highway, Inverness 34450. Located on the river at the County Line Bridge in an area of the Withlacoochee known as a mini Everglades, this is a classic Florida seafood shop with a huge choice of seafood plus steaks, chops, burgers, and side dishes. A specialty is grouper, prepared your way and served with all the trimmings. Shrimp, lobster, scallops, oysters, clams, crab cakes, and farm-raised catfish also highlight the menu. The fisherman's platters are belt-busters, especially the Shipwreck Special, consisting of a half-pound sirloin steak, a lobster tail, and tons of trimmings. Order a round of gator bites with tangy mustard sauce for the table. For dessert, have the lime pie. Hours are Sunday noon to 8:00 P.M. and Tuesday through Saturday from 11:00 A.M. $-$$$. (352) 637-5888.

The Gathering. 724 U.S. 41 South, Inverness 34450. This eatery is as comfortable as the family parlor, with comfort foods to match. Bring the family for casual dining on family favorites. Open 4:00 P.M. until closing Thursday through Sunday. (352) 344-8476.

Stumpknockers. 110 West Main Street, Inverness 34450. This is a great location on the downtown square, with another location overlooking the river at the bridge on State Road 200 between Inverness and Ocala. The name, incidentally, applies to a small breamlike fish found in Florida rivers. Most people come here for the hot, crisp, deep-fried catfish featured in all-you-can-eat specials every night. Order from a menu that also features seafood and steaks, fries, sandwiches, and salads. The river location is open for dinner daily except Monday; the downtown restaurant is open for lunch and dinner except Monday. $-$$. (352) 726-2212 downtown or (352) 854-2288 on the river.

WHERE TO STAY

Best Western Citrus Hills Lodge. 350 East Norvell Bryant Highway, Hernando 34442. This is a quiet country spot where you'll find reliable Best Western quality. Stop for the night in a standard or deluxe room with Jacuzzi, take a swim in the heated pool, have your hair done or get a massage in the salon, and go on your way after a free continental breakfast. Every room has a coffeemaker; a microwave or refrigerator is available. The concierge can arrange tennis or a round of golf nearby. $$. (352) 527–0015.

The Crown Hotel. 109 North Seminole Avenue, Inverness 34450. The Crown is a delightfully old-fashioned thirty-four-room hotel with brass bedsteads, hearty dining in Churchill's (see Where to Eat), and a British pub. Modern amenities include private baths, a swimming pool, air-conditioning, telephone, color TV, and parking for your horseless carriage. A showcase in the lobby holds replicas of the glittering crown jewels of England. Ask about packages, suites, and the seventh-night-free promotion. Pets are permitted for $10 per pet per night. $$. (352) 344–5555.

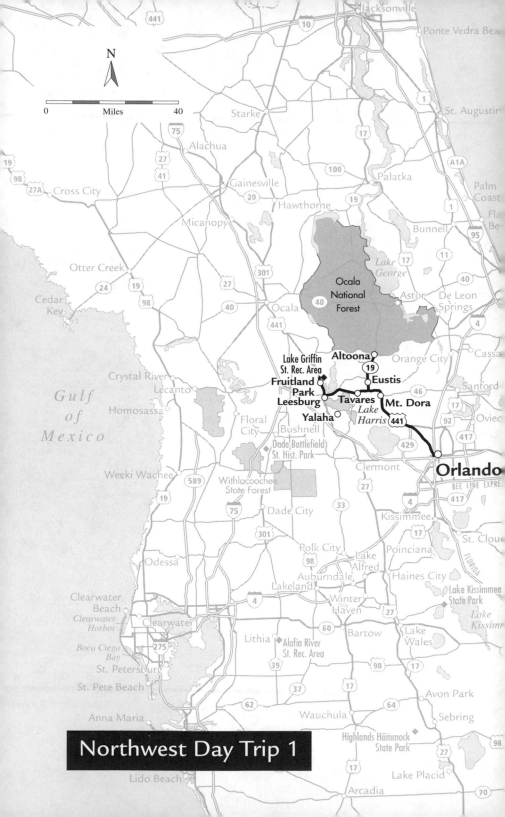

Northwest Day Trip 1

NORTHWEST DAY TRIP 1

Mount Dora · Tavares · Leesburg

Leave Orlando headed northwest on U.S. 441, or the Orange Blossom Trail, through Apopka to Mount Dora. Continue west on U.S. 441 to Tavares, then Leesburg. Return the same way, or check a map for alternative routes such as State Road 48 around Lake Harris or U.S. 27 south out of Leesburg to Route 50, then east into Orlando.

Sample an area that is filled with lakes, miles of green countryside, and still enough rural flavor to give you a rest from city life. Stay in a highway motel, an upscale hotel or inn, or a rustic fish camp.

MOUNT DORA

Even though it has been gripped by the giant tentacles of Orlando, Mount Dora still has an old-fashioned downtown and the quaint, quiet charms of the village it once was. Relive the past by booking a room at the Lakeside Inn and walking the shaded streets to shop and dine. In the old days, visitors arrived on the train and walked to the hotel, only a few footsteps away, while hand wagons followed with their mountains of baggage. Northerners (including President Calvin Coolidge, who spent a month here in 1930) came to stay the season, complete with their servants and all the steamer trunks it took to keep them in fashion for weeks. The yacht club on the lake is Florida's first, dating to 1913 and rebuilt after a fire in 1966. It's the scene of periodic antique boat shows and daily boat rides aboard the *Mount Dora Star*.

Downtown is bordered by Clayton, Liberty, McDonald, and Tenth Streets. To browse the antiques district, you'll find most shops between Alexander and Tremain Streets on Third through Seventh Avenues. The city has more than a dozen individual shops, a nice contrast to the enormous antiques-fest at Florida Twin Markets, also known as Renninger's Antique Center, on U.S. 441, which is also a must for serious antiquers.

There really is a Lake Dora, although the "mount" is a local joke celebrated in T-shirts that proclaim, I CLIMBED MOUNT DORA. The lake sits below the lawns of the Lakeside Inn, a sparkling expanse of sweetwater that is still a paradise for boating, fishing, and nature and sunset watching.

WHERE TO GO

Chamber of Commerce. Alexander at Third Street, Mount Dora 32757. Located in the old train depot, the chamber provides a window on quaint yesterdays, when Florida visitors came by rail. Pick up brochures and ask friendly locals where to dine, shop, and sleep. One brochure describes a self-guided 3-mile driving tour past green parks and historic mansions dating to the 1880s and early 1900s. Another lists and maps the antiques shops and boutiques. Hours vary, but the depot is usually open business hours. (352) 383-2165; www.mtdora.org.

Mount Dora Cannonball. Alexander and Third Streets, Mount Dora 32757. The Cannonball offers an hour-long ride in a vintage rail car pulled by a 1913 oil-fired steam engine. The Mount Dora Scenic Railway's cars have appeared in movies including *Rosewood* and on the TV miniseries *North and South*. Hours vary seasonally, so call ahead and then get to the station at least ten minutes early. Adult tickets are $10.00, seniors age 55 and older are $9.00, and children age 12 and under are $6.00. (800) 625-4307 or (352) 383-4368.

Palm Island Park. Tremain Street, Mount Dora 32757. Located between Third and Fourth Avenues this park covers twelve acres of wetlands accessed by boardwalks. You'll probably see alligators, otters, herons, ospreys, coots, ducks, woodpeckers, and much more wildlife among the cypress, oaks, maples, and palms. The park also has mulched nature trails, picnic areas, and a picturesque lighthouse. Open from 7:30 A.M. to a half hour after sunset. Free admission. (352) 383-2165.

WHERE TO SHOP

Garden Topia. 125 West Sixth Avenue, Mount Dora 32757. As the name implies, this place is a gardener's utopia. Start exotic plants from seeds. Shop for statuary, pots, and decorative pieces that will turn your garden into a showplace. Buy dried flowers, gifts, books, garden furniture, or a unique birdbath. Shop indoors and out, on ordinary days or during special events such as the organic farmers' market, Christmas open house, and craft days. Open every day 10:30 A.M. to 5:00 P.M. and in evenings during special occasions. (352) 383-2280.

    Renninger's Antique Center. 20651 Highway 441, Mount Dora 32757. The center is one of the largest gatherings of antiques dealers in the state. Most stalls are open 10:00 A.M. to 5:00 P.M., and the center's liveliest on weekends, although a good selection of dealers are here every day. Shop for antiques, collectibles, and rarities in every category from soup tureens to nut bowls. (352) 383-8393 or (800) 522-3555.

WHERE TO EAT

Beauclaire Restaurant. 100 North Alexander Street, Mount Dora 32757. Located in the Lakeside Inn, the Beauclaire is sedate and lovely in its Gatsby-era garb. It's a favorite for its Sunday brunch as well as for elegant dinners, lingering lunches, and pleasant breakfasts. Start dinner with a dozen steamer clams in a succulent broth or the hearts of palm salad with shrimp. From the list of seafood, pasta, poultry, and meat entrees, try the Chicken Georgia with peaches and pecans, seafood St. Jacques, grilled swordfish, or rack of lamb. Lunchtime favorites include chicken potpie, hot roast beef sandwich, and corned beef Reuben. Other choices range from soup to the Vegi-Sandwich. Open daily for breakfast, lunch, and dinner. Reservations are suggested at any time and are essential for Sunday brunch. $-$$. (352) 383-4101.

    Goblin Market. 331 North Donnelly Street, Mount Dora 32757. The Goblin is a tiny, bookish place with fewer than a dozen tables and personal service from owners and chef. Start with a fragrant soup or the escargot en croute followed by fresh grouper in potato crust, roasted chicken, or one of the chef's daily specials based on the best of what the marketplace offered that morning. Beer and wine are served, and the restaurant is smoke-free. Open daily except Sunday for lunch and dinner. $$$. (352) 735-0059.

WHERE TO STAY

Darst Victorian Manor. 494 Old Highway 441, Mount Dora 32757. The Darst looks like a Queen Anne mansion, but it's newly built with modern touches that have won it an AAA four-diamond rating. Five suites all have private baths; two have fireplaces. Watch sunsets on the lake, explore the area, go antiquing, seek out the area's smart restaurants, or play golf at one of Mount Dora's two country clubs. Tea and a country breakfast are included in rates. $$-$$$. (352) 383-4050; www.bbonline.com/fl/darstmanor.

Dreamspinner. 117 Diedrich Street, Eustis 32726. This bed-and-breakfast inn offers seven guest rooms housed in a stately home built in 1881 in the center of Eustis, a few miles north of Mount Dora. Relax in the romantic gardens or on the wraparound veranda, play a game of croquet on the lawn, and sleep in a room furnished with antiques and fine art. Afternoon tea, wine and cheese, and breakfast are all included. Well-behaved pets are welcome. $$$. (352) 589-8082.

Fiddlers Green Ranch. 42725 West Altoona Road, Altoona 32702. The ranch is located north of Mount Dora on the southern border of Ocala National Forest. Rent a cabin or villa with up to three bedrooms. Bring groceries; every unit has a full kitchen, laundry room, and living-dining room. Vacation dude ranch style with trail rides into the forest, overnight campouts with a barbecue dinner, campfire entertainment, and chuck wagon breakfasts. The ranch also has a swimming pool and gift shop. Bring your pet if you like. $$-$$$. (352) 669-7111 or (800) 94-RANCH.

Emerald Hill Inn. 27751 Lake Jem Road, Mount Dora 32757. This spacious ranch house on a high overlook above Lake Victoria offers five guest rooms and personal service from hosts who live here. Escape to a country setting shaded with live oak trees, magnolias, and cypress. The included continental breakfast is served in the Florida room. $$-$$$. (352) 383-2777 or (800) 366-9387; www.bbonline.com/fl/emeraldhill.

Lakeside Inn. 100 North Alexander Street, Mount Dora 32757. The inn is in the heart of town, a few blocks from the main street overlooking the lake that attracted wealthy Northerners to winter here more than a century ago. Headquarter here while you "do" the antiques district, stroll streets straight out of yesteryear, and try the town's trendy restaurants. Dine in the inn's restaurant, snack at the pool bar, enjoy happy hour in the lounge, enjoy live entertainment after dinner some nights, play tennis day or night, and bring your boat if you like. Dockage is free to hotel guests. Rooms and suites are available in the main hotel, which has a spacious front porch with rockers. Or stay at Lakeside Landings Bed & Breakfast, where guests take breakfast at the inn. Ask about packages. $$–$$$. (800) 556–5016 or (352) 383–4101; www.lakeside-inn.com.

TAVARES

Early settlers stopped short when they saw the beauty of this area, surrounded by lakes that are still the star of the tourism show here. A number of operators offer sight-seeing, dinner, and luncheon cruises on the lakes and old canals that were dug generations ago for the lumber trade. Driving through on U.S. 441, you'll see signs offering a number of cruises and boat rentals, or stay at the Mission Inn (see West Day Trip 1) and cruise Lake Harris aboard their antique yacht, *La Reina*.

WHERE TO GO

Bartholomew's Yesteryear Cruises. 12423 Highway 441, Tavares 32778. Cruise through scenic lakes aboard an old-fashioned riverboat or a silent electric boat. Have dinner or lunch while you sightsee. Call ahead for reservations, which are essential. (352) 343–7047.

Discovery Gardens. 30205 State Road 19, Tavares 32778. Discover nine gardens in a parklike setting. The goal is to teach visitors about horticulture and landscape design, but there's also pleasant self-guided strolling in a fragrant setting that changes day by day, season by season. Open every day 9:00 A.M. to 4:00 P.M. (352) 343–4141.

WHERE TO STAY

Lake Harris Lodge. 119 Lake Park Road, Tavares 32778. This is nothing fancy, just an RV park where you can rent a space for your RV or stay in a cottage that has all the basics for eating and sleeping after a day on the lake. All the fish camp basics are here: boat rental, bait and tackle, a store selling basic supplies, and a launch ramp you can use for a fee. Fishing guides are available. $-$$. (352) 343-4111.

LEESBURG

WHERE TO GO

Lake Griffin State Recreation Area. 3089 Highway 44/27, Fruitland Park 34731. The park is 2 miles north of Leesburg, an ancient oak hammock where city-weary folks can fish, canoe, launch a boat, picnic, or camp in developed sites that have water and electric hookups. A 1,000-foot canal connects the recreation area to Lake Griffin. The area is open 8:00 A.M. to sunset every day. State park fees apply. (352) 360-6760.

WHERE TO SHOP

Dr. Fergie's Fruit Market. U.S. 27 and Fourteenth Street, Leesburg 34748. Stop along the highway to buy fresh citrus in the sunshine of the Bahamian owner's smile. Open Monday through Saturday 8:00 A.M. to 6:00 P.M. (352) 787-6771.

WHERE TO EAT

Yalaha Country Bakery. 8210 County Road 40, Yalaha 34797. The bakery is southeast of Leesburg, perfectly situated for a country drive into a slice of Bavaria. The bakery and restaurant are German to the core, serving sandwiches on crusty European-style breads. Buy breads from the wood-fire brick oven to take home. Open Monday through Friday 8:00 A.M. to 5:00 P.M. $. (352) 324-3366. Check the Web site at yalahabakery.com for news of Saturday concerts, usually jazz or Big Band sound. Sandwiches are sold until 4:30 P.M.

WHERE TO STAY

Big Cypress Cottages Resort. 408 Ice Cream Road, Leesburg 34748. This is a simple fish camp offering twelve rustic cottages and boat rental. Bring your boat and use the launch ramp for a fee, or rent a boat here. Bring everything with you, including food, bait, and tackle—and don't forget your fishing license. $-$$. (352) 787-1282.

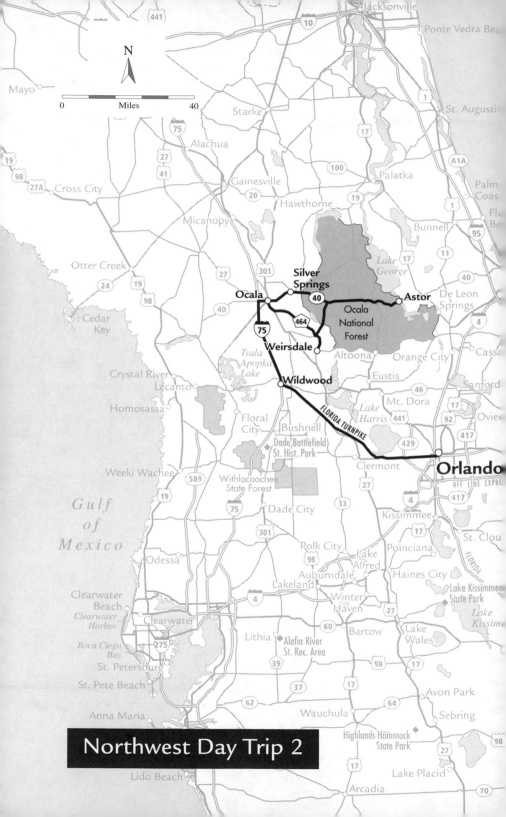

Northwest Day Trip 2

Today it's a busy crossroads city, growing explosively with modestly priced retiree developments, but just a generation ago, Ocala was a small town serving the dozens of sprawling horse farms stretching from one county line to another. Its neighbor, Silver Springs, has been inhabited since long before European settlement. Moist forests with their chattering monkeys and lush, green tangle look like a movie set and, in fact, have been used repeatedly by Hollywood. Take the Florida Turnpike north to Wildwood, then I-75 to Ocala.

OCALA

WHERE TO GO

Appleton Museum of Art. 4333 East Silver Springs Boulevard, Ocala 34470. Located on State Road 40, this is an outstanding museum, starting with the stately building, grounds, and fountains. Collections are a mixture of this and that but are dazzling and unique. See African pieces, pre-Columbian art, and masterworks from all eras and media. Special exhibits and visiting shows are seen throughout the year. The gift shop alone is worth the trip. Admission is $6.00; hours are 10:00 A.M. to 6:00 P.M. every day. (352) 236–7100.

Don Garlits Museum of Drag Racing. 13700 Southwest Sixteenth Avenue, Ocala 34470. This museum is a project of the "Big Daddy" of drag racing, whose enormous collection of classic and vintage cars is on display here. In the museum, see memorabilia depicting the history of drag racing. Open daily 9:00 A.M. to 5:00 P.M. Admission is $12. (352) 245-8661; www.garlits.com.

Marion County Museum of History. 307 Southeast Twenty-sixth Terrace, Ocala 34471. This museum showcases Seminole Indian clothing and artifacts, a 1,500-year-old canoe, artworks, and other displays depicting the history of this ancient area. Hours vary, but it's usually open Friday and Saturday 10:00 A.M. to 2:00 P.M. Admission is $2.00. (352) 629-2773.

Silver River State Park. 1425 North East Fifty-eighth Avenue, Ocala 34470. Located on State Road 35 at the headwaters of the Oklawaha River, this park is one of the state's great wilderness reserves. It's the home of fourteen different habitats, laced with trails and dotted with clear, cold springs. Visit the pioneer park and museum, hike trails, or canoe the river. There are no other facilities. The museum and education center are open only on weekends and some holidays 9:00 A.M. to 5:00 P.M. State park fees apply. (352) 236-1827.

WHERE TO EAT

Arthur's. 3600 Southwest Thirty-sixth Avenue, Ocala 34470. Located in the Hilton, Arthur's is worth a special trip for an intimate dinner or a memorable Sunday brunch. When you make reservations, indicate whether you want a quiet booth or a table overlooking the pool and gardens. Fine cuts of beef are a house specialty, but everything is done with a knowing touch for seasonings, herbs, and a hint of Haiti—or is it New Orleans? There's always a fresh catch of the day, salmon, and a good choice of dishes for carnivores and vegetarians alike. Desserts are showy and delicious. Open for dinner daily and brunch on Sunday. Reservations are strongly recommended. $$$. (352) 854-1400.

BageLicious Bakery & Cafe. 2459 Southeast Twenty-seventh Avenue, Ocala 34474. Located in Shady Oaks Mall, this is a handy place to grab a quick breakfast or a bag of sandwiches to take on a picnic or trail ride. Or stop here for lunch while you're shopping the mall. Nosh on New York–style bagels, pastry, a burger, a salad, or a sandwich. $. (352) 237-6511.

Bella Luna Cafe. 3425 Southwest College Road, Ocala 34474. This eatery is Italian to the core. Start with bruschetta, snails, or

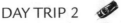

mussels, followed by the chef's special *pasta e fagioli* soup and one of the crisp salads. Choose your main dish from a long list of pastas, risotto, chicken, fish, beef, or veal dishes. There's also pizza and a nice choice of children's favorites. Call for hours and reservations. $$-$$$. (352) 237-9155.

Blackwater Inn. State Road 40 at U.S. 17, Astor 32102. The Blackwater is a country inn overlooking the St. Johns River, well worth the forty-five-minute excursion out of Ocala because the drive takes you across the entire waist of the Ocala National Forest. The waterfront tables are hard to get, but every table has a good view of the river, bridge, and colorful parade of passing boats. Seafood is the star of the extensive menu, with a huge choice of ocean and freshwater fish, crab, oysters, and shrimp prepared many ways, with all the trimmings. The choice of soup, salads, chicken, steak, and other dishes is very good, and the big salad bar provides plenty of choices for those who want to pick and choose. **Williams Landing**, upstairs over the inn, is best for burgers and snacks. Both have a full bar. Note the location at Routes 17 and 40, because the inn is also handy when you are day-tripping north or northeast out of Orlando. Just east of the inn, note the large live oak tree and a marker at the site where naturalist William Bartram landed in the eighteenth century. Open for lunch and dinner daily except Monday. Reservations are highly recommended. $-$$$. (352) 759-2802.

Carmichael's Restaurant. 3105 Northeast Silver Springs Boulevard, Ocala 34470. Carmichael's is a favorite for its attractively priced Sunset Dinners served Monday through Saturday 4:30 to 6:30 P.M. Home-style dinners include meat loaf, top sirloin, chicken parmagiana, Salisbury steak, liver and onions, and chicken and dumplings. Open for breakfast, lunch, and dinner Monday through Saturday and lunch and dinner Sunday. Reservations welcome. $-$$; (352) 622-3636; www.carmichaelsrestaurant.com.

WHERE TO STAY

Ocala Silver Springs Hilton. 3600 Southwest Thirty-sixth Avenue, Ocala 34470. This property is the city's best business hotel, a highrise with a marble lobby and a piano bar for a romantic pre- or postdinner drink, a superb restaurant, a business center, and a good location handy to both downtown and the interstate. Order from room service, use the putting greens or tennis courts, swim in the pool, or play volleyball. Some rooms have a minibar, refrigerator, and/or whirlpool bath. (352) 854–1400; www.hilton.com.

Seven Sisters Inn. 820 Southeast Fort King Street, Ocala 34470. This Victorian showplace in Ocala's historic neighborhood has been showered with awards and honors. The inn serves a bracing breakfast filled with gourmet scents and new tastes and does all the things that B&B lovers dote on. Upstairs, a loft is roomy enough for a family. Special events include the occasional murder mystery weekend or cooking class. Ask about special packages such as a candlelight dinner just for you. $$–$$$. (800) 250–3496.

Shamrock, Thistle & Crown. Mail address: P.O. Box 524, Weirsdale 32195. This property is located on County Road 42, 3 miles east of U.S. 441/27 between Ocala and Leesburg. Sleep in a romantic three-story Victorian mansion built around 1887. Stay in a whirlpool suite with fireplace or the Victorian cottage. All rooms have private bath, coffeemaker, and TV with VCR. Included in the rates are a full breakfast, cider or hot drinks, shortbread, chocolates, and a morning newspaper. $$–$$$. (352) 821–1887 or (800) 425–2763; www.shamrockbb.com.

SILVER SPRINGS

To get to Silver Springs travel east of Ocala on State Road 40.

WHERE TO GO

Silver Springs. 5656 East Silver Springs Boulevard, Silver Springs 34488. Located on State Road 40, this is Florida's oldest theme park, dating to 1878 when the first glass-bottom boats began providing tourists a glimpse of a pristine underwater world of grottos, silvery fish, and artesian springs that spill millions of gallons of water every day into the Oklawaha River. There is still plenty here for the nostalgia buff who mourns the old Florida. Take a glass-bottom boat tour. Stroll unspoiled footpaths lined with native plants and brilliant annuals. See alligators, gars, turtles, manatees, Florida panthers, native and imported bears, and wild monkeys that still roam free in the forests along the "lost river." Kids can play in Kids Ahoy! Playland. Movie fans can spend a cool, quiet hour in the museum, where movie clips show dozens of scenes that were shot here. They range from commercials to Tarzan movies and snippets of *Creature from the Black Lagoon.*

You'll really need more than one day to take all the cruises and the Jeep Safari, see the shows, watch the wildlife, shop the stores, and try the restaurants. Hours are limited in winter, so call ahead. Admission is $31.95 for adults and $22.95 for guests under 48 inches tall. Children ages two and younger are free. Ask about a combination ticket for Silver Springs and Wild Waters, and the twelve-month OnePass, which is a sensational deal because it covers not only unlimited general admission but also concerts and special events. Concerts, scheduled late March through September, feature top stars and groups such as Tanya Tucker, Glen Campbell, Roy Clark, and the Guy Lombardo Orchestra. There's an annual Corvette Show in November and a month-long Festival of Lights in December. (352) 236-2121; www.silversprings.com.

Wild Waters Water Park. 5656 East Silver Springs Boulevard, Silver Springs 34488. Another attraction on State Road 40, Wild Waters invites the family to dare the 60-foot-high Twin Twister flume and seven other thrill slides and rides. For little ones, the Caribbean Sprayground provides gentle fountains and mists; the Tad Pool is for wading. Splash in the wave pool, play volleyball, or dry out in a giant video arcade and game room. Lockers, rest rooms, and a kennel for the dog are available. Three restaurants serve burgers, pizza, hot dogs, and the like, and the Shiver Shack has ice cream treats. Suntan products, swimwear, and beach togs are sold in the shop. Make a day of it April through September 10:00 A.M. to 5:00 P.M., sometimes later during special events. Adult admission is $22.95, children ages 3 to 10 pay $19.95, and parking is $5.00 unless you have a pass. Ask about annual passes and combination tickets for Wild Waters and Silver Springs. (352) 236-2121.

WHERE TO STAY

Holiday Inn Silver Springs. 5751 East Silver Springs Boulevard, Silver Springs 34488. This is a plain-Jane inn, clean and comfortable, across the street from Silver Springs attractions. It's an ideal headquarters for a weekend at the theme park and water park, especially during the blockbuster country concerts staged regularly. The twenty-four-hour restaurant is a plus, and the inn is kept up to date with dataports, cable TV, microwaves and refrigerators, and a business center. (352) 236–2575 or (800) 465–4329.

Rosslor Manor. Mail address: P.O. Box 687, Silver Springs 34489. Directions to this fifty-acre riding estate will be given when you make reservations. Overnight in a large, luxurious guest room, take afternoon tea, and tour the grounds in a horse-drawn carriage. Innkeepers can arrange pleasure or trail riding, instruction in classical dressage, horseback picnics, or hunter-jumper courses. Fish the estate's private pond for bass or bream, or walk wildlife trails among live oaks draped in Spanish moss. Continental breakfast is included in the rates. $$–$$$. (352) 236–4219; www.rosslor.com.

OCALA NATIONAL FOREST

This is such a vast area with so many recreation opportunities, you could come here time and again and never tire of the nature show, crystal springs flowing into narrow rivers, spring-fed swimming holes, and miles of woodlands abuzz with birds and insects. Ocala National Forest consists of swamp, acres of prairie and pinewoods, countless springs, plus lakes, rivers, streams, hunting reserves, and a 66-mile portion of the Florida Trail. This wilderness is highly sensitive to nature's whims, so be aware of water levels, fire danger levels, winds, and currents.

There will be times when some lands aren't accessible due to flooding, some waterways too rough (especially Lake George, which is very large, shallow, and subject to quick buildups in high winds), or campfires not permitted because of the fire hazard. This is an ever-changing, ever-evolving landscape—always new, always exciting, always challenging. To the casual visitor, especially one who expects the towering trees and mountains of western forests, the flat sameness of this national treasure might seem featureless. Listen and watch. Let it reveal itself to you, and you'll find a natural drama that is filled with beauty and excitement.

State Road 40 runs through the middle of the national forest between Barberville and Ocala. Much of its western border is the Oklawaha River. Just east of Ocala on Route 40, the Ocala National Forest Visitor Center offers information, souvenirs, and invaluable

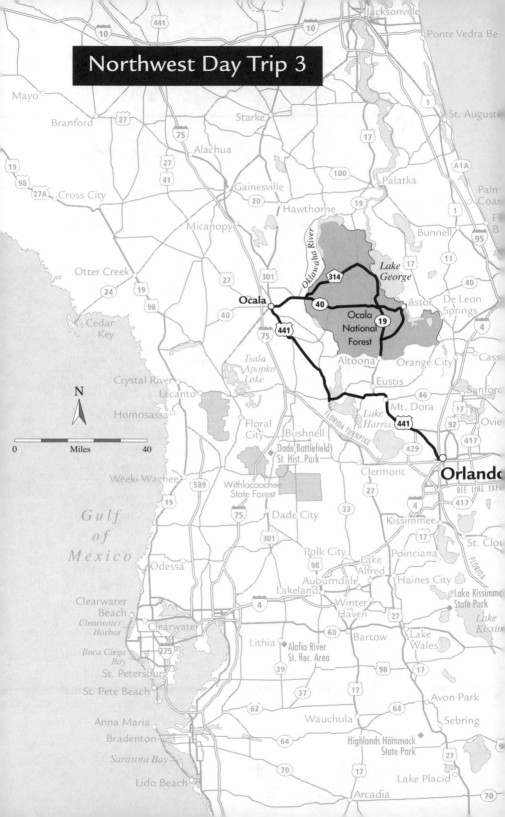

advice. Countless spots in the forest offer fishing, and many areas are set aside for hunting in season. Myriad rules apply throughout the forest, most of them based on respect for the environment and common sense in regard to personal safety. Leave a trip plan with someone at home. Familiarize yourself with the area's hazards, including poisonous snakes, insects, and plants. Keep small children well in hand. Bring a camp stove, since firewood may be in short supply. Be especially vigilant about cooking fires. If you start a forest fire, you are financially liable.

For information, write the Seminole Ranger District, 1551 Umatilla Road, Eustis 32726 (352-357-3721) or the Lake George Ranger District, Route 2, Box 701, Silver Springs 32688 (352-625-2520). Many areas are free. Fee areas include Fore Lake, Mill Dam, Juniper Springs, Alexander Springs, Clearwater Lake, Lake Dorr, and Salt Springs.

WHERE TO GO

Alexander Springs Recreation Area. This area is off State Road 445, which runs south off Route 40 at Astor Park. Launch a canoe to float the spring run, camp in a developed campground with rest rooms and a dump station (no hookups), swim off the salt-white beach, and hike the Timucuan Indian Trail along waters that were sacred to the ancients. A concession stand sells ice and staples and offers rental canoes.

Big Scrub is in the southwest corner of the national forest. A campground offers drinking water and rest rooms.

Clearwater Lake is on the southern edge of the national forest off Route 42 near Paisley. It's a campground where you can also swim, walk an interpretive trail, and launch a boat. Rest rooms, drinking water, and a dump station are available.

Johnson Field is east of Rodman Dam on the northern border of national forest. Come here to camp, picnic, or launch a boat. There are rest rooms but no showers.

Juniper Springs and **Fern Hammock Springs** are on Route 40 just west of Route 19. Swim in the springs and canoe the spring "run" at Juniper Springs, which also has camping, rest rooms and showers, and a barrier-free nature trail.

Lake Dorr is on Route 19 just north of Route 42 in Lake County in the southern half of the national forest. The recreation area has campsites, drinking water, swimming, a picnic area, rest rooms, a boat launch, and showers.

Lake Eaton Sinkhole Trails are found south of Route 314 off Road 79. Leave your car in the parking area and walk the half-mile loop to the sinkhole, which is 450 feet around and 80 feet deep, or add the 1.2-mile longer trail that reaches the sinkhole then joins the shorter trail. A boardwalk and stairs let you hike to the bottom of the sink.

Mill Dam Lake off Route 40 is a popular fishing hole offering camping, drinking water, swimming, a picnic area, boat launch, and rest rooms. Hike the interpretive trail.

Salt Springs Recreation Area is just north of the intersection of Routes 19 and 314. Camp, swim, picnic, or launch a boat. The site has drinking water, rest rooms, showers, and a dump station.

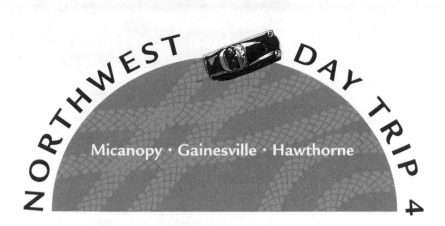

Micanopy · Gainesville · Hawthorne

The fastest way to get to this area from Orlando is on the Florida Turnpike north, then I–75 north to Micanopy off U.S. 441 into Gainesville. From Gainesville, drive southeast on Route 20 to Route 2041 and Route 325 and watch for the Marjorie Kinnan Rawlings site on the way to Hawthorne.

MICANOPY

You'll think you're in another time zone when you drive into Micanopy (say *mick-an-OH-pea*), named for an Indian chief. Timucuan Indians had a thriving community here before Europeans arrived, and it's said to be the oldest continuously occupied inland settlement in the state. When naturalist William Bartram visited here in 1774, he found a Seminole village. Not long after Florida became a U.S. territory, a trading post was established here. Browse the antiques centers and have a meal in one of the restaurants or a picnic on a park bench in the grassy median that divides the main street.

Driving through, note the Town Hall, which is also the public library. It was built as a schoolhouse in 1895. Note old homes that were built in Victorian times, some of them elegant; others simple and utilitarian, suited to frontier life. You'll pass the Presbyterian Church, built in 1870 for a congregation established in 1854, the Herlong Mansion, now an inn, and the line of old banks and

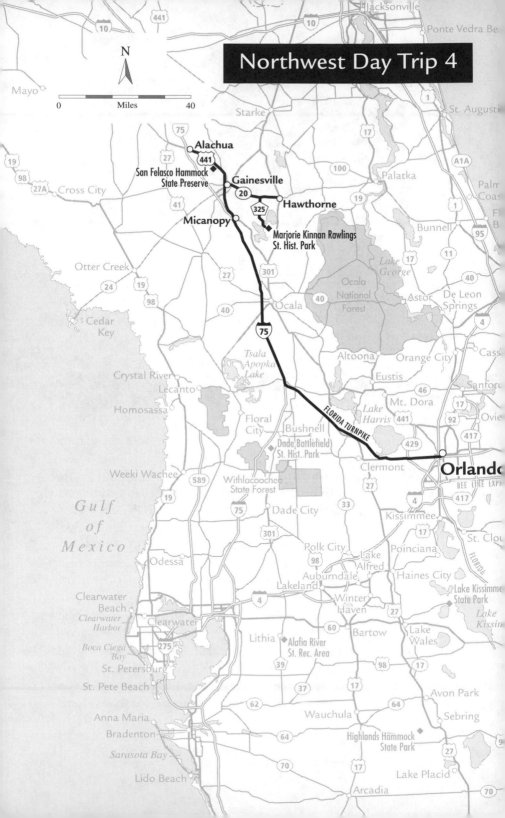

mercantiles that are now occupied by restaurants and antiques shops. If you have time, ask the way to the cemetery, where the oldest grave was dug in 1826 for a man born in 1737.

WHERE TO GO

Micanopy Historic Society Museum. Cholokka Boulevard at Bay Street, Micanopy 32667. Located in the old Thrasher Warehouse, built in 1890, this collection takes you back through the history of a busy little country town that has changed little with the centuries. The Coca-Cola sign on the north wall was painted in the 1920s. The bookstore alone is worth a special visit. Open Friday through Sunday 1:00 to 5:00 P.M. for a modest admission. (352) 466-3200.

Prairie State Preserve. Route 2, Box 41, Micanopy 32667. The preserve is 10 miles south of Gainesville on U.S. 441; watch for signs off I-75. Within this 20,000-acre world of wildlife and lakes, you can boat, hike more than 20 miles of trails, fish, picnic, camp, or train your binoculars on the abundant bird life. Many migratory birds winter in this natural paradise, so dedicated bird lovers come back time and again to add to their lists. Herds of horses and American bison roam the land. Climb the observation tower for the best vista. The visitor center is open every day 9:00 A.M. to 5:00 P.M.; the park is open every day 8:00 A.M. to sunset. Call ahead for a schedule of ranger-led activities. A small admission is charged. (352) 466-3397.

WHERE TO STAY

Herlong Mansion. 402 Cholokka Boulevard, Micanopy 32667. This is a Greek Revival mansion surrounded by live oak trees dripping Spanish moss where hosts offer a variety of accommodations in rooms, suites, and cottages decorated in Victoriana. Ask for a fireplace, whirlpool tub, kitchenette, or refrigerator, and specify whether you want a TV and/or VCR. Not every room has electronic intrusions. Borrow a book from the home's library and relax on the veranda or in the garden. Breakfast is included. $$-$$$. (800) HERLONG or (352) 466-3322; www.herlong.com.

Shady Oaks. 209 Cholokka Boulevard, Micanopy 32667. This three-story mansion has a wide wraparound porch to catch the breezes. The most romantic room is Victoria's Suite. Some rooms have a hot tub, TV, and/or VCR. Call at least three days in advance, and hosts will serve a candlelight supper in your suite, make dinner reservations at a nearby restaurant, or have a picnic hamper ready for your local explorations. Breakfast is included in rates. $$–$$$. (352) 466–3476; www.shadyoak.com.

GAINESVILLE

The University of Florida is the elephant in the living room, the city's blessing and curse. Football games bring in 85,000 fans for big week-ends, and the city's population swells and sinks by more than 30,000 depending on whether classes are in session. When fans and students are in town, it's hard to get restaurant and hotel reservations—and impossible to find a parking space. On the other hand, the university is a travel destination in itself—a world of museums, cultural events, and exciting, youthful action.

For a quiet walk that costs nothing, write ahead (see Regional Information) for a free walking tour map through the Northeast Historic District. You'll see a timeline of Southern architecture from the 1880s through the 1930s, including the Murphree House, where William Jennings Bryan was entertained, and Gracy House, where prohibitionist Carrie Nation stayed. She gave the children little wooden axes as souvenirs of her crusade to destroy saloons. From Micanopy follow U.S. 441 north to Gainesville.

WHERE TO GO

Devil's Millhopper State Geological Site. 4732 Millhopper Road, Gainesville 32611. Located on State Road 232, this is like no other locale in the state. A 120-foot-deep, 500-foot-wide sinkhole opened here eons ago, allowing species that are found nowhere else in Florida to live in the cool, dark depths. In fact, the name of the county, Alachua, is Native American for sinkhole, or "large jug." Walk down the 232 steps to the bottom of the sinkhole, observing waterfalls and rare plants along the way. Guided walks are offered at 10:00 A.M. on Saturday. Displays in the visitor center explain this geological phenomenon. Bring a picnic to enjoy on the grounds. It's generally open 9:00 A.M. to sunset but closes at 5:00 P.M. October through March. A small admission is charged. (352) 955–2008. Just west of here a few miles is **San Felasco Hammock State Preserve**, almost 7,000 acres of pine and hardwood forest with sinkholes, creeks, wildlife, rare plants, and 10 miles of marked hiking and horseback riding trails. (352) 462–7905.

Florida Museum of Natural History. Mail address: P.O. Box 112710, Gainesville 32611. Located at Southwest Thirty-fourth Street at Hull Road, this museum is a star in the state's tiara, a repository of natural treasures native to Florida. More than twenty-five million specimens are in the collection. See fossils, skeletons of prehistoric creatures, rare plants, seashells, butterflies, and much more. The Collectors Shop offers scientific games for children and nature-related souvenirs for adults. Admission is free. Open Monday through Saturday 10:00 A.M. to 5:00 P.M. and Sunday and holidays 1:00 to 5:00 P.M. Closed Christmas and Thanksgiving. (352) 846–2000.

Fred Bear Museum. I–75 at Archer Road, Gainesville 32608. This museum is a tribute to the man who founded Bear Archery. Displays of stuffed animals and mounted heads aren't for everyone, but the collections of artifacts from around the world, including primitive art and 2,500-year-old arrow points, are interesting and educational. Open daily except major holidays 10:00 A.M. to 6:00 P.M. Admission is $5.00 for adults, $4.00 for seniors, $3.00 for children ages six to twelve, and $12.00 for a family of two adults and two children under age 12. (352) 376–2411.

Kanapana Plantation House. Located west of Gainesville on Archer Road. Call for directions and an appointment. The house is not open to passersby. This is one of a handful of antebellum plantation houses that can still be found in central Florida—an enormous Cracker-style house that has been restored to the way it looked when it centered a big cotton plantation before the Civil War. Admission is charged and reservations are required. (352) 338–9162.

Matheson Historical Center. 513 East University Avenue, Gainesville 32601. The center is of interest to all history buffs and a must for postcard collectors. In the center's collection are more than 18,000 postcards, 1,200 stereo-view cards, and 2,500 books about Florida history. See rare old maps and prints. Admission is charged. Open

Tuesday through Friday 9:00 A.M. to 1:00 P.M. and Sunday 1:00 to 5:00 P.M. Closed Saturday and Monday. (352) 378-2280.

Mill Creek Farm. Country Road 235-A, Alachua 32615. The farm is a retirement home for horses, a labor of love in a beautiful setting. Learn about the volunteers who work so hard to make a home for more than eighty horses whose working life is over and the ten dogs, all of them with their own hard-luck stories, who stand guard over them. Admission is two carrots, but bring a whole bag if you can. You get to feed them to the horses, so the more carrots, the more friends you'll make. Open Saturday 11:00 A.M. to 3:00 P.M. (386) 462-1001.

Morningside Nature Center. 3540 East University Avenue, Gainesville 32601. The nature center is a 278-acre living-history farm, operating just as it might have in North Carolina a century ago. You'll see a cabin dating to 1840, farm buildings, an heirloom garden, barnyard animals, a barn, and a schoolhouse. Seven miles of trails and boardwalks lead through the woods and sand hills, where you'll see more than 130 species of birds, 225 wildflower species, and countless critters to watch at the animal observatory. Every day is different, depending on what's going on in the farmer's life and what special programs or exhibits are on the schedule. Open every day 9:00 A.M. to 5:00 P.M. Free. (352) 334-2170.

Samuel P. Ham Museum of Art. Hull Road at Southwest Thirty-fourth Street, University of Florida, Gainesville 32600. This is one of the state's largest art museums. It's filled with changing exhibits and permanent collections of American masters, African arts, and pre-Columbian works. One visit isn't enough because something is always going on, from lecture series to films and performances. Admission is free. Hours are Tuesday through Saturday 11:00 A.M. to 5:00 P.M., Saturday 10:00 A.M. to 5:00 P.M., and Sunday 1:00 to 5:00 P.M. The gift shop closes at 4:30 P.M., and no one is admitted after 4:45 P.M. (352) 392-9826.

Sante Fe Community College Teaching Zoo. 3000 Northwest Eighty-third Street, Gainesville 32600. This is the only community teaching zoo in the nation that houses mammals, reptiles, amphibians, birds, and endangered species from all over the world. Zookeepers lead the tours, so it's a great place to bring children who are seriously interested in animals, endangered species, or animal husbandry. During the week visit by appointment, or come on Saturday and Sunday 9:00 A.M. to 2:00 P.M. Free. (352) 395-5604.

WHERE TO EAT

Ale House & Raw Bar. 3950 Southwest Archer Road, Gainesville 32610. This is an old-fashioned sports bar where you can watch the games on forty TVs while scarfing down a hearty burger and crispy fries. Do serious damage to a big steak, a bowl of pasta, or a platter of wings or seafood. Have one of the twenty-five draft beers, or try one of the bartender's daily drink specials. Open Monday through Saturday 11:00 A.M. to 2:00 A.M. and Sunday noon to 11:00 P.M. $-$$$. (352) 371-0818.

Banyan's Restaurant. 7417 West Newberry Road, Gainesville 32611. Banyan's is revered for its all-you-can-eat seafood buffet on Friday and its prime rib specials on Saturday. Stop in for the breakfast and lunch buffets, the weekend brunch, or dinner followed by the 9:00 or 10:00 P.M. show at Coconut's Comedy Club, which has its own telephone (352-332-2224). Open daily 6:30 A.M. to 10:00 P.M. $-$$. (352) 332-7500.

Calico Jack's. 3501 Southwest Second Avenue, Gainesville 32611. This is a college hangout with a sports bar ambience and special prices on beer and seafood. Order crawdads by the pound, oysters, sandwiches, wings, shrimp, crab, or burgers. If you're headed for a game, call ahead and they'll pack up everything you need for a tailgate party. Live music plays Friday night. $-$$. Open every day 10:30 A.M. to 2:00 A.M.

Chuckwagon Country Skillet. Williston Road at I-75, Gainesville 32610. This is the place for a hearty family meal with a different all-you-can-eat special every day. Cooking is country style: beef stew, chicken and dumplings, catfish and fixings, meat loaf with mashed potatoes, and pot roast. Desserts are special, especially the pies. Open every day 6:00 A.M. to 9:00 P.M. $. (352) 336-5677.

Cuban Express Cafe. 101 Northwest Twenty-third Avenue, Gainesville 32611. The father-son owners here know Cuban food. Have a Cuban sandwich, black beans and rice, roast pork, *arroz con pollo,* fish, or the pot roast with Cuban accompaniments such as yellow rice and plantains. Open Monday through Friday 11:00 A.M. to 7:00 P.M. and Saturday noon to 3:00 P.M. $. (352) 381-0074.

David's Barbecue. 5121 Northwest Thirty-ninth Avenue, Gainesville 32611. Where there's smoke, there's great barbecue, so pull into the Timber Village Shopping Center for a pig sandwich, barbecued chicken with all the fixings, or a big barbecue dinner platter with ribs, chicken, beef, or a combination. Portions are massive, which makes the place popular with football players. Breakfasts are quick, hot, and sized for fullbacks. Open every day 7:00 A.M. to 9:00 P.M. $-$$. (352) 372-1555.

Farah's. 1120 West University Avenue, Gainesville 32601. Farah's has a Mediterranean look and feel, with a menu to match. Have one of the wraps, a gourmet hamburger, a Black Angus steak, pasta, fresh seafood, or the chef's special of the day. There's a full bar, and live jazz plays on weekends. Ask for a table in the enclosed patio overlooking the avenue, or get out of the spotlight for an intimate meal in the back of this attractive room. Open Monday and Tuesday 11:00 A.M. to 10:00 P.M. and Wednesday through Saturday 11:00 A.M. to 11:00 P.M. $$-$$$. (352) 378-5179.

Gator Greats Restaurant. 201 Southeast Second Avenue, Gainesville 32601. Located in Union Street Station in the heart of downtown, this is a favorite gathering place after the game or any time when Gator fans are in the mood for Black Angus steaks, a big salad bar, and a baked potato. Pasta and seafood are also on the menu, and there's a full bar. Open for lunch and dinner; call for hours and reservations, which are essential. Valet parking is free. $$-$$$. (352) 378-5494.

The Melting Pot. 418 East University Avenue, Gainesville 32601. This spot is best known for its fondues—a good spot for family and friends to stick a fork in it together and have a leisurely, fun-filled meal. Order one of the main dish fondues with chicken, beef, cheese, or seafood, all served with fresh vegetables, then wade into the chocolate fondue for dessert. Reservations are recommended. Open Sunday through Thursday 5:30 to 10:00 P.M., Friday and Saturday to 11:00 P.M. $$. (352) 372-5623.

Porter's. University Avenue at Main Street, Gainesville 32601. Porter's is where people celebrate with a great steak or lobster. Have the filet mignon, roasted duckling, prime rib, scallops, shrimp, the fresh catch of the day, or the chef's specialty du jour. The Sunday brunch is famous for its "benedicts"—eggs or crab cakes—plus prime rib, eggs Wellington, and rafts of salads and desserts. Have a drink at your table, or stop first at the friendly, woody bar. Open for lunch Monday through Saturday 11:00 A.M. to 2:00 P.M., dinner every night 5:00 to 11:00 P.M., and Sunday 11:00 A.M. to 3:00 P.M. $$$. (352) 372-5623.

Publix Supermarket. 3720 Northwest Thirteenth Street, Gainesville 32600. This supermarket has a sushi bar, where you watch as chefs create wonderful sushis in many flavors, then pick up a package to take to your hotel room or picnic. Everything is natural and ready to eat. If you have a special request or want a large quantity, call ahead. The supermarket also has a deli with hot and cold take-out dishes. $. (352) 335–3785.

Steve's Cafe American. 12 West University Avenue, Gainesville 32601. The cafe is a wisp of New Orleans jazz and pizzazz, transplanted to this university city. Have rack of lamb, fresh fish with a special sauce, chicken, or shrimp. The building, which dates to the late 1800s–early 1900s, is a jewel. The wine list is impressive, and Steve also offers a long list of foreign and domestic beers. Hours vary, so call ahead. $$–$$$. (352) 377–9337.

Third Place Pub & Grill. 5323 Southwest Ninety-first Terrace, Gainesville 32611. Located in the Haile Village Center, this place has something for everyone, so take the entire family. There's a children's menu, takeout, a locally popular brunch, and an eclectic menu ranging from offbeat sandwiches, salads, and gargantuan beefburgers to such nightly specials as a mixed grill of duck breast, filet mignon, and homemade sausage. Arrive in time for happy hour specials. Open Monday through Thursday 11:00 A.M. to 9:00 P.M., Friday to 10:00 P.M., Saturday 9:00 A.M. to 2:00 P.M. and 5:00 to 10:00 P.M., and Sunday 9:00 A.M. to 2:00 P.M. The bar is open 4:00 P.M. to midnight. $–$$$. (352) 378–0721.

WHERE TO STAY

Best Western Gateway Grand. 4200 Northwest Ninety-seventh Boulevard, Gainesville 32606. Reserve a room, minisuite, executive suite, or the presidential suite at this three-story inn. Every room has dataports and cable TV; some have refrigerator and microwave. Dine in the Key West Grill & Lounge, swim in the pool, soak in the outdoor whirlpool, and get your workout in the fitness room. Meadowbrook Golf Club is next door, so ask about golf packages. Ask, too, about special rates for seniors, groups, military and hospital personnel, or those on university business. Business and laundry services are available. $$. (352) 331–3336 or (800) 528–1234.

Econo Lodge. 2649 Southwest Thirteenth Street, Gainesville 32608. This property is a 6-block walk from the campus and is within walking distance of several restaurants. There's a swimming pool, dataports in every room, and cable television as well as a complimentary continental breakfast. Pets are welcome. $. (352) 332-2346 or (800) 446-6900; www.econolodge.com.

Holiday Inn University Center. 1250 West University Avenue, Gainesville 32601. Located on U.S. 441, this is a reliable choice for business or vacationing with its restaurant, lounge, twenty-four-hour coffee shop, barber and beauty shops, and central location. The rooftop swimming pool is Olympic size and is surrounded by a football field–size sundeck. Rooms are attractively appointed with desks, user-friendly desk chairs, and dataports. (352) 376-1661 or (800) 465-4329.

Magnolia Plantation Bed & Breakfast. 309 Southeast Seventh Street, Gainesville 32607. This B&B offers five rooms in a romantic Victorian mansion, plus three cottages. Have wine and cheese with the host each afternoon. You will be sent on your way the next morning with a grand breakfast. Rooms are all different, so discuss the choices when you reserve. Some units have a fireplace, VCR, refrigerator, and/or telephone. With restrictions, pets are allowed. If you want a massage, one can be arranged. $$$. (352) 375-6653; www.magnoliabnb.com.

Reitz Union Hotel. Mail address: P.O. Box 118505, Gainesville 32611. Stay in the heart of the University of Florida campus in this handy hotel on Museum Road. The hotel offers thirty-six rooms and suites, free continental breakfast, and that precious commodity on campus—free parking. $–$$. (352) 392-2151.

Red Roof Inn. 3500 Southwest Forty-second Street, Gainesville 32608. This popular chain motel is conveniently located at exit 75 East off I-75. It's a good spot for a comfortable room or suite, a swim, and a comfortable price. Pets are welcome. Restaurants are nearby. $$. (352) 336-3311 or (800) 843-7663.

Residence Inn by Marriott. 4001 Southwest Thirteenth Street, Gainesville 32608. This is an up-market hotel with touches of home. Ask for a one- or two-bedroom suite with or without a fireplace. Kitchens are fully equipped, pets are allowed on payment of a fee, and breakfast and hospitality hour are included in the price. Work out in the fitness center, and enjoy the pool and whirlpool. Walk to Bivens Nature Center, or drive to most points of interest in less than fifteen minutes. $$–$$$. (352) 371–2101 or (800) 331–3131; www.residenceinn.com.

Sweetwater Branch Inn. 625 East University Avenue, Gainesville 32607. This is an elegant Victorian palace, where fourteen rooms have been filled with antique furnishings and groomed for the fussiest business or pleasure visitor. Some rooms have hot tubs; most have a fireplace and plush Oriental rugs. $$$. (352) 373–6760 or (800) 451–7111; www.sweetwaterinn.com.

Super 8 Motel. 2000 Southwest Thirteenth Street, Gainesville 32608. This no-frills motel offers a complimentary continental breakfast. Weekly rates are available; transportation to university, hospitals, and airport can be requested. If you're in town on university or hospital business, ask about discounts. $. (352) 372–3654 or (800) 800–8000.

University Centre Hotel. 1535 Southwest Archer Road, Gainesville 32607. This property is for those who prefer a high-rise city hotel with easy access to the airport, university, sight-seeing, the interstate, and Shands Hospital. Take a room or suite, swim in the pool, have your hair done, and park under cover in the garage. The hotel has its own restaurant and lounge, but it's also handy to other dining. Don't miss the hotel's buffet lunch Monday through Friday ($), with a different country featured each day. $$–$$$. (352) 371–3333 or (800) 824–5637.

University of Florida Hotel, a Doubletree Hotel. 1714 Southeast Thirty-fourth Street, Gainesville 32607. This is a full-service hotel with everything convenient for the business or leisure traveler. Swim in the pool, eat in the restaurant, order from room service, relax in the lounge, and shop for souvenirs and sundries in the gift shop. Dataports are in every room. The hotel also has suites, including a luxurious presidential suite. Ask the concierge about transportation to the campus, airport, hospitals, and business center. Doubletree's trademark is the freshly baked chocolate chip cookies that greet every guest on check-in. $$–$$$. (352) 378–0070.

Villager Lodge–University. 1900 Southwest Thirteenth Street, Gainesville 32608. This ninety-one-room lodge is large enough to offer services and small enough to provide special touches such as a free continental breakfast daily. Ask about weekly, monthly, and senior rates. Transportation to the campus, hospitals, and airport is offered. There's a swimming pool but no restaurant. Pets are permitted. $$. (352) 372-1880 or (800) 328-7829.

HAWTHORNE

From Gainsville, take Route 20 east into Hawthorne.

WHERE TO GO

Hawthorne Museum and Cultural Center. Johnson Street at Southeast Fourth Avenue, Hawthorne 32640. This museum once housed the New Hope United Methodist Church. Built in 1907, the building now showcases the works of local artists and artisans, as well as relics of the community's past. A modest admission is charged. Open Friday through Sunday 1:00 to 5:00 P.M. (352) 481-4436.

Marjorie Kinnan Rawlings House. Route 3, Box 92, Hawthorne 32640. This home is southeast of Gainesville on Cross Creek. Marjorie Kinnan Rawlings, author of the beloved books *The Yearling* and *Cross Creek,* lived in this rustic, country cottage in the 1920s, an escape from her pressure-cooker life in New York. The house itself, built between 1880 and 1900, is furnished as it was during her years here. You'll see her typewriter, books, kitchen, and even the hidden bar where she had to hide her liquor, which was illegal during Prohibition. Marjorie was known to her neighbors as a quirky, feisty, and complex woman whose strong personality can still be felt at this site. Thanks to dedicated volunteers, the kitchen garden and other plantings are preserved as she left them. There's a picnic table, so stop for lunch, a hike through the nature trail, and a look at the home even if it isn't open. Tours are given Thursday through Sunday at 10:00 and 11:00 A.M. and hourly 1:00 to 4:00 P.M. Admission is $3.00 for adults and $2.00 children ages 6 to 12. No tours are given in August and September. (352) 466-3672.

Homosassa · Crystal River ·
Cedar Key

Gushing springs, ancient Indian relics, seas of manatees floating
freely in pristine waters. They add up to a part of Florida unlike any
other. From Orlando, take the Florida Turnpike north to I-75 and
jog north for just one exit, then turn west on Route 44 to Lecanto.
Turn south on Route 490, crossing U.S. 19-98, and into Homosassa
and Homosassa Springs. Returning, you might leave Cedar Key on
State Road 24 to Alternate 27, which joins I-75 just north of Ocala.

This day trip covers a lot of territory. You'll enjoy it much more
with an overnight in one of these lovely towns.

HOMOSASSA

Homosassa and Homosassa Springs are just south of Crystal River,
close enough to combine in one weekend.

WHERE TO GO

Homosassa Springs State Wildlife Park. 4150 South Suncoast
Boulevard, Homosassa 34446. This park showcases native Florida
wildlife from manatees to alligators and crocs. It's one of the few
places in the state where you're sure to see a manatee any day of the
year. Some are here for rehab before their return into the wild; others
will spend their lives here, unable to fend for themselves. Stroll
nature trails to look for deer, black bears, bobcats, river otters, and
cougars, plus bird life ranging from colorful flamingos to majestic

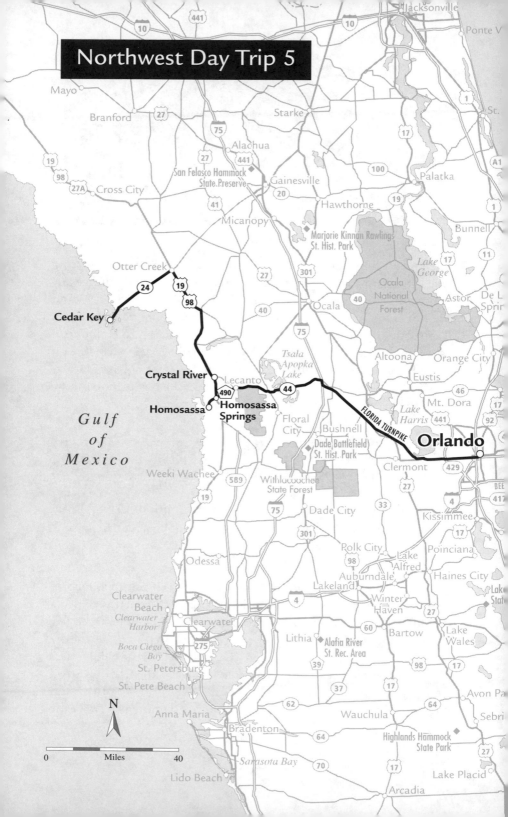

Jacksonville

Ponte V

Mayo

Branford

Starke

St.

Cross City

San Felasco Hammock
State Preserve

Gainesville

Palatka

Alachua

Hawthorne

Micanopy

Marjorie Kinnan Rawlings
St. Hist. Park

Bunnell

Otter Creek

Ocala
National
Forest

Lake
George

Astor

De L
Sprir

Cedar Key

Ocala

Crystal River

Lecanto

Tsala
Apopka
Lake

Altoona

Orange City

Homosassa

Homosassa
Springs

Eustis

Mt. Dora

Gulf
of
Mexico

Floral
City

Bushnell

Lake
Harris

FLORIDA TURNPIKE

Orlando

Weeki Wachee

Dade Battlefield
St. Hist. Park

Clermont

Withlacoochee
State Forest

Dade City

BEE

Kissimmee

Odessa

Polk City

Poinciana

Lake
Alfred

Haines City

Auburndale
Lakeland

Clearwater
Beach

Clearwater
Harbor

Clearwater

Winter
Haven

Lithia

Alafia River
St. Rec. Area

Bartow

Lake
Wales

Boca Ciega
Bay

St. Petersburg

St. Pete Beach

N

Anna Maria

Bradenton

Lake
Stat

Avon Pa

Sebri

Wauchula

Highlands Hammock
State Park

0   Miles   40

Sarasota Bay

Lido Beach

Arcadia

Lake Placid

birds of prey. See the museum, the gift shop, and the underwater observatory. Programs are scheduled throughout the day, so arrive early and plan to spend all day. Food is available at the Wildside Cafe, or bring a picnic to eat in the Garden of the Springs. The park is open daily 9:00 A.M. to 5:30 P.M.; tickets are sold until 4:00 P.M. Admission is $7.95 for adults and $4.95 for children ages 3 to 12. A kennel is available for pets. (352) 628–5343.

River Safaris and Gulf Charters. 10823 Yulee Drive, Homosassa 34487. This outfit is owned by Captain Dennis Lowe, a fifth-genera-tion west coast Florida fishing guide, and his family. Let them plan your trip on Crystal Springs or Blackwater Rivers, sunsets on the Gulf, fishing expeditions to all the captain's secret hotspots, or an airboat ride through wetlands alight with wildlife. Or take the family to the St. Martins Keys for the wildlife sightings. In Homosassa Springs, take Yulee Drive off Highway 19 (by the Burger King), then go 2 miles to the stop sign, then left for 1 mile. The Lowes offer a variety of boat tours and fishing trips, all led by licensed captains, and they also have canoes, johnboats, and pontoon boats for rent. Bait, tackle, snacks, and supplies are sold here; there's an art gallery and gift shop, too. (352) 628–5222 or (800) 758–3474.

WHERE TO EAT

Charlie Brown's Crab House. 5297 South Cherokee Way, Homo-sassa 34448. Located at the Homosassa Riverside Resort (see Where to Stay), this place is famed for its Maryland-style crab cakes, grouper, prime rib, sirloin, daily pasta specials, and Dirt Pie for dessert. They'll also be glad to cook your catch for you. Call for hours. $$. (800) 442–2040 or (352) 628–2474.

Seagrass Pub & Grill. 10386 Halls River Road, Homosassa 34487. If you're arriving by boat, this eatery is at Marker #7 on the river. Make a meal out of the big choice of appetizers, or order them all in a sampler that serves up onion rings, mozzarella sticks, poppers, and beer-battered vegetables. Have a whole-meal salad with chicken or shrimp or a garden salad to go with a basket filled with your choice of foods. Choose the Black Angus burger, grilled chicken, shrimp, grilled kielbasa, fried ravioli, clam strips, or a prime rib sandwich with fries or macaroni salad. Hours vary, so call ahead. $–$$. (352) 628–3595.

WHERE TO STAY

Homosassa Riverside Resort. 5297 South Cherokee Way, Homosassa 34448. The resort sits on serene waters where you can while the day away doing absolutely nothing. Or fish, dive, take a river tour, swim with manatees, rent a pontoon boat or canoe, take an airboat ride, or sign on for a sunset cruise. This isn't the Ritz, but it's comfortable and homey, with standard and king rooms overlooking the Homosassa River. Efficiencies have a microwave and refrigerator. Kitchenette suites have a full kitchen. All units have cable television and telephone.

Hang out in the Monkey Bar, a tiki bar that overlooks Monkey Island, or the Yardarm Lounge with its floor-to-ceiling window on the river. Dining is in Charlie Brown's Crab House (see Where to Eat). Shop in a cluster of boutiques selling toys, gifts, candles, silks, jewelry, and home accessories. Only a mile away, the wildlife park at Homosassa Springs is one of the state's best manatee sanctuaries, where you can watch them from an underwater room. Ask at the resort about the canoe and kayak trails that stretch from Crystal River to Chassahowitzka. $$. (800) 442–2040 or (352) 628–2474; www.homosassariverside.com.

MacRae's of Homosassa. Mail address: P.O. Box 318, Homosassa 34487. Located at 5300 South Cherokee Way, on the Homosassa River, MacRae's is a fish camp that has been here since 1917. Book a motel room or fully equipped apartment, and slip back a century or two while you explore this primeval paradise. Fish inshore or in the Gulf, dive with manatees, paddle waters filled with bird life, or call for a tee time at a nearby golf course. Boats, canoes, paddleboats, and pontoon boats are available for rent. Seafood restaurants are within walking distance; Crumps, known for its seafood and spirits, is just across the river. $–$$. (352) 628–2602. Call between 7:00 A.M. to 6:00 P.M.

CRYSTAL RIVER

Crystal River is on the Gulf, west of Inverness. From Homosassa, return to U.S. 19–98 for the trip north to Crystal River. Sweetwater springs boil up into the bay, creating a habitat that is irresistible to manatees. It's a unique destination for scuba divers, and the Indian mounds make it a unique destination for history hunters, too.

WHERE TO GO

Crystal River State Archaeological Site. 3400 North Museum Point, Crystal River 34429. This site is steeped in mystery. Who were the people who lived here? How and why did they build these mounds? What happened to them? What is the meaning of the carved stones they left behind? Archaeological excavations have been going on here since 1903, so allow several hours for hiking the nature trail; touring the midden, ceremonial, and burial mounds; and seeing the displays in the visitor center. State park admissions apply. Call ahead for open times. (352) 795–3817.

Crystal River National Wildlife Refuge. 1502 Southeast Kings Bay Drive, Crystal River 34429. The refuge covers Kings Bay, where 72-degree spring waters flow twelve months of the year. Manatees can be found during the coldest months, generally December through February. Dive trips, snorkeling, and boating have to be arranged through private companies nearby. Canoeing the Crystal River is also popular; a number of outfitters rent canoes, or bring your own, which can be launched at most canoe liveries for a fee. Admission is free. The refuge is open during daylight hours. (352) 563–2088.

Rock Crusher Canyon. 275 South Rock Crusher Road, Crystal River 34429. The "canyon" is an old rock quarry that forms a natural amphitheater where music rocks and resounds. Big-name groups appear in concert throughout the summer. Luncheon shows are priced $20 to $25; dinner shows are $20 to $30. You'll hear a great concert while dining on a three-course meal that ends with Creole bread pudding with whiskey sauce. It's also an RV park with a swimming pool, clubhouse, hiking trails, instant telephone hookup, and pads for 400 rigs. Find out what's on the concert schedule at (352) 795–1313 or www.rockcrushercanyon.com.

Yulee Sugar Mill Ruins State Historic Site. 3400 North Museum Point, Crystal River 34428. This was once the site of a thriving sugar plantation owned by David Levy Yulee, born in the West Indies and no stranger to a life of power and affluence. When the Civil War broke out, he chose to throw in his lot with the Confederacy. His mansion was burned by Union forces, and his mill fell to ruin. Today the imposing limestone mill has been partially restored to serve as the focal point of a picnic site and a pleasant roadside stop. Open 8:00 A.M. to sundown daily.

WHERE TO SHOP

The Shoppes of Heritage Village in historic downtown Crystal River are clustered around Highway 19 at Citrus Avenue. Browse shops selling toys, custom jewelry, collectibles, antiques, gifts, apparel, and party supplies; have lunch at the cafe. Hours vary shop to shop, season to season, so call ahead. (352) 795-8630.

WHERE TO EAT

Cracker's Bar & Grill. 502 Northwest Sixth Street, Crystal River 34423. This spot overlooks Kings Bay. Laze away an hour or two in the Tiki Hut, then dine on sumptuous seafood platters or a grilled rib-eye steak. Start with a soup or chowder, or nosh on alligator chunks, deep-fried mozzarella, stuffed shrimp, or calamari. Choose from a cornucopia of side- and main-dish salads plus burgers and hot and cold sandwiches. Kids can choose clams with french fries, a hot dog, chicken fingers, spaghetti, or grilled cheese. Have a brownie sundae or peanut butter pie for dessert. Open for lunch and dinner every day, or ask about carryout. $$. (352) 795-3999.

    Half Shell's Oyster Bar & Restaurant. 773 Northeast Fifth Street, Crystal River 34429. This is the place for freshly shucked oysters, sold by the half dozen, dozen, or bucket. Or choose from a wide palette of seafood specialties, steak, chicken, pasta, or a vegetarian option. Crawfish are prepared Cajun style and sold by the pound and half pound. Order the shrimp platter, chicken wings by the dozen, stuffed oysters, crab cakes, hot sandwiches, a variety of burgers including fish or oyster burgers, salads, kids' favorites, and a nice list of sides to order a la carte. Ask about peel-and-eat specials in season, combo platters, and landlubber favorites, especially the twin pork chops or the steak served with sizzling peppers and onions. Open for lunch and dinner Tuesday through Saturday. $$-$$$. (352) 563-5255.

WHERE TO STAY

Best Western Crystal River Resort. 614 Northwest Highway 19, Crystal River 34428. The resort offers rooms and efficiencies handy to the waters and wiles of Kings Bay. Every room has a coffeemaker, clock radio, iron and ironing board, hair dryer, safe, and dataport telephone. Swim in the pool, soak in the whirlpool, have a drink in the tiki bar, shop in Sea Treasures, book an airboat ride or a scuba expedition in the full-service dive shop, and dine casually in the waterfront restaurant. Hotel hosts can arrange tennis, golf, tarpon fishing, canoeing, and other pleasures. $$-$$$. (352) 795-3171 or (800) 435-4409; www.seawake.com.

    Plantation Inn & Golf Resort. Crystal River 34429. This complete, 200-acre resort has something for everyone, including divers and golfers. This is the home of the Florida Women's Open, many state PGA tournaments, and the Original Golf School, one of the nation's most successful teaching programs. The twenty-seven-hole championship golf course, designed by Mark Mahanah, has twenty-one water holes, sloped greens, and plenty of challenges. Swim in the resort's swimming pool or with manatees in the wild. Rent a boat for fishing or sight-seeing. Units with kitchen are available. The restaurant has plantation decor and a comprehensive menu of seafood and standards. $$$. (800) 632-6262 or (352) 795-4211; www.plantationinn.com.

CEDAR KEY

From Crystal River, go north on U.S. 19–98 to Otter Creek and take Route 24 southwest to Cedar Key. The ride is part of the fun. You'll see parts of Florida you never knew existed, and the drive out the long causeway to the island is a float through a wonderland of wildlife and waterfowl. Strolling the sleepy streets of the island, it's hard to imagine that Cedar Key was once a thriving seaport and a seething center of wartime activity. So important was salt to the war effort (to preserve meat for the troops), Cedar Key was an early target for Union troops. They attacked from the sea, captured this strategic center, and cut off much of the South's access to supplies brought here by blockade runners.

After the war, lumbering continued to support island residents, who denuded the forests almost down to the last toothpick. Cedar, one of the chief wood products, was harvested for making the pencils you probably used in grammar school. The sea provided fish and tons of oysters. In time, highways and railroads were built elsewhere, deeper harbors were required as ships grew larger, and little Cedar Key languished, battered by the occasional hurricane. Now it has bounced back, a favorite with travelers for its funky, world's-end ambience.

WHERE TO GO

Cedar Key State Museum. Mail address: Box 538, Cedar Key 32625. The museum is found at the northern point of the C-shaped island. Take Gulf Boulevard north, then go east on Hodges Drive to Whitman Drive. See one of the state's great collections of seashells as well as relics from the island's boisterous past. The museum is open 9:00 A.M. to 5:00 P.M. daily except Tuesday and Wednesday. A small admission is charged. (352) 543–5350.

Cedar Key Scrub State Reserve/Waccasassa State Preserve. Mail address: P.O. Box 187, Cedar Key 32625. The preserve is 6 miles east of Cedar Key on State Road 24. The vast Gulf Hammock was once dominated by forested islands threaded by tidal creeks; this 4,000-acre reserve is all that remains. Still, it's a wildlife wonderland bordered by the Waccasassa River, available to visitors on a first-come, first-served basis for hunting, boating, fishing, and hiking. There is a small picnic area off State Road 24, 6 miles east of Cedar Key, and service roads can be used as hiking trails. Bring your binoculars, and be prepared to be wowed by sightings of raccoons, black bears, bald eagles, wild turkeys, and gaggles of other bird life. Open 8:00 A.M. to sundown. (352) 543–5567.

WHERE TO EAT

The Island Room at Cedar Cove. State Road 24 at Second Street, Cedar Key 32625. Located in the Cedar Cove Beach and Yacht Club, this is a good choice for drinks and dinner with a view of the sun sinking into the Gulf. Crab cakes are a specialty of the house. Another is grouper, cooked and sauced in a variety of luscious ways. Or try the Chicken Savannah made with roasted pecans. The wine list is impressive and international. Open for dinner daily and Sunday brunch. Reservations are recommended. $$-$$$. (352) 543-5666.

WHERE TO STAY

The Island Place. First Street at C Street, Cedar Key 32625. This is a rustic condo complex of one- and two-bedroom self-catering apartments within walking distance of the marina and grocery store. Everything you need to do your own cooking is here, or call for delivery from a list of the island's many excellent restaurants. Units have washer, dryer, microwave, cable TV, and a private balcony with a view of the most razzle-dazzle sunsets in Florida. The resort has a swimming pool and hot tub. Hosts can arrange fishing, boating, shelling, or sight-seeing. $$-$$$. (352) 543-5306 or (800) 780-6522.

Regional Information

DAY TRIP 3 (Also see West Volusia Tourism.)

NORTH

DAY TRIP 1

Seminole County Convention & Visitors Bureau
1230 Douglas Avenue #116
Longwood, FL 32779
(407) 665–2900 or (800) 800–7832
www.visitseminole.com

Sanford Main Street, Inc.
209-B West First Street
P.O. Box 1741
Sanford, FL 32772
(407) 322–5600
www.sanfordmainstreet.com

DAY TRIP 2

Cassadaga Spiritualist Camp
Box 319
Cassadaga, FL 3270
(386) 228–2880

West Volusia Tourism
(800) 749–4350
www.naturalflorida.org

St. Johns River Country
101 North Woodland Boulevard,
Suite A-308
DeLand, FL 32720
(386) 734–0575 or (800) 749–4350
www.naturalflorida.org

Putnam County Chamber of Commerce
1100 Rein Street
Palatka, FL 32177
(386) 328–1503

NORTHEAST

DAY TRIP 1

Chamber of Commerce
115 Canal Street
New Smyrna Beach, FL 32168
(800) 541–9521

Southeast Volusia Historical Society
P.O. Box 968
New Smyrna Beach, FL 32170

New Smyrna Beach Visitors Bureau
2242 State Road 44
New Smyrna Beach, FL 32168
(866) 397–6976
www.newsmyrnabeachonline.com.

DAY TRIP 2

Daytona Beach Convention & Visitors Bureau (walk-ins)
1801 West International Speedway Boulevard

Daytona Beach, FL 32118
(800) 854-1234 or (386) 253-8669
www.daytonabeach.com

Daytona Beach Convention &
Visitors Bureau (mail requests)
126 East Orange Avenue
Daytona Beach, FL 32114
(800) 854-1234 or (386) 255-0415

Flagler County Tourist Development
Council
1200 East Moody Boulevard, Suite 1
Bunnell, FL 32110
(800) 881-1022 or (386) 437-0106

DAY TRIP 3

St. Johns County Convention &
Visitors Bureau
88 Roberia Street, Suite 250
St. Augustine, FL 32084
(800) OLD-CITY or
(904) 829-1711
www.VisitOldCity.com

Jacksonville and the Beaches
201 East Adams Street
Jacksonville, FL 32200
(800) 733-2668 or (904) 798-9111

EAST

DAY TRIP 1

Space Coast Office of Tourism
8810 Astronaut Boulevard,
Suite 102
Cape Canaveral, FL 32920
(800) 936-2326 during business
hours;
(800) 872-1969 automated line
www.space-coast.com

SOUTHEAST

DAY TRIP 1

Indian River County Chamber of
Commerce
1216 Twenty-first Street
P.O. Box 2947
Vero Beach, FL 32961
(561) 567-3491
www.vero-beach.fl.us/chamber

DAY TRIP 2 (Also see Space
Coast Tourism.)

Kissimmee-St. Cloud Convention
& Visitors Bureau
1925 East Irlo Bronson Memorial
Highway
Kissimmee, FL 34740
(800) 333-KISS or (407) 847-5000
www.floridakiss.com

SOUTH

DAY TRIP 1

(Also see Kissimmee-St. Cloud.)
Lake Wales Area Chamber of
Commerce
340 West Central Avenue
Lake Wales, FL 33850
(863) 676-3445
www.lakewaleschamber.com

DAY TRIP 2

Avon Park Chamber of Commerce
28 East Main Street
Avon Park, FL 33825
(863) 453-3350
www.apfla.com

Convention & Visitors Bureau of
Highlands County
309 South Circle Street
Sebring, FL 33870
(863) 385–1316 or (800) 255–1711
www.highlandscvb.com

DAY TRIP 1

Central Florida Convention & Visitors Bureau
P.O. Box 61
Cypress Gardens, FL 33884
(800) 828–7655 or (863) 298–7565
www.sunsational.org

DAY TRIP 2 (See Central Florida Convention & Visitors Bureau.)

DAY TRIP 3

Tampa Bay Convention & Visitors Bureau
400 North Tampa Street #2800
Tampa, FL 33610
(800) 4–TAMPA or (813) 223–2752
www.visittampabay.com

DAY TRIP 4

St. Petersburg/Clearwater Convention & Visitors Bureau
14450 Forty-sixth Street North #108
Clearwater, FL 33756
(877) 352–3224 or (727) 464–7200
www.floridasbeach.com

DAY TRIP 5

Sarasota Area Visitor Information Center
655 North Tamiami Trail
Sarasota, FL 34236

(941) 957–1877 or (800) 522–9799
www.sarasotafl.org

The Center has a branch office at 5947 Clark Center Avenue in the Albritton Grove Market. The office provides information on Sarasota, Longboat Key, Lido Key, Siesta Key, Casey Key, Venice, Manasota Key, Englewood, and North Port

Anna Maria Island Chamber of Commerce
5337 Gulf Drive North
Holmes Beach, FL 34271
(941) 778–1541
www.annamariaislandchamber.org

Bradenton Area Convention & Visitors Bureau
(Mail address only; specify Bradenton area information.)
12290 Treeline Avenue
Fort Myers, FL 33913
(800) 4–MANATEE or (941) 729–9177
www.flagulfislands.com

DAY TRIP 1

Lake County Convention & Visitors Bureau
20763 U.S. Highway 27
Groveland, FL 34736
(800) 798–1071 or (352) 429–367
www.lakecountyfl.com

Greater Dade City Chamber of Commerce
14112 Eighth Street
Dade City, FL 33525
(352) 567–3769
www.dadecitychamber.org

DAY TRIP 2

Greater Hernando County
  Chamber of Commerce
101 East Fort Dade Avenue
Brooksville, FL 34601
(352) 796-0697

DAY TRIP 3

Citrus County Tourist Development
  Council
801 Southeast U.S. Highway 19
Crystal River, FL 34429
(352) 527-5223 or (800) 587-6667
www.visitcitruss.com

Pasco County Office of Tourism
7530 Little Road
New Port Richey, FL 34654
(800) 842-1873 or (727) 847-8990

NORTHWEST

DAY TRIP 1

Mount Dora Chamber of Commerce
Alexander at Third (in the Old
  Seaboard Coast Line Depot)
P.O. Box 196
Mount Dora, FL 32757
(352) 383-2165

Lake County Convention &
  Visitors Bureau
20763 U.S. Highway 27
Groveland, FL 34736
(800) 798-1071 or (352) 429-3673
www.lakecountyfl.com

DAY TRIP 2

Ocala/Marion Chamber of
  Commerce
110 Silver Springs Boulevard
Ocala FL 34470
(352) 629-8051
www.ocalacc.com

DAY TRIP 3 (See Ocala.)

DAY TRIP 4

Visitors and Convention Bureau of
  Alachua County
10 Southwest Second Avenue
Gainesville, FL 32601
(352) 374-5260
www.visitgainesville.net

(Visit the Welcome Center at exit
  77 on I-75.)

DAY TRIP 5

Cedar Key Chamber of Commerce
Box 610
Cedar Key, FL 32625
(352) 543-5600
www.cedarkey.org

Citrus County Tourist Development Council
801 Southeast U.S. Highway 19
Crystal River, FL 34429
(352) 527-5223 or (800) 587-6667
www.visitcitruss.com

GENERAL INFORMATION

Visit Florida
550 Technology Park
Lake Mary, FL 32746
(888) 7-FLA-USA
www.flausa.com

Official Florida Vacation Guide
c/o Miles Media
3675 Clark Road
Sarasota, FL 34233
(888) 7-FLA-USA
(Contact this organization to request
  the *Official Florida Vacation Guide*.)

Florida RV Trade Association
401 North Parsons Avenue, Suite 107
Brandon, FL 33510
(800) 330-7882 (Florida only) or
    (813) 684-7882
www.frvta.org
(Contact this group for the *Official
RVers Guide,* including campground listings.)

Florida Association of RV Parks
    and Campgrounds
1340 Vickers Drive
Tallahassee, FL 32303
(850) 562-7151
(Write or phone for a list of
    commercial campgrounds.)

Office of Greenways and Trails
Mail Station 795
325 John Knox Road, Building 500
Tallahassee, FL 32303
(850) 487-4784
(Write for information hiking,
    biking, and equestrian trails and
    state and national forests.)

Florida Department of
    Environmental Protection
Recreation Trails Program
3900 Commonwealth Boulevard
Tallahassee, FL 32399
(850) 487-4784
(Write for information on canoe
    trails.)

Festivals and Celebrations

Note: Contact numbers can change from year to year. Your best bet is to call tourism information numbers for the cities or counties listed in Regional Information. Dates are always subject to change.

JANUARY

Garage Sale, Sebring. Find bargains galore during an event that calls itself the country's largest garage sale. Sebring does it again every April. (863) 471–5104.

Indian River Native American Festival, New Smyrna Beach. Celebrate Florida's rich and varied tribal history from pre-Columbians through the Seminole era. Visiting tribes add color with dancing, feasting, native dress, and games. (386) 424–0860.

Sarasota Film Festival. The festival screens movies indoors and out as locals and celebrities mingle at parties and special events. (941) 364–9514.

FEBRUARY

Auto and Antique Winterfest, Zephyrhills. This event at Festival Park is highlighted by an antique and car show and auction. (813) 920–7206.

Calusa Wood Carvers Show, New Port Richey. This annual event features master carvers and their works. Vendors from all over the country are here to sell tools and woods. (727) 848–8721.

Mount Dora Art Festival, Mount Dora. One of the leading art events of the region, this festival draws about a quarter of a million visitors on the first full weekend of the month. (352) 383–2165.

Roaring 20s, Sebring. Dress like a flapper, show up in a tin Lizzie, and enjoy all that jazz. (863) 471–5104.

MARCH

12 Hours of Sebring Grand Prix of Endurance, Sebring. This is one of international auto racing's most sought-after events, attracting big-name drivers, manufacturers, and fans. Reserve accommodations early because more than 100,000 race fans stream into this small town. (863) 655-1442.

Annual Easter Surfing Festival, Cocoa Beach. This becomes the surfing capital of Florida for two weekends, depending on the date of Easter. (321) 452-5352.

Antiques Show and Sale, Ormond Beach. The Casements, once the home of John D. Rockefeller, is a wonderful setting on the river with exciting antiques to see or buy. (386) 441-0585.

Azalea Festival, Palatka. This is central Florida's biggest azalea event, even though the azaleas themselves may be past their prime if it has been a warm winter. A queen is crowed and there are pageants, parades, food and midway attractions; always the second weekend of March. (386) 328-1503.

Bach Festival Concerts. Featuring the stellar Bach Festival Chorus and Chamber Orchestra, concerts are staged in several venues this month. Works of other early composers are also featured. (863) 324-7535.

Chasco Fiesta, New Port Richey. Enjoy one of the state's oldest Native American festivals. (727) 842-7651.

Cincinnati Reds Spring Training, Sarasota. The Reds train here all this month. (941) 954-4101.

Daytona Beach Garden Show, Daytona Beach. The big Ocean Center fills with mountains of blooms plus plants for sale and seminars that sharpen your own gardening skills. (386) 252-1511, extension 2569.

Grant Seafood Festival, Melbourne. This is one of the state's leading seafood blowouts. Another seafood festival, **SeaFeast,** takes place at Port Canaveral. (800) USA-1969.

Kumquat Festival, Dade City. Experience honest, small-town wackiness with kumquat cooking, concerts, arts, crafts, and food booths. (352) 567-3769.

Pioneer Heritage Days, Lake Placid. Remember the good ol' days. Don a bonnet or straw hat and your best gingham, and join the celebrations. (800) 255-1711 or (941) 465-4331.

Sarasota Jazz Festival, Sarasota. One of the state's long-established, high-profile jazz events features internationally known musicians. (941) 366-1552.

Spring Break, takes over Daytona Beach most of this month with beer, babes, and bawdy behavior. Either come here to join the fun, or run the other way. (386) 854-1234.

APRIL

Blessing of the Fleet, St. Augustine. Blessings take place in many Florida seaports this month, a ceremony that goes back centuries. In St. Augustine, the Bishop of the Diocese of St. Augustine performs the rite on Palm Sunday starting at noon with a procession from the Cathedral Basilica to the Cathedral. Pleasure boats and commercial craft participate. (800) OLD-CITY.

Cabbage and Potato Festival, Hastings. This agricultural community 18 miles west of St. Augustine hosts a delightfully cornball, old-Florida event with feasting, street entertainers, arts, games, and contests. Admission is free. It's usually held the last weekend of the month. (386) 692-1420.

Easter Skydiving Boogie, Zephyrhills. Hundreds of skydivers gather for fun and competition. Dates vary with Easter. (800) 404-9399. Another "boogie" is held on Thanksgiving weekend and over Christmas.

Garage Sale, Sebring. Here's a second helping of the country's largest garage sale, also held in January. (863) 471-5104.

Indian River Festival, Titusville. This wet and wild funfest features contests, a wacky raft race, food, and music. (321) 267-3036.

La Musica International Chamber Music Festival, Sarasota. This festival attracts top musicians from Europe and throughout North America. (941) 364-8802.

Melbourne Art Festival, Melbourne. More than 275 top artists and exhibitors show their paintings, jewelry, woodworking, sculpture, and textiles. (321) 722-1964.

Rhythm and Ribs Festival, St. Augustine. This yearly festival features championship barbecue, live jazz, and great local wines. It's held at St. Francis Field on Castillo Drive; shuttles run from downtown at San Sebastian Winery. (904) 829-5565.

Shark's Tooth Festival, Venice Comb the beach at the self-proclaimed Shark's Tooth Capital of the World to see how many teeth you can find, then stroll among food and crafts vendors. (941) 412-0402.

Spring Arts and Crafts Festival, St. Augustine. The festival is held at the Special Events Field on Castillo Drive. Free shuttles run from downtown. Eat, drink, and view the works of more than a hundred artists. (800) OLD-CITY.

Tico Warbird Air Show, Titusville. This show features vintage and modern military aircraft in rousing stunts and flyovers. (800) USA-1969.

MAY

Blue Crab Festival, Putnam County. This festival continues over the three-day Memorial Day Weekend. (386) 325–4406.

Civil War Reenactment, New Smyrna Beach. Relive the times yearly in Old Fort Park. (386) 409–8076.

Memorial Weekend Cathedral Festival, St. Augustine. Held Friday through Monday on the grounds of the Mission of Nombre de Dios, the festival features arts, crafts, games, rides, entertainment, food, and fireworks. (386) 824–2806.

Memorial Day weekend also marks the start of St. Augustine's Summer Concert Series, sponsored by the Jazz Society. Free concerts are held downtown in the Plaza at 7:00 P.M. every Thursday through Labor Day.

Mother's Day Native American Powwow, Dade City. Held along the Withlacoochee River, the powwow features Indian dancing, singing, arts, and crafts. (352) 521–4104.

JUNE

Greek Landing Day Festival, St. Augustine. Celebrate the first colony of Greeks in North America. The festival is held in late June at St. Photius National Greek Orthodox Shrine, 41 St. George Street. Admission is free. (386) 829–8205.

Sarasota Music Festival, Sarasota. This two-week chamber music celebration features world-renowned artists. (941) 953–4252.

JULY

Fourth of July is celebrated throughout central Florida, but droughts in recent years have caused a cutback or cancellation of some fireworks. For information on St. Augustine's Bayfront blowout, call (800) OLD-CITY.

Florida International Festival, Daytona Beach. This festival centers around the London Symphony Orchestra, which calls Daytona Beach their summer home. Classical and popular music are celebrated for two weeks. Buy season tickets well in advance. (386) 257–7790.

AUGUST

Fais-Dos-Dos Cajun Festival, Cocoa. Enjoy Cajun food, crafts, dancing, and music. (321) 632–7445.

Playwrights Festival, St. Augustine. The Limelight Theater presents original plays selected in a statewide competition on the first and second weekends. (386) 825-1164.

SEPTEMBER

Caladium Festival, Lake Placid. Hundreds of acres of these ornamental plants grow in the area and are celebrated with arts, crafts, music, and fun. (941) 465-4331.

Days in Spain/Founders Day, St. Augustine. Spanish dancing, period costumes, music, and entertainers re-create the founding of the nation's oldest city. On the grounds of the Nombre de Dios Mission, a sacred reenactment of the first mass held in the New World is offered. (904) 825-1010.

Family Salsa Festival, Melbourne. A city park fills with good music, spicy food, cool drinks, contests, and games. (321) 253-0363.

Labor Day Bluegrass Festival is held at the Sentoma Youth Ranch between Brooksville and Dade City. Money is raised for the ranch, where youths are housed. Make reservations for camping. (352) 754-3082.

Pioneer Florida Day, Dade City. Celebrate at the Pioneer Florida Museum with costumes, reenactments, children's activities, and demonstrations of Cracker crafts. (352) 567-0262.

OCTOBER

Airport Extravaganza, Melbourne International Airport. The extravaganza celebrates aviation with flyovers, static displays, old warbirds, business displays, and food and souvenir vendors. (321) 724-5400.

Biketoberfest, Daytona Beach. The city and county for miles around fill with ear-busting motorcycles and their sometimes bizarrely dressed riders. Drive carefully; these are fast machines that aren't always easy to see. (386) 854-1234.

The Colony's Annual Stone Crab, Seafood, and Wine Festival brings in celebrity chefs who celebrate the yearly stone crab season in this resort's gourmet restaurants and around the grounds. Reserve early and stay the weekend. (800) 426-5669.

Cracker Day, St. Augustine. Enjoy bluegrass, banjos, and barbecue in the St. Johns County Fairgrounds off State Road 207 near St. Augustine. (800) OLD-CITY.

Mount Dora Bike Festival, Mount Dora. This festival is three days of rides, contests, and picnicking for riders of all levels—including families—on picturesque streets and rural roads that *Bicycling* magazine named one of the planet's top fifty bicycling destinations. (352) 383-2165.

Polish American Festival, Titusville. Serve up Polish dancing, crafts, and great food. (321) 264–9877.

Rattlesnake Festival, San Antonio. See professionals handle rattlesnakes at this yearly gathering. The party includes foods, crafts, music, and fun. (352) 588–4444.

St. Armand's Circle Art Festival. More than 200 national and international artists show their works in this chichi shopping center. (941) 388–1554.

Seminole Indian Florida Pioneer Festival, Brevard Community College, Cocoa Beach. Learn about the tribe made up of runaway slaves and Indians from assorted tribes, who made war on settlers and have not signed a surrender to this day. (321) 632–1111.

NOVEMBER

Art Festival, Sebring. It's one of the best regional art festivals in the South with paintings, photographs, gifts, food, and festivities for all ages. (863) 471–5104.

Birthplace of Speed Celebration, Ormond Beach. Commemorate the days when gentlemen raced on the beach sands. The two-day event features a gaslight parade, antique car show, swap meet, antique auto races, and much more. (386) 677–3454.

Bug Jam, Dade City. The jam brings together hundreds of Volkswagens for viewing, parts swapping, and camaraderie. (813) 996 6306.

Great Chowder Debate, St. Augustine. Every year at Conch House Marina, 57 Comares Avenue, St. Augustine, the "debate" serves up barrels of the best seafood chowder ever created. (904) 829–8646.

Greek Festival, Daytona. Held in the spectacular gold-domed St. Demetrios Greek Orthodox Church, the festival features authentic food, music, dance, and crafts. (386) 252–6012.

Nights of Lights, St. Augustine. More than a million tiny, twinkling lights burn along the bay and downtown. It starts mid-November and continues through January, with various ceremonies and programs throughout. (800) OLD–CITY.

Space Coast Art Festival, Cocoa Beach. This is one of the oldest, largest art shows in Florida. See extensive displays of paintings, photography, glass, sculpture, and weaving. (321) 784–3322.

Turkey Run Car Show and Swap Meet, Daytona International Speedway. This is one of the year's biggest events for car fanciers.

DECEMBER

Christmas Boat Parades feature boats sparkling with lights that reflect in the water. They're held in most waterfront communities, including Anna Maria, Cocoa, DeLand, Edgewater, and Sarasota Bay.

Grand Illumination, St. Augustine. Bring a candle and join the parade to the plaza to hear the governor's proclamation at Government House, 48 King Street. Soldiers fire muskets, and the Christmas season is serenaded with ancient carols. (386) 794-7682. **British Night Watch Weekend** is part of the centuries-old celebration, a two-day event with a cast of British soldiers and citizens reenacting ceremonies that took place during the British occupation. Later in the month, usually about the second weekend, boat parades begin. St. Augustine's **Regatta of Lights** floats along the Bay of Lions and the Castillo de San Marcos. (904) 829-1770.

ONGOING EVENTS

The second Saturday of every month is **East Coast Cruiser Night** on Canal Street in New Smyrna Beach, 6:00 to 9:00 P.M. Antique cars, street rods, and other interesting iron make the scene, while people party and listen to live music.

The last Thursday of every month is **Gallery Stroll** in downtown DeLand. Visit a half dozen art galleries, linger over a glass of wine in one of the pubs, and have dinner in one of the restaurants.

Every Saturday morning on Lemon Avenue, Sarasota hosts a **Farmers' Market** downtown.

Living history events are portrayed on Sunday afternoon January through mid-April at **Historic Spanish Point,** Osprey. (941) 966-4215.

Circus Sarasota performs in season at the Sarasota Fairgrounds. (941) 355-9335.

On the first Friday of the month, 6:00 to 9:00 P.M., join a **Friday Walk** of Palm Avenue, Sarasota, to visit shops, galleries, and restaurants. Special events include live music, gallery openings, and special menus. (941) 365-7414. On the fourth Friday, the same sort of event takes place at **St. Armand's Circle** (941) 388-1554.

About the Authors

Janet Groene and her husband, Gordon Groene, are a full-time travel writer and photographer team who live in central Florida. Assignments take them worldwide, but they have also traveled their home state for more than thirty years in their cars, RV, private plane, and sailboat. They've written thousands of newspaper and magazine features and more than a dozen books, including *Romantic Weekends Central and North Florida, Florida Guide, Caribbean Guide, Puerto Rico and the Virgin Islands,* and *52 Florida Weekends.* They are members of the American Society of Journalists & Authors and Boating Writers International.

Janet is also a member of the Society of American Travel Writers and Outdoor Writers Association of America. Among her awards is the Distinguished Achievement in RV Journalism Award. Both Groenes hold the NMMA Directors Award for boating journalism.